The
SURVIVOR
Personality

For Charles Maclean,
with much appreciation for
all the work you do for
others.

also by Al Siebert:

Student Success: How to Succeed in College and Still Have Time for Your Friends (Timothy L. Walter, co-author)

The Adult Student's Guide to Survival and Success: Time For College (Bernadine Gilpin, co-author)

The SURVIVOR *Personality*

Al Siebert, Ph.D.

Practical Psychology Press – Portland, Oregon

Practical Psychology Press
P.O. Box 535
Portland, OR 97207

Book Design: Kristin Pintarich
Cover Design: Robert Steven Pawlak

Printed using soy based ink by Thomson-Shore, Inc.
Printed in the United States of America.

Publisher's Cataloging in Publication
        (prepared by Quality Books, Inc.)
Siebert, Lawrence A., 1934-
        The survivor personality / by Al Siebert.
        p. cm.
        Includes bibliographical references and index.
        Preassigned LCCN: 93-083431
        ISBN: 0-944227-06-6

1. Life change events.   2. Life skills--Handbooks, manuals, etc.
3. Self-help techniques.   I. Title.

BF637.L53S54 1993   158.1
                                     QBI93-290

CONTENTS

1 Life is Not Fair—
  And That Can Be Very Good For You   1

2 Learning About Survival   11

3 Playful Curiosity:
  Learning What No One Can Teach   15

4 Flexibility: An Absolutely Essential Ability   23

5 Needing to Have Things Work Well:
  The Synergy Imperative   35

6 Empathy is a Survival Skill   43

7 The Survivor's Edge: Intuition, Creativity, Imagination   51

8 The "Good Child" Handicap   65

9 Thriving   79

10 How To Be Positive About Negative People   97

11 How to Handle Yourself With Angry People   113

12 The Roots of Resiliency: Your Inner "Selfs"   129

13 Self-Managed Healing   139

14 Surviving Emergencies and Crises   165

15 Surviving Disasters:
   Mother Nature vs. Human Nature   181

16 Learnings From Survivors of Torturous Conditions   199

17 The Serendipity Talent:
   Turning Misfortune into Good Luck   221

18 Surviving Being a Survivor   229

19 Our Transformation to the Next Level of Development   235

   Appendix A: Guidelines for Listening to
     Survivors of Extreme Experiences   249

   Appendix B: Guidelines for Thriving During
     Job Loss and Job Search   253

   Chapter Notes and References   257

   Recommended Reading   266

   Index   267

   Acknowledgements   273

CHAPTER ONE

LIFE IS NOT FAIR— AND THAT CAN BE VERY GOOD FOR YOU

When you are hit by adversity or have your life disrupted, how do you respond? If you lost your job, developed a serious illness, or faced a personal crisis, how well would you cope?

Different people react to adversity and disruptive change in different ways. Some become despondent. Others feel victimized. They complain about how they were wronged. Some get angry and lash out trying to hurt anyone they can.

A few, however, reach within themselves and find ways to make things turn out well. These are life's best survivors, those people who have an amazing capacity for surviving crises and extreme difficulties. They are durable and resilient in distressing situations. They regain emotional balance quickly, adapt and cope well. They thrive by gaining strength from adversity, and often convert misfortune into good luck.

Are life's best survivors different from other people? No. They survive better because they are better at using the inborn abilities possessed by all humans.

Learning Survivor Skills

If you are like most people, you have not had good coaching on how to handle adversity, crises, or constant change. This book shows you how. It is a manual on how to build skills that will be available to you during disruptive changes and crisis. By practicing survivor skills and increasing your range of responses you will be ready to cope well with whatever comes your way. This book shows how to learn to:

- regain emotional stability when your life is knocked off track.
- cope with unfair developments in an effective way.
- increase your self-confidence for handling disruptive changes.
- break free from childhood prohibitions that prevent many people from effective coping.
- thrive during difficult transitions.
- develop a talent for serendipity.

The following true story is an example of someone turning a devastating blow into good fortune. The story begins in 1926, the year a 25 year old illustrator and one of his older brothers started a cartoon animation studio. Because they were among the first to master the art of moving picture cartoons, their studio received a big, one year, renewable contract from a New York film distributor, Charles Mintz, to produce a cartoon series named "Oswald the Lucky Rabbit."

Mintz, who owned the rights to the character, sent his brother-in-law, George Winkler, to California to watch production activities. Winkler spent many weeks at the studio getting to know the animators and learning production procedures.

As the highly successful first year drew to a close, the illustrator took his wife with him on a train to New York where he expected to renegotiate a longer, more profitable contract with Mintz. In New York, the meeting with Mintz did not go as expected. Mintz surprised him. Mintz said that he and his brother would have to work for a lower fee if they wanted to renew the contract. He was shocked. He knew he could not produce the cartoons with less money.

As they argued, he discovered what Mintz was up to. Winkler had persuaded Mintz to take over production of the Oswald cartoons. During his visits to the California studios, Winkler had secretly arranged to hire away several of their best animators. Mintz and Winkler believed they could cut costs and increase their profits by producing the series themselves. Their strategy in the negotiations was to get him to give up his right to renew the Oswald contract.

They succeeded.

He felt shocked, angry, and hurt as he and his wife, Lillian, left New York for the long train ride home. He had trusted Mintz and Winkler. He had trusted his employees. He had honored his part of the contract and expected to be treated fairly in return. He had worked many long nights and weekends to meet production deadlines.

Now, without warning, the highly successful cartoon series was taken away from him. He would no longer be the producer of the series he worked long and hard to develop. His studio had lost its only big account.

Turning Disaster Into Opportunity

The young illustrator did not react like a victim to the raw deal pulled on him by Mintz and Winkler. During the train ride back to Hollywood, he reflected on his situation. What if he created his own cartoon character instead of waiting to be hired to work on other people's ideas?

His first illustrating job had been at a commercial art studio housed in an old building in Kansas City. During long hours at the drawing board, he used food crumbs to train a mouse that lived in the building. He called the mouse Mortimer.

What about Mortimer the Mouse as a cartoon character?

Lillian said the name Mortimer sounded too stuffy. This mouse needed a friendlier, more playful name.

What about Mickey? (Yes, the young illustrator in this story is Walt Disney!) Walt liked the name Mickey. He began making sketches for a new cartoon series.

Back at the studio he and his brother decided to take advantage of a new technology that added sound to motion pictures. He charged into his new project with enthusiasm.

The rest, of course, is history. In 1928, in New York City, the Disney studios held the premier showing of an animated cartoon starring Mickey Mouse. The new cartoon was an immediate success. Oswald the Rabbit soon disappeared from theaters and Mickey Mouse went on to become one of the greatest cartoon personalities of all time.

Walt Disney converted Mintz and Winkler's unethical conduct and treachery into one of the best things that ever happened to him. If you look around, you will find that many successful people have similar stories. Their stories may not be as dramatic as this one, but they will be similar in the way they made a bad situation turn out well.

Discovering Survivors

My interest in survivors began in 1953, when, after my sophomore year in college, I joined the paratroopers. I was sent to Ft. Campbell, Kentucky, and assigned to the 503rd Airborne Infantry Regiment for basic training. As part of the 11th Airborne Division, the 503rd had returned from Korea after suffering heavy losses in combat. We were told that only one in ten men had come back alive.

We heard stories about the 503rd. This was the unit that parachuted onto Corregidor Island during World War II and recaptured it from the Japanese. These were jungle fighters—tough, unstoppable, and deadly. They would be our training cadre, and we were nervous about what our training would be like. Talk of mean, screaming drill sergeants spread through the barracks.

When we started basic training, however, the sergeants and officers were not what we had expected. They were tough but showed patience. They pushed us hard but were tolerant. When a trainee made a mistake, they were more likely to laugh and be amused than to be angry. Either that, or to bluntly say, "In combat you'd be dead now," and walk away.

Combat survivors, it turns out, are more like Alan Alda playing Hawkeye, the mischievous, non-conforming surgeon in the M.A.S.H. television series than they are like the movie character Rambo. In fact, the commanding officer of SEALS training at the Naval Special Warfare Center said in a magazine interview, "The Rambo types are the first to go."

During our training I noticed that combat survivors have a sort of personal radar always on "scan." Anything that happens, or any noise draws a quick, brief look. They have a sort of relaxed awareness. I began to realize it wasn't just luck or fate that these were the few who came back alive. *Something about them as people had tipped the scales in their favor.*

They did not exhibit a self-centered "survival of the fittest" attitude. Quite the contrary. They had such strong self-confidence they didn't have to act mean or tough. They knew what they could do and apparently didn't feel the need to prove anything to anyone. We trainees knew that if we had to go into deadly combat, these were the fighters we'd want to be with.

A Practical Definition

Later, when I was a graduate student in psychology, I learned that the mental health profession did not seem to know about people who hold up well under pressure. After graduation I started my own personal research to understand life's best survivors. To focus my efforts, I developed a list of four criteria.

People with survivor personalities are those who:

- have survived a major crisis or challenge;
- surmounted the crisis through personal effort;
- emerged from the experience with previously unknown strengths and abilities; and
- afterwards find value in the experience.

Using these four criteria as a frame of reference, I listed some questions I wanted to answer:

- How do some survivors of horrible experiences manage to be so happy?
- Is there a basic pattern of personality traits that survivors share? If so, what are the traits?
- What about their uniqueness? How can a person be similar to others and yet be a unique individual?
- Is the survivor personality inborn? Is it learned?
- If it is learned, why do so many people grow up without learning it?
- What percentage of people have survivor personalities?
- What are survivors like when they aren't surviving? Is there a way to spot such people when things are peaceful?

A Map-Developing Odyssey

One benefit from a good education is learning how to learn. I kept a curious and open mind as I read autobiographies and interviewed hundreds of people—survivors of the World War II Bataan Death March; Jewish survivors of the Nazi holocaust; ex-POWs and Vietnam veterans; survivors of cancer, polio, head injury, and other physically challenging conditions; survivors of co-dependency, abuse, alcoholism, and addictions; parents of murdered children; survivors of bankruptcy, job loss, and other major life-disrupting events. I became curious about public employees who remain cheerful and dedicated to their work even while being maligned by the people they serve.

With a quiet mind I absorbed whatever people told me. I allowed the territory to create its own map for me. I gradually began to sense some patterns, some predictable qualities and ways of reacting. I stopped being surprised, for example, to hear survivors laugh at themselves about some stupid thing they did.

I learned that most survivors are ordinary people with flaws, worries, and imperfections. When people call them heroes they disagree. "We just did what any reasonably sensible people would have done," say two women who were lost for a week in the mountains during freezing winter weather. "We aren't heroes," they keep saying to people awed by their survival.

I learned that a few people are born survivors. They are the natural athletes in the game of life. Just as some people are born musicians, writers, artists, or singers, some people are gifted in living. The rest of us need to consciously work to develop our abilities. Just as we would have to take lessons and practice diligently to become artists or musicians, we have to work at learning how handle job pressures, difficult people, conflict, negative situations, unwelcome change, and crises.

I learned that some of life's best survivors grew up in horrible family situations, and that many of the people least skillful at coping with life's difficulties have come from ideal homes. Many of the best people in our world have been through experiences that no public school could get away with arranging. They have been strengthened in the school of life. They have been abused, lied to, deceived, robbed, mistreated, and hit by the worst that life can throw at them. Their reaction is to pick themselves up, learn important lessons, set positive goals, and rebuild their lives.

I learned that people seldom tap into their deepest strengths and abilities until forced to do so by a major adversity. As Julius Segal, the distinguished survivor researcher has said, "In a remarkable number of cases, those who have suffered and prevail find that after their ordeal they begin to operate at a higher level than ever before....The terrible experiences of our lives, despite the pain they bring, may become our redemption."

Lt. Commander Charlie Plumb, for example, was a navy pilot shot down early in the Vietnam war. He was held in a prison in Hanoi for six years in a stone cell 8 feet by 8 feet in size. He had no window to look out and nothing to read. He was frequently hog-tied, repeatedly beaten, and subjected to gruelling interrogations. Yet, in retrospect, when he talks about his experience as a POW, he says "It's probably the most valuable six years of my life. Amazing what a little adversity can teach a person....I really felt there was some meaning to that, to my experience itself."

Thriving vs. Self-Victimizing

I became curious about a fascinating difference in people. Some, like Charlie Plumb, can go through a torturous experience and say "It was horrible, but it was the most valuable experience of my life." At the other extreme, some people who are healthy, employed, and living in safe communities with their families, complain about their lives as though they were being tortured.

The victim style is revealed in statements that repeat this complaint: "If only other people would change, my life would be better." There's nothing wrong with that belief, of course, because it's true. Each of us can name several people who would make things better for us if only they would change how they act. It is extremely unlikely, however, that others will voluntarily change themselves to make your life easier. You are the only person on the planet that you can really do something about. Fortunately, you were born with an ability to learn how to handle unfair situations and distressing experiences. You can learn how to respond effectively to life's challenges. You can acquire a learning/coping response as an alternative to feeling like a victim who blames others.

A Teaching Challenge For Me—A Learning Challenge For You

Years of observing and learning about life's best survivors has convinced me that:

- A survivor style develops out of everyday habits that increase chances of survival should it become necessary.
- A survivor style can be learned, but it can't be taught as one would teach a sport or skill.
- People trained to act, think, and feel as instructed cannot cope with life's unexpected challenges as well as a person with a self-discovered personality.

A frustrating situation for a teacher! How can I teach what can't be taught? How can I offer expert advice about survivorship when people who try to do what an "expert" says actually *lower* their chances of coping well with unexpected difficulties?

My way of handling this teaching and learning challenge is to explain the situation and offer coaching tips on how to manage your own learning. If you've read many "self-help" or "self-improvement" books, you may have noticed that the authors often start by saying that none of the existing self-help books worked very well for them. It was only after they compiled their own list of habits or principles that they finally found the way to greatness, effectiveness, excellence, prosperity, wealth, love, power, and good digestion. Their book, they say, will save you from the time and struggle of reading any other books.

The effectiveness or workability of any plan, however, *comes from the learning struggle*. Through trial and error you learn what works and what doesn't work for you. The best self-improvement comes out of real life, everyday experiences, not from books or workshops that tell you *what to learn*.

Thus, my approach is to provide guidelines on *how to learn* good surviving, coping, and thriving skills. This is a book of *useful questions and practical guidelines, it is not a book of instructions*. It is a manual for discovering inborn abilities that no other human being can reveal to you. Only you can discover them. In the school of life the responsibility is on the learner, not the teacher.

What We Will Cover

Curiosity is one of the most important survivor qualities. Asking questions about how things work leads to practical understanding that can be transferred to new and unexpected situations. That is why **Chapter 2** shows how to manage your *learning about survivorship* by being curious about survivors.

Chapters 3 through 7 cover *how and why some people become better survivors than others*. These chapters show how a survivor personality emerges from ways of feeling, thinking, and acting that parents and teachers typically do not encourage in children.

Be forewarned that because I have spent many years teaching introductory psychology, most chapters contain an explanation of the psychological principles involved. Skip those parts if you only want the guidelines for handling a specific situation. Understanding the underlying principles, however, is best in the long run. If you understand how the psychological principles of cause and effect work, you can apply the principles to a wide variety of new, unexpected situations.

SELF-DEVELOPMENT SUGGESTIONS: At various places in the book you will come across a suggestion in an insert like this one. If you want to get the most out of the book, take time to do the suggested activity.

The biggest challenge for most people trying to cope with difficult situations is breaking free from inner prohibitions that act as *invisible emotional handicaps*. Most children are born with the inner motivation for developing a unique survivor style, but something happens to them during childhood that disrupts the natural process of self-motivated learning. The problem traces back to the way parents and teachers turn boys and girls into "good boys" and "good girls." This phenomenon is examined in **Chapter 8**.

The escalating pace of life has created numerous challenges facing many people today—too much pressure, too much change, negative people, angry people, and becoming unemployed. **Chapters 9 through 12** contain specific guidelines for handling difficult people and difficult situations in ways that makes you stronger. In each case the coping effort shows *how to thrive* by converting the difficulties into valuable personal growth.

What about life and death situations? **Chapters 13 through 16** offer insight into what others have done when thrown into the worst possible circumstances. While there is no prescription for survival in crises, disasters, and torturous conditions, we can *learn from what others have gone through*. The value in learning about many kinds of survival is that one person's way of surviving cancer, for example, may carry just the right clue for someone struggling with months of unemployment.

The best survivors are those who find a way to convert misfortune into good luck. **Chapter 17** explains why a *talent for serendipity* is one of the best overall indicators of a survivor personality, and how it can be developed.

There is no way of existing on this planet that does not have its drawbacks. **Chapter 18** lists some of the *difficulties survivors encounter* because they are survivors.

And lastly, during my study of survivors I stumbled onto something quite unexpected. **Chapter 19** describes how the *human race appears to be in a transformation* to its next level of development. Our increasingly unstable, more difficult world is breaking our society out of old, rigid ways of thinking and doing things. People are being forced by the cross currents of change, uncertainty, chaos, and unexpected adversities into a more complex level of adapting, coping, and thriving.

It is not essential that you agree with this last speculation, however. The purpose of this book is to show you what you can do when your life is disrupted, how you can gain strength from adversity, and how life's unexpected, unwanted, distressing, unfair experiences can lead to a better life for you.

CHAPTER TWO

LEARNING ABOUT SURVIVAL

The best way to learn about survival is to *talk* with survivors. Reading books and articles about survivors can be informative and inspiring, but published stories are almost always incomplete. Reports of survivor stories rarely include the person's self-talk during the ordeal, seldom include step-by-step descriptions of how they problem-solved situations, and may not report any actions that would upset the public.

Private interviews—off the record—will fill in missing details and give you a more complete understanding. To survive, the person may have done something they seldom mention, or would not want others to know. They may have done or said something funny that they rarely tell anyone.

For example, a Vietnam combat veteran, a former army officer, told me that leeches would attach to his legs when he took patrols through rice paddies and marshy areas. His practical solution to the leech problem was to write home and have his mother send him a large pair of women's pantyhose, the kind advertised as indestructible. These pantyhose worked so well at keeping the leeches off, that other soldiers would take him aside and privately ask if he could get a pair for them. He said he gave out several hundred pair of the pantyhose—always with discretion and an air of secrecy.

Most survivors have such stories. That is why, if you can arrange to meet and talk with people who have survived difficult experiences, you will gain more from this book.

The following questions will help you identify individuals to consider for interviews:

- Who have you heard about at work or in your community who has survived a major difficulty? Is this person someone who is happy and enjoys life despite their experience?
- Who, among the people you know, has referred to a bad experience in their past as one of the best things that ever happened?
- If you had to ask someone you know to help you through a survival situation, who would you choose?
- If your organization needed to put several of its best people on a highly important project, who do you hope would agree to take responsibility?

Prepare for your interview by writing down a few questions you want to ask. Toward the end ask what they learned from their experience or why it was valuable for them. You may want to ask "Is there one ability more important than others for survival?" Compare the answers you get with what I report.

NOTE: If the survivor you are going to interview has been through an extremely distressing experience, prepare yourself by reading the appendix titled "Guidelines for Listening to Survivors of Extreme Experiences."

Inquire about previous life experiences that may have prepared them for this—*and be ready for some surprises*. Psychiatrist E. James Anthony, for example, was curious about "children at high genetic risk for psychosis." He conducted a number of studies and, to his amazement, he says, he found that about ten percent of "these children with psychotic parents were not simply escaping from whatever genetic transmission destiny had in store for them, and not merely surviving the milieu of irrationality generated by psychotic parenting; they were apparently thriving under conditions that sophisticated observers judged to be highly detrimental to a child's psychosocial development and well-being."

Anthony discovered that these children were invulnerable to the hereditary factors and environmental conditions working against them. His studies showed them to be "good copers," resilient, self-confident, and creatively competent.

Anthony refers to his discovery of "invulnerable" children as "a serendipitous finding." The lesson here is this: resist making assumptions about survivors and realize that you don't know what you might discover unless you inquire for yourself.

From your interviews try to learn what it is about survivors that gives them the ability to know what to do, what not to do, how to handle unexpected developments, and how to get the right things done.

Do they talk to themselves when under pressure? Do they hold any goals in mind?

Let the person being interviewed talk about anything he or she happens to think of. Listen and absorb how this person thinks, feels, and acts. Listen to the kinds of questions they ask.

Here is a tip: To understand life's best survivors requires a new way of thinking about people, because *it isn't what a person is like, it is how a person interacts with situations that determines survival*. Allow the relationship between how this person does things and their being a survivor gradually unfold for you.

Lee Iacocca, for example, in writing about his time as president of the Ford Motor Company, says that he ate many business meals with Henry Ford, the Chief Executive Officer. Iacocca says "Henry's standard meal was a hamburger. He would rarely eat anything else." After ordering a hamburger Henry would usually complain that "no restaurant he had ever been to could make a hamburger the way he liked it—the way it was prepared in the company's executive dining room."

Iacocca was curious. One day when they were eating lunch in the executive dining room at company headquarters, he went into the kitchen to speak to the chef. He said "Henry really likes the way you make hamburgers. Can you show me how?"

"Sure" the chef said, "but you have to be a great chef to do it right, so watch me very carefully." The chef took an inch-thick New York strip steak out of the refrigerator, put it through the meat grinder, fashioned it into a patty, and slapped it onto the grill. The chef smiled and said "Amazing what you can cook up when you start with a five-dollar hunk of meat!"

This amusing, behind-the-scenes anecdote reveals that Lee Iacocca has a curious mind. Even while immersed in multi-million dollar corporate plans and projects, he took time to find out why this chef was the only one who could make a hamburger that Henry Ford liked.

Is there a relationship between Iacocca's curious nature and his ability, later, to bring the Chrysler corporation back from the brink of bankruptcy? I believe so. As you will see in the next chapter, one of my consistent findings about life's best survivors is that they have a playful curiosity. They love learning how things work.

CHAPTER THREE

PLAYFUL CURIOSITY: LEARNING WHAT NO ONE CAN TEACH

What does a toddler do when it isn't hungry, sleepy, or sick? Does it just sit and do nothing? No. A healthy child walks, crawls, and runs around getting into things. It opens cupboard doors, pulls out pans and bangs them. It gets into mother's purse. It takes toys apart. It puts small objects into its mouth to see what they taste and feel like. It plays with anything it can get its hands on.

To play is to learn—nature's way.

Learning How Things Work: Experimenting with Life

At meal time, when a baby waves her hand around and knocks her milk over, this is what Selma Fraiberg describes as "a young scientist replicating an experiment." The baby wants to see if once again the giant beings that control its life will move around, make noises, and make another container with white sloshy stuff appear.

Playing and experimenting are closely linked to human survival. Human infants are not born with the same ability to survive on their own as the young of other animals. Humans need more time to learn how to care for themselves than members of other species. The noteworthy principle here is that the more the young of a species are born ready to survive on their own, the less they can learn later in life.

Maria Montessori, internationally recognized as an outstanding educator of children, said that a child's playing "is effortful, and leads him to acquire the new powers which will be needed for his future."

Years ago Robert W. White explained that because "so little is innately provided" to humans, "much has to be learned about dealing with the environment...." What is called child's play, "Involves discovering the effects he can have on the environment and the effect the environment will have on him. To the extent that these results are preserved by learning, they build up an increased competence in dealing with the environment."

How Humans Learn What They Can Do

Each person's growth and development is influenced by three different kinds of learning. One is the inner, self-motivated, self-managed learning that comes directly from experience. It is the learning that results from the inborn urge to explore and play.

Another kind of learning occurs from imitating those around us. Through "modeling" we acquire the action patterns of others.

A third kind of learning is controlled and directed by others. Unfortunately, when teachers, parents, and other adults do too much training, instructing, and educating, the child is pulled away from his or her inborn capacity for self-managed learning. The adult efforts overpower and inhibit the child's capacity for self-managed learning. This is why some students show up in school and passively wait to be taught, why some employees show up at work and passively wait to be told what to do. That is how they were raised. They became conditioned to look to others for instructions on what to think, feel, and do.

Locking a child into a prescribed way of acting, thinking, feeling, and talking early in life may make things comfortable for the adults who are raising him or her, but the child then becomes like an animal born with predetermined behavioral patterns. It is blocked from self-managed learning and changing later in life. In a rapidly changing world, a person stuck in a fixed pattern is less able to adapt.

It is important to understand that the inborn predisposition to ask questions tends to be suppressed by adults, rather than encouraged. Think back to when you were a child. Were you praised for pestering your parents with questions? Did teachers thank you when you interrupted the lesson they were teaching with questions about something else? Probably not. Have you ever been to a high school commencement where a graduating senior was honored for being the best student in the class at asking questions? I've asked hundreds of audiences that question and no one has ever raised a hand.

In most homes and schools, asking questions is not viewed as a skill or talent to be cultivated, not nearly as much as learning answers. This, even though life's best survivors ask lots of questions—good questions, impudent questions, disruptive questions.

People with a survivor style are like curious, playful children who never "grow up." They retain from childhood their curiosity about what exists.

They love learning how things work. They may be delighted, laugh, and grab anyone nearby to show them. It is not unusual for a friend to be greeted with, "Guess what I just learned!" A woman once called to tell me, "I just found out why the afternoon TV shows are called soap operas! It's from the days when the programs for housewives were sponsored by the laundry soap companies! I never knew!"

Such people often approach something that attracts them in a playful way, because for them playfulness and learning how things work are closely linked. They enjoy playing with situations, people, and their own experiences.

The life-long child asks: "How does this work?" "What is that?" "What if I did such and such?" "What would happen if I acted in another way?" "What if I tried something different?"

Discovering Cause and Effect Relationships

Experimenting and playing show a person the relationship between what they did and what happened as a result. Having experienced this relationship, they may repeat the action to confirm that the same outcome occurs. Or they may try a variation to observe if the outcome changes.

Experimenting leads to first-hand knowledge of relationships between events. *If such and such is done, then* certain outcomes usually occur. *If*, for example, a boss tries to take credit for the crew working hard to meet a deadline, *then* the workers usually get even through the grapevine and the next time don't work as hard. Experimenting enables a person to see for himself or herself. To experiment is to learn from one's own experience.

Playful people putter, tinker, or just plain fool around. Robert Fulghum, for example, writes about how he likes sorting clothes when they come out of the dryer because "there's lots of static electricity, and you can hang socks all over your body and they will stick there." He says that once, when his wife discovered him covered with warm socks, she "gave me THAT LOOK. You can't always explain everything you do to everybody, you know."

Curiosity can lead a person to find out what they can get away with. When told about a certain rule, they may break it just to see what will happen. Sometimes they conduct secret experiments. Someone might have an affair, for example, just to find out what it is like.

Playful people may appear to be wasting their time, but their playing leads to learning about themselves and the world. Robert Fulghum proved this when he wrote *All I Really Need to Know I Learned in Kindergarten*, a book that jumped to the top of the best-seller list in the United States and remained there for many weeks.

Becoming Competent

Answers we discover for ourselves frequently work better than what others tell us. Life's best survivors are not especially bothered when what they see and think does not fit with the way that others think. They will experiment with different ideas or points of view to find out what works best. They seem less interested in *who* is right, they are more interested in connections between cause and effect. Furthermore, they continually seek information and new ideas that will explain how things work and how to make things work better.

The really competent people in every sphere of human activity are those individuals who go beyond their teachers. They learn what they are taught, may try imitating what someone else does well, and then continue to learn what no one else could teach them. In contrast, *people who follow instructions on how to be successful are seldom as successful as they could be.*

Think about several of the most capable people you know. Are they effective primarily because of a class they took or a training program they went through? No. Effectiveness, competence, skillfulness, and mastery result from self-motivated, self-managed learning.

Becoming Life Smart

The psychologists who created IQ tests ran into a problem. The average 17 or 18 year old could do as well *or better* on intelligence tests than could people 30 or 40 years old. Try as they would, psychologists could not construct an IQ test where adults got better scores than high school juniors and seniors.

In terms of a person's ability to handle life's challenges well, intelligence tests don't measure smartness. If the tests did, an uneducated taxi driver would get a higher score than a professor on how to survive on the streets of a big city. Having a high IQ is much different from being life smart. No recent graduate with a Masters in Business Administration could have assumed the presidency of Chrysler Corporation and brought it back from the brink of bankruptcy, as Lee Iacocca did. That took someone with years of experience.

How do people become smarter and smarter as the years go by? How is it that a person can get better and better decade after decade?

Getting smarter year after year comes from retaining a childlike, playful curiosity, from practicing the ability to be guided by feelings, and learning from experience. It comes from asking questions and searching for answers; from experimenting with life, even being willing to look foolish and make mistakes. Such an orientation to the world and to one's experiences enables a person to develop an increasingly accurate understanding of their world, and leads to increasingly better skills.

How to Learn From Experience

A specialist in vocational rehabilitation once said to me, "In the schools you go to as a child, you sit in classes where first you learn the lesson, then you take the test. In the school of life it is the opposite. First you take the test, then you learn the lesson."

He is right. The question is, how do you learn directly from experience? Here are some guidelines:

- You have some sort of planned or unplanned experience.
- If you are upset, express your feelings; clear your emotions.
- Reflect on the experience, replay it in your mind as an observer. Avoid explanations that either justify or condemn what happened. You don't learn when you rationalize, justify, or criticize what you have done.
- Describe the experience. Tell a friend; write about it in a journal.
- Ask what can be learned from the experience. If such a thing were to happen again, what would you do next time?
- Imagine yourself talking or acting in a more effective way next time.
- Rehearse doing it the way you desire.

Take some time to think about something difficult that you went through, such as a divorce or a distressing break-up with someone. By following the steps listed above you can learn about yourself. Trace back to early clues you ignored. Decide what to do and not do *the next time*. When you process experiences in this way, you will increase your self-confidence for handling similar situations better in the future.

Laughing Goes with Learning

Laughing about something learned is an excellent sign that valuable learning has occurred. Learning that results in personal growth is emotional as well as mental. The kind of learning associated with increasing life-competence happens in the body, not just in the mind.

Laughing as a reaction to learning means that healthy emotional learning is taking place. Insightful learning, especially about one's self, can be a delightful experience. It stays with you a long time—much longer than information you memorized for a class.

Playfulness and Laughing are Survival Skills

Captain Hawkeye Pierce, the character played by Alan Alda in the popular television series *M.A.S.H.*, was a good example of someone who used his playfulness for emotional survival. Hawkeye knew that as a M.A.S.H. (Mobile Army Surgical Hospital) surgeon, his primary responsibility was to use his medical skills with the sick and wounded. As a draftee who viewed the Korean War as an insanity, he maintained his emotional stability by playing with his circumstances.

In the midst of death and wasted lives he invented ways to laugh and play. He would break military rules, but would never violate his professional standards. When the "gung-ho" doctor, Major Frank Burns, would threaten Hawkeye, Hawkeye would usually laugh and find a way to embarrass the Major.

Life-competent people often do that—laugh at threats. They react like a martial arts master might respond to an attack by a child. And their amused laughing may be all it takes. They are so non-threatened, it is disarming.

Playing and laughing go together. Playing keeps the person in contact with what is happening around them. A playful spirit lets the person maintain an attitude of "this situation is my toy. I'll play with it as I wish." A friend of mine said she went to the hospital with one of her friends who had to have a breast removed because of a malignant tumor. When the woman was brought back from surgery and began to recover from the anesthesia my friend asked, "How are you?" The woman looked down at the bandages on her chest and said, "I'm all right, I still have 'vage.'"

"You what?" my friend asked.

"They took 'clea' but I still have 'vage,'" she said, laughing.

My friend told me, "I knew immediately that with a sense of humor like that, she was going to be fine."

Benefits of Self-Managed Learning

Curiosity, questions, playing, experimenting, and laughing are the way to learn valuable lessons and develop new abilities throughout your life. The benefits you gain from self-managed learning include being able to:

- look forward to the next incident with positive, even eager anticipation. People who dwell on unpleasant past experiences without learning from them enter similar situations ready to be victimized again.
- build self-confidence and become more willing to take risks. You know that you now have a better chance to handle things well, but if things do not work out, you will still gain by learning something useful.
- try out guidelines suggested by others to see how well they work for you. Then adapt and modify the guidelines to fit with your style, your situation, and your purposes.
- get better and better as the years go by. You are a constant learner in the school of life. You become more and more "life smart."
- be the first to adapt, or create a new way of doing something. You do not have to wait for others to solve problems and teach you the solutions.
- learn new ways to be employable or provide a new service or product in a shifting, changing, unstable world.

Learning is a way of life for life's best survivors. In a world where change is constant, learning is an *essential* survival skill. The ability to ask new questions, learn from experience, pick up useful methods from others, change, and adapt is linked with another survival skill—being flexible.

CHAPTER FOUR

FLEXIBILITY: AN ABSOLUTELY ESSENTIAL ABILITY

A former student of mine, a nurse named Gayle, brought a teenage girl named Rosyann to talk with me on a warm, sunny, Saturday afternoon. Gayle stayed outside while Rosyann sat on a large foot stool in my living room talking with me about being kidnapped by her father and spending almost eight years with him in California before being found and returned to her mother.

We talked for almost two hours. Rosyann told me about her sadness when she left her friends, how she handled coming back to live with a mother she barely remembered, and what it was like to come back to a small town in Oregon after living most of her life on the streets of large California cities.

When it was time for Rosyann to leave, she started to stand up but then paused. She said, "There's one thing that puzzles me..."

"What's that?" I asked.

She looked down and fiddled with her shoe. "I know I'm social," she said, keeping her head down. "I like being with people a lot. But sometimes I'm anti-social. I have to get away from people and don't want anyone near me."

She glanced up and scanned me to check my reaction. I sensed her caution. Here was a street-smart teenager taking a risk telling a shrink a secret about herself.

I had to think fast. "Good!" I said. "I'm glad to hear that! It means you are very mentally healthy!"

Her eyes lighted up. She broke into a big grin and said, "Wow! You mean I'm not schizy?"

"No. Just the opposite. You are more mentally healthy than most people. I'm really pleased to hear that you have both kinds of feelings."

"Whew," she said, letting out a big sigh. "I've worried about being a schizo."

"Not at all," I said as we stood up. "Good survivors like you have all kinds of opposite feelings. You'll notice more as you get older."

She grinned at me and shook my hand with both of hers.

As I watched Rosyann and Gayle walk away, with Rosyann gesturing and talking about our meeting, I thought to myself "Whew. I'm glad I had enough presence of mind to say the right thing."

Many times I don't think of what I should have said until sometime later, but this time I did. My years of experience had prepared me for this moment.

What was going on in the last exchange between Rosyann and myself? It had to do with my discovery that life's best survivors sometimes feel like misfits, and that a key source of their strength is viewed by some people as emotional instability.

Before I explain, take a few moments to check off the traits you possess and add any important ones not listed at the bottom. While much valuable information about survivorship comes from talking with others, many clues lie within you. Which of the following traits do you recognize in yourself?

_____	sensitive	_____	tough
_____	strong	_____	gentle
_____	cowardly	_____	courageous
_____	mature	_____	playful
_____	humorous	_____	serious
_____	distant	_____	friendly
_____	self-confident	_____	self-critical
_____	trusting	_____	cautious
_____	dependent	_____	independent
_____	impulsive	_____	well-organized
_____	happy	_____	discontent
_____	cooperative	_____	rebellious
_____	proud	_____	humble
_____	selfish	_____	unselfish
_____	involved	_____	detached

____	lazy	____	hard-working
____	logical	____	creative
____	calm	____	emotional
____	shy	____	bold
____	loving	____	angry
____	consistent	____	unpredictable
____	messy	____	neat
____	optimistic	____	pessimistic
____	_____	____	_____
____	_____	____	_____

The Basis for Survivor Flexibility

Survivors puzzled me at first. They are serious and humorous, hard-working *and* lazy, self-confident *and* self-critical. They are not one way *or* the other, they are *both* one way *and* the other.

This was a hard mental barrier to break through. Most tests of personality view a person as either one way or another, not both. *Psychology Today* magazine, for example, conducted a survey asking readers to indicate the qualities of an ideal male. The questionnaire listed pairs of qualities and asked readers to choose between them. It asked: "Is an ideal male extroverted *or* introverted? Critical *or* nonjudgmental? Always self-confident *or* self-doubting?" and so on. Surveys such as this force you to respond only to the choices they present. A form returned with "all of the above" or "it depends on the situation" written on it is viewed as invalid and thrown out.

Books are written describing people as being "optimists" *or* "pessimists," as type A personalities, *or* type B. Yet many survivors are both optimistic *and* pessimistic, hard working as well as lazy. How can a person be both one way and the opposite? What is the a relationship between being a survivor and having paradoxical personality traits?

When I ask survivors if there is any quality or trait that contributes most to being a survivor, they usually answer without hesitation. They say either "flexibility" or "adaptability."

That makes sense, but then I wondered, "How do you *do* flexibility? What makes mental and emotional flexibility possible?"

We find an answer in the writings of T.C. Schneirla, a scientist famous for his studies of animal behavior. After years of research he concluded that for any creature to survive it must have the ability to move toward or away from anything near it. The creature must be able to move toward food and safety or away from danger. Schneirla described the ability to approach as well as to withdraw as being a "biphasic pattern of adjustment."

Biphasic patterns of movement are possible for us because of opposing muscular systems in our bodies. We have control over our physical actions because flexor and extensor muscles work against each other. Our ability to move our hands and place them exactly where we want comes from having muscles in controlled opposition to each other.

This balanced oppositional control is like having a reverse gear in a car. Without it, the car gets stuck in places where forward progress is blocked. Balanced opposing forces are at work when we ride in an elevator. The elevator can be stopped where we choose because of the counter-balancing weight that hangs down in the shaft on the other side of a large pulley. Construction cranes, the tall ones, are another example of a counter-balanced system. A massive weight counter-balances the lifting arm.

Just as we can move our bodies in many different ways because of our opposing muscular systems, we can have contradictory emotions because the sympathetic and parasympathetic nervous systems work in controlled opposition. The parasympathetic nervous system enables us to respond with relaxed, peaceful contentment, while the sympathetic nervous system enables us to have a "fight or flight" reaction in other situations. These counter-balanced nervous systems give us a range of different reactions to different circumstances. Because we have two nervous systems working in controlled opposition, we can run toward something in joy or away in fear. Because we can do *both*, we have some choice over responding in one way *or* the other.

Mental and Emotional Flexibility

Physiological principles usually have counterparts in personality. What is true of the body is often reflected in the mind. The equivalent in personality of counter-balanced nervous systems and muscle systems are oppositional traits of personality—the paradoxical qualities—that enable an individual to respond in both one way and another.

Biphasic personality traits increase survivability by allowing a person to be one way or its opposite in any situation. To have biphasic traits is to be more adaptable rather than being "either one way or another." It is to be proud *and* humble, selfish *and* unselfish, cooperative *and* rebellious. The long-term AIDS survivors being followed by *Parade Magazine*, for example, are all seen as having "spirituality and irreverence."

Response Choices

Pairs of biphasic, paradoxical, or counter-balanced traits are essential to a survivor style because they give you choices about how to respond. Look back at the checklist. See how many *pairs* you checked off. The more pairs of traits you recognized in yourself, the more likely it is you have survivor qualities. If you added other items to the list, that's even better. The list is not meant to be complete. It never could be. The list is presented to demonstrate the biphasic principle.

People who hold up well in what I call "cross-fire" jobs usually have many paradoxical qualities. A cross-fire job is one in which you are caught between many people making demands on you, while you remain open to handle emergencies and surprises. On a daily basis you must handle strong pressure from many different sources. To do this well requires being able to respond in different ways to different pressures, reacting creatively to each person, event, and circumstance.

To respond in the same fixed way to all situations reduces your ability to adapt to changing events and circumstances. The ability to respond in a variety of ways gives you choices and makes you much more adaptable—even though having biphasic qualities may feel strange.

One of the readers of the first draft of this book, a former head nurse in a hospital psychiatric unit, said in her written response to this section, "I appreciate the paradoxes—it's good to know it's not weird. I used to puzzle myself about being conservative-liberal, generous-stingy, serious-silly, quiet-gregarious, interested-bored, involved-aloof...."

Why is Flexibility So Vital?

The important thing is having many such pairs of traits, what ever they may be. The longer the list of pairs of paradoxical or biphasic traits descriptive of you, the more complex you are, and, typically, the better you are at successfully dealing with any situation that develops. The people involved in my survivor personality research project agree. These real-life survivors say that more than any other strengths, being flexible and adaptable are central to a survivor personality.

Why does having a complex personality increase your survival chances? Having a variety of available responses is crucial when handling variable, unpredictable, chaotic, or changing conditions. Successful people in any profession know that it is better to have many possible responses than to be limited to a few.

Adaptation is the key to survival in nature as well as among people. Two biologists, in commenting upon successful patterns of survival in the animal and plant kingdom, wrote:

> The plants and animals that survive in their progeny are the lucky ones. They hold the winning combination: a successful pattern fitting one place and time, and the ability to modify the pattern in the correct direction as fast as the environment changes. The luckiest of all have an adaptation ready, still unused, as though prepared for alteration that has not yet come. They gain a head start in the altered world. Less fortunate are those whose pattern limits them to a single situation. They vanish forever....

The One Way Mistake

If you look at someone who does not handle life well it is often because this person always thinks, feels, or acts in only one way and would never consider the opposite. Many people are so taken with the idea of being self-starters, for example, they lose sight of the need for the counter-balancing skill of being a self-stopper.

A person who can only act in one way has little self-control, and therefore must be kept in check by external forces. Have you ever known a person who didn't know when to stop talking? Such a person keeps going and will continue until the listener finally terminates the conversation. The less a person can consciously do the opposite of their favored pattern, the more helpless and subject to external forces they are.

Many college students act as though they only have two choices about studying. At one extreme is the "bookworm" who only stops studying when the library closes and time runs out. At the other extreme is the "party animal" who sees studying as an unpleasant interference to parties, dates, campus activities, beach and ski trips, athletics, and other socializing. Students who get the most out of college, however, are able to both study and play. They study effectively, stop, and then have time for other important activities.

A Vietnam veteran working as a salesman asked me about why he would have periods of many days when he was not able to make himself do anything. He said when he was on a roll he could go for many hours. His water filtering device was such a hot item he could go into a cocktail lounge at 1 AM and sell units to the bartender and several customers. But he'd sometimes run out of energy and couldn't leave his apartment for days.

The problem? He didn't know how to stop himself, take a break, and rest. His body would protect itself and take control at a level stronger than his will power.

In my workshops for managers I often have participants get into small groups and list the qualities of the "best" and the "worst" manager they've ever known. When the groups read their lists, it is clear that an effective manager is very flexible. Such a person adapts well. Excellent managers are both people oriented and focused on results. They are both friendly and task oriented.

General H. Norman Schwartzkopf many counter-balanced qualities during the Gulf War. He was described as being both "more demanding and more trusting than was customary." He was "very concerned about the life of each individual" under his command *and* very focused on destroying the enemy. He was in firm control *and* gave his field commanders great latitude in decisions. A French general said "He appeared to be something of a brute. But then people realized that…he was extraordinarily sensitive."

Both Tough and Gentle

Abraham Maslow, an outstanding teacher and known as one of the founders of humanistic psychology, could be tough when he had to. After the World War II, a number of foreign students enrolled in Maslow's classes at the university where he taught. He found that many of these students had authoritarian ideas about what a teacher should be like. He said:

> The authoritarian students preferred, required and functioned best under an authoritarian teacher. Any other kind of teacher was regarded as not quite a real teacher and was taken advantage of, couldn't keep control, etc. The correct thing to do with authoritarians is to take them realistically for the bastards they are and then behave toward them as if they were bastards. That is the only realistic way to treat bastards. If one smiles at them and assumes that trusting them and giving them the key to the pantry is going to reform them suddenly, then all that will happen is that the silver will get stolen and, also, they will become contemptuous of the "weak" Americans, whom they see as spineless, stupid, unmasculine sheep to be taken advantage of. I have found whenever I ran across authoritarian students, that the best thing for me to do was to break their backs immediately; that is, to affirm my authority immediately, to make them jump, even to clout them on the head in some way that would show very clearly who is the boss in the situation. Once this was accepted, *then* and only then could I become slowly an American and teach them that it is possible for a boss, a strong man, a

man with a fist, to be kind, gentle, permissive, trusting, and so on.

It is impressive to note that Maslow was comfortable acting in a way contrary to what he would have preferred to do. He did what was necessary to teach students with different values. He did not experience the use of authoritarian methods as inconsistent with his dedication to the development of human potential. He saw it as one of many teaching methods. He understood that the *effect* of an action is what counts, not the social correctness of the action.

Does this revelation mean that Maslow was secretly "an authoritarian?" Not at all. It means that he could be both permissive and autocratic to achieve his teaching goals. The method he chose to use depended on his reading of the students in his classes.

Thinking of People as Nouns or Labels Impairs Thinking

To understand the nature of life's best survivors, it is important to examine a second barrier to understanding people. The first barrier is the tendency to think in *either/or* terms rather than *both/and* about personality qualities. The second barrier is to use nouns or labels when describing people. We are living in a world where it is common to hear people called "optimists," "liberals," "extroverts," "alcoholics," "schizophrenics," and "co-dependents." Turning people into such nouns, however, is a child's way of thinking. It limits understanding. It strips away what is unique about an individual and restricts the mind of the beholder to inaccurate generalizations.

A more effective way to view people, and one that allows better understanding, is to assume that every person is more complex, more unpredictable, and more unique than any label. To assume a person is more complex than any theory opens up the possibility that a person can be both one way and the opposite.

An advantage of *describing* what people feel, think, and do instead of labelling them with a noun, is that when a person changes from one situation to the next, we can be comfortable with his or her shift instead of getting upset when they don't stay consistent with the way we have categorized them.

Developing Emotional Flexibility

If being more emotionally flexible seems desirable, a practical question to ask is: "*How* does a person develop a range of biphasic or paradoxical abilities so important to flexibility and thus to survival?"

For adults, the course of development depends on one's starting point. When a person dislikes conflict, his or her developmental path is to learn how to be firm and confrontive.

For the person with a non-confronting and permissive style, it takes years to become more firm and direct with people. Why years? Because deciding to add a counter-balancing opposite ability can be very difficult. To be more effective, one must consider acting in ways he or she has ridiculed or condemned others for.

To a person raised to avoid conflict, people who fight and are forceful are perceived in negative ways, as not all right as human beings. If one is forceful and competitive, then conciliatory people are seen as wishy-washy scaredy-cats.

Such one-way perceptions, regardless of content, are examples of polarized thinking in which we feel repugnance for our disliked opposites, for our anti-models. Thus, when an unassertive person is urged to learn assertiveness, their reaction is usually, "I couldn't do that." Why not? Because to be assertive is to act like one of those despised authoritarians.

Similarly, when a fear-inducing, tough-acting person is told to be more appreciative or to be a good listener, the inner reaction is, "No." For an autocratic person to listen well, express sincere appreciation, and be influenced by subordinates would be to act like a despised, weak, gutless person who gets shoved around.

Emotional aversions for one's anti-models run deep in the subconscious and are not easy to overcome. It takes a combination of frustration and courage to become more paradoxical—frustration when one's habitual approach doesn't work well in some situations, and courage to see that what one has previously despised in others may in fact have some merit. We will go into this process in more depth in chapters 8 to 11.

It Isn't Easy Being Multi-Faceted

Moshe Feldenkrais, the renowned originator of body-movement techniques that foster better physical integration, observed that "reversibility is the mark of voluntary movement." An action that cannot be reversed is involuntary. It is reflexive and is not under conscious control. If you always respond one way and never in the opposite way, you will sometimes be helpless to stop yourself from reflexively doing or saying something that you later regret.

Many people with opposing or counter-balanced personality traits, however, have been told that there is something wrong with them. People with rigid thinking can't handle complex people very well, and often view them as defective. Women, in general, have more paradoxical traits than men, and have more survivor personality traits. Yet for many decades American businessmen kept women out of executive positions. They claimed that women were too unpredictable and unstable to be trusted with real responsibility. When a woman in a responsible position proved to be highly effective, men would often see her as "different, not like most women." Either that, or they would decide she was more like a man than a woman.

SOME QUESTIONS TO REFLECT ON:

Is being paradoxical something you are comfortable with?

When you were growing up were you allowed to be inconsistent in your thoughts, feelings, and actions?

Were you instructed to think, act, or feel in one way only? What happened when you had inconsistent feelings or thoughts?

When someone you know acts, feels, or thinks in contradictory ways, do you stay relaxed? Tolerant of their inconsistencies?

From your knowledge of survivors can you verify the paradoxical or biphasic traits in them?

In some instances the biggest struggle for people with paradoxical traits is that they suspect that the negative views others have of them are accurate. One summer I was invited to repeat a workshop I had done the year before at a health education conference. The subject was "Indicators of Psychological Fitness." When we started, I asked for comments from the group about why they chose to attend my session. A woman in her mid-twenties stood up and said, " Last year I learned in your workshop that I wasn't schizophrenic. You helped me see that it is *healthy*, not sick, to have two opposite feelings." She stared into my eyes and with a feeling of deep appreciation added "I needed that. You'll never know how much I needed that. I came back to learn more this year."

Another time, after I finished giving a talk about the survivor personality to a professional women's group, one of the women took me aside. She shook my hand with vigor and said, "Thank you! You've cured me of my mental illness."

"How did I do that," I asked, "in a thirty minute talk?"

"I've been trying to hide what I believed was a mild case of schizophrenia. Tonight you showed me that I'm not mentally ill, I'm mentally healthy. I'm *cured* thanks to you!"

I remembered what these two women had said to me when I saw Rosyann glance at me to see how I would react to her disclosure about being both social and anti-social. That is how I knew what she was concerned about.

We come now to some new questions. What is the difference between a person whose unpredictable, paradoxical nature makes him or her effective and a person whose unpredictable nature makes him or her an energy drain on others? How can a person be both unpredictable and effective?

What gives playful, paradoxical people a sense of direction? How do they know what to do in situations they have never faced before? And how do they know what *not* to do? How do they know what would not work? If having paradoxical traits provides options about ways to respond, what determines choices?

Answers to these questions can be found by examining a strong motive in life's best survivors. It is the need to have things work well.

CHAPTER FIVE

NEEDING TO HAVE THINGS WORK WELL: THE SYNERGY IMPERATIVE

You can own a powerful personal computer, but if you do not know how to use either it or the software, of what value is it? Similarly, you can have all sorts of abilities and personality traits, but if you do not know how to use them well, what good are they?

When you hire someone for a repair job, you expect the person to have a variety of tools. But it is even more important that the person be good at trouble-shooting and fixing things. This is illustrated in the story about the man who fixed a plumbing problem by hitting a pipe with a hammer. His bill for $100 was itemized: "$5 for hitting the pipe—$95 for knowing where to hit."

People best at surviving are good trouble-shooters. They are handy. They are inventive. They often come up with amazingly easy solutions to difficult problems because they want and need for things to work smoothly and easily.

Needing For Things to Work Well

The need to have things work well explains much about why some people are better survivors than others. The need for good synergy is a central, motivational principle in their lives. This motivation helps explain why, when necessary, they can succeed with a situation that no other person has ever faced.

Their sense of knowing when things are working well and when they are not doesn't, however, come from following rules or memorized techniques. It comes from an inner awareness or feeling about nature's laws and principles. They have a good sense of what Mihaly Csikszentmihalyi calls "flow." When things are not working well, these people do not complain; instead, they feel an urge to make improvements.

Joanne Hazel, the psychiatric nurse who wrote to me about her paradoxical nature, is an excellent example of how a person with a survivor personality takes action when things are not working well. When her two daughters were in elementary school, she decided to retire, stay home, and be "mom." Joanne's daughters were both very bright, and she wanted to participate in their growth and development.

Joanne became frustrated, however, when she found that the school district did not have a good program for the talented and gifted. Her meetings with teachers, principals, and superintendents got little positive results. She talked with parents of other gifted children but could not get much support from them.

Did she give up? No. Did she write letters complaining about the school district? No. She campaigned, got elected to the school board, and a short while later became its chairman. (Her choice of titles.)

Her position gave her authority over the school district superintendent. It also gave access to the State Superintendent of Education and to many resources. Through her efforts, within several years her school district had an excellent program for talented and gifted students.

When things are working well, life's best survivors drift into the background. They may appear to be lazy or inattentive, but this is not the case. Their attitude is typically, "Why should a person spend energy when it isn't necessary?" They do not have to show off their strengths. They do not need to manipulate events to try to claim credit for successes. When things are working well, they understand that intruding into the actions of others would be disruptive and energy-draining. Interference for the purpose of personal gain causes a waste of human energy, time, and resources, and that disturbs people who like to have things work well.

At work they may seem to have soft, easy jobs. That is often true. Their jobs are easier because they worked very hard to get things that way. Somehow when they are around, meetings run more smoothly, people work together better, equipment runs efficiently, and work is done more pleasantly.

Synergistic Humans

Ruth Benedict, a cultural anthropologist, is credited as the first person to use "synergy" as a way to describe human activities. She used the term to explain differences she had observed in the quality of life between cultures. She said:

> I shall need a term for the gamut, a gamut that runs from one pole, where any act or skill that advantages the individual at the same time advantages the group, to the other pole, where every act that advantages the individual is at the expense of others. I shall call this gamut *Synergy*, the old term used in medicine and theology to mean combined action. In medicine it means the combined action of nerve centers, muscles, mental activities, remedies, which by combining produced a result greater than the run of their separate actions.
>
> I shall speak of cultures with low synergy, where the social structure provides for acts that are mutually opposed and counteracted and of cultures with high synergy, where it provides for acts that are mutually reinforcing.

Benedict's ideas are applicable to groups as well as cultures. High synergy exists in an organization when minimum effort results in cooperative and effective action. Low synergy exists when it takes excessive effort to get even routine matters done.

Trying to get something done in a low synergy organization is like driving a heavily loaded truck and trailer down the highway with all the tires flat. Working in a high synergy organization is like cruising along the highway in a well-tuned sports car.

High synergy provides greater results than could be predicted from looking at the individual members. With an athletic team, for example, a group of *good* players can combine their talents to create an *outstanding* team. The synergy comes from the positive interaction of the different individuals to create results beyond what each person could produce alone. Low synergy produces less in the way of results than would be predicted from looking at the individuals, as is the case of certain all-star games where a group of individual superstars do not play well together as a team. *Synergy is an outcome of how individuals interact.*

An example from agriculture might be useful. Research into the effects of different fertilizers has led to some fascinating results. In certain experiments, for example, phosphates increased crop yield in a test plot by 10%. Nitrogen in a nearby plot increased crop yield 15%. But when the phosphates and nitrogen were spread together over a third test plot, the crop yield increased not by 25% (the sum of the effects of the two fertilizers individually) but by 40%. The extra 15% gained by using the two together is a positive interaction effect—that's synergy.

The Synergistic Personality

People with survivor personalities might just as easily be described as having synergistic personalities. The term used for describing the way the person interacts with the world is not important. It is the same personality style.

The link between survivorship and being a competent, synergistic human is as follows—when things are working well, such a person:

- sits back and let things run themselves.
- expends much less energy than people do who are struggling.
- has chunks of optional time for being curious about the early signs of new developments.
- devotes attention to the little things that count.
- spots early indications of potential trouble and takes action to prevent it.
- works on future happenings so that when they occur things fall into place easily.
- is more relaxed, feels better and enjoys "working" as good exercise.
- puts high quality time and energy into emergency developments without having other basic matters interrupted.
- responds to an emergency or crisis with an attitudinal reflex of both expecting and needing for things to work out well.

The Need for Good Synergy is a Selfish Need

One of the most noticeable qualities of people in whom the synergy motive is strong is that they volunteer to help out when there is trouble. People with survivor personalities are foul-weather friends. When things are working well, they may drift about seeming to be uninvolved; but when there is trouble, they show up, ready to lend a hand or take charge. Why? Why do they make themselves available in times of difficulty?

They do this, in part, to deal with bothersome feelings. When other people are in pain, they feel it. When life is going well for others, they feel better. Their effort to eliminate a problem or reduce pain or distress in another person has a selfish component.

Thus the need for good synergy is as selfish a motive as any other. The more well integrated a person's thoughts, feelings, and actions become, the more the person needs a pleasantly functioning world in which to live. Being exposed to discordant, unstabilizing, energy-draining, disruptive people or conditions can be painful. Thus, working to make things better for others is not an unselfish activity. Many years ago the Spanish philosopher Jose Ortega y Gassett wrote, "Contrary to what is usually thought, it is the man of excellence, and not the common man, who lives in essential servitude."

The need for good synergy in people with the survivor style is paradoxical, because *they make world a better place for themselves by devoting themselves to making it better for others.* They are both selfish and unselfish at the same time. They have resolved what Abraham Maslow called the "selfish-unselfish dichotomy." They have achieved a state of selfish altruism.

Maslow stated:

> In highly developed, psychiatrically healthy people, self-actualizing people, whichever you choose to call them, you will find, if you try to rate them, that they are extraordinarily unselfish in some ways, and yet also they are extraordinarily selfish in other ways....
>
> High synergy from this point of view can represent a transcending of the dichotomizing, a fusion of the opposites into a single concept.

In other words, synergistic individuals act unselfishly for selfish reasons. They must, for their own good, take action to improve discordant, energy-draining situations. Actions that result in things working better lead to feelings of satisfaction and may be profitable as well. The two are not incompatible.

Anthony Robbins, famous for his inspirational speeches, books, and tapes, says "I am totally and completely focused on delivering to my audience what they really need." He says, "If you are totally sincere, if you really care about people, and give your all, you succeed." At the age of 32, Robbins has had the immeasurable satisfaction of helping thousands of people discover how to improve their lives, and his businesses currently bring in over $50 million a year. He benefits both emotionally *and* financially.

Low and High Synergy Managers

The synergy concept provides a useful framework for explaining the difference between the effects obtained by those managers with a controlling, autocratic style and the effects obtained by managers who successfully run flatter organizations where teams of people work autonomously. *Low synergy* results when a boss sets the goals, uses threats, interferes with the way people work, exerts tight control, tries to solve all the problems, and attempts to make people perform well. *High synergy* results when a manager has everyone participate in goal setting and problem solving, and leaves people *free* to do their jobs as they think best.

Some Disadvantages

Is being synergistic the ideal? Not always. No way of operating is without its problems. There can be a disadvantage from being too synergistic. A former college classmate who had become a department manager in a state agency told me about a problem she had. She was too effective! She had developed her people so well and had her department running with such efficiency that when some upper level administrators or politicians came through and saw such a relaxed, friendly group of workers, they decided her department did not have enough work to do.

She had documented that her department produced more work per person, of higher quality, with fewer errors and at a faster rate than any comparable unit. But still she heard about upper level grumbling that her people did not *appear* to be working hard enough. She later resigned, took her retirement money, and opened a pasta place in a mall. More fun for her but a great loss to the state.

A more serious difficulty is sometimes encountered by people who uncover dishonesty, unethical, or illegal activities in their organizations and report their findings to upper management. They expect management to take corrective action, but in many instances the "whistle-blower" becomes targeted as a trouble-maker. Articles and books have documented hundreds of cases in recent times, in which dedicated, conscientious, loyal employees have been harassed, demoted, sent for psychiatric evaluations, transferred to meaningless positions, or fired as a consequence of speaking out about something wrong in their organizations.

Thus it is that efforts to correct something not working well can, as with the other survivor traits, create problems with others. (The term "whistle-blower" is defined and discussed in more depth in the chapter on "Surviving Being a Survivor.")

Becoming More Synergistic

If developing synergistic skills is seen as desirable, how can a person do that? Here are some suggestions:

- Approach new, unstable, or difficult situations with this question in mind: "How can I interact with this so that things turn out well for everyone?"
- Look for creative ways to help make things work well. Ask others "What would you like to have happen?" Volunteer in a way that lets others refuse your help if they wish.
- Recognize and admit that you have selfish reasons for wanting to have things to work well for others.
- Don't tell anyone that what you are doing is only for their own good.
- Search for ways to convert difficulties into an opportunity to make things better.

- Realize that it is all right to be successful at what you do and paid well for it *without working hard!*
- Learn the difference between *allowing* things to work well and trying to *make* things work well.
- Ask yourself what you are uniquely qualified to do in your current life situation that would be useful for others. Jim Dycr, who retired after 31 years as a state employee, founded a foster parents association. He did this he says, "because I know how bureaucracy works. I know how to interpret rules for the good of people."

Developing synergistic skills requires being open to new experiences and wanting to take effective action. As you gain more experience, the habit of looking for ways to have things turn out well becomes reflexive. When potential problems or emergencies arise, you react almost instinctively as you absorb information and act to meet the challenge at hand.

The need for good synergy helps explain why there is no good personality test for the survivor personality. The best assessment of a synergistic person is to look at how well things are working around him or her. The survivor personality traits are determined more by the situation than by fixed inner habits. That is why they show so many paradoxical qualities.

Wanting and needing to have things work well for everyone means that you must have an accurate understanding of what other people feel and think. This brings us to a uniquely human survival skill. That skill is empathy.

CHAPTER SIX

EMPATHY IS A SURVIVAL SKILL

Ken Donaldson was held in a Florida mental hospital against his will for fifteen years. During that time he received no treatment for his alleged mental illness. Ken wrote letters to many authorities and many attorneys asking for help. He got it. Ken, who attributes his obstinate nature to his Pennsylvania Dutch heritage, was the first mental patient in the nation to win a Supreme Court case against a mental hospital and the physician in charge.

I wrote to Ken after the verdict was announced and asked him, "Why were you successful in getting help, while so many thousands of other mental inmates have their letters ignored?"

He wrote back, "Always I had borne in mind how the recipient would look at the letter."

Empathy Development

Ken had empathy for the readers of his letters. Empathy is the ability to accurately comprehend what another human thinks and feels. It is a special form of learning. Being curious, letting in new information, and experiencing feelings enable you to develop an accurate, empathic sense of what is going on in others.

It is important to distinguish empathy from sympathy. A sympathetic reaction occurs when one person *takes on* the same feelings as another. When a friend experiences a personal loss and you cry with them, that is sympathy. To empathize is to understand and recognize the feelings of someone else without *having* the same feelings.

A student nurse received a letter from her boyfriend at another college. He wrote to say that since they were going to schools in different cities, she should go ahead and date other guys. He said he wanted to date some girls on his campus and he would see her during the next holiday. She felt devastated. She thought they had an understanding about being unofficially engaged.

As she sat on her bed crying, her roommate came in and asked what was wrong. The girl showed her roommate the letter and the roommate started crying too. A friend from across the hall came in, found out what had happened, and started crying with them. Both friends had a sympathetic reaction, they felt the student nurse's pain as their own.

Later that afternoon the student nurse had to report for duty on a hospital ward. The head nurse took one look at her and called for a nursing instructor. The instructor then took the student into a conference room to find out what had happened. When the instructor learned about the boy friend's letter, however, she did not burst into tears. She was supportive, remained calm, and asked questions to determine if the student could do her ward assignments without upsetting patients with her personal problem. The nursing instructor had empathy for the student nurse.

The best survivors "read," and accurately comprehend what is going on in others. The empathic reading of another person comes from asking such questions as: "How does that person feel?" "What does she see?" "What might he do?" "How does that person experience me?" These questions open one's mind to understand another person's needs, fears, views, and so on.

To understand the relationship between empathy and survival, look at people who have been under the domination, threat, or control of others. Women, for example, have managed to survive for centuries in a world where men have held official power. As a result, women have learned how to understand men much better than men have ever understood women. In my seminars, male supervisors and managers have asked, "How do you understand women?" Never once, however, has a woman asked, "How do you understand men?"

Whenever someone is subjected to the control of others, it is essential for them to understand the people in power. In most organizations, workers understand the managers much better than the managers understand the workers. This explains why workers who do not want to cooperate with change have so many ways of thwarting management's efforts.

Empathy explains one of the differences between being intelligent and being "street-wise." People in control often do not live by the same laws and rules they force on others. Because their safety is a "given," they don't need to be as tuned in to the information that empathy would reveal to them.

Empathy Avoidance is Not Smart

Many administrators and executives confuse sympathy with empathy. Fearful of the consequences of having a *sympathetic* reaction to workers, they avoid exposure to worker's views and feelings. As a consequence, they are often at a strategic disadvantage, and are stunned when they are outsmarted by groups who understand them better than they understand themselves. When people in authority take steps to avoid understanding those who are trying to appeal to them, the power of their authority erodes.

In the competition between corporations for sales and market position, the side that best understands the customer has the advantage. As competition has heated up in recent years, sales organizations have had to give up trying to make customers buy the way they want to sell. They have had to sell the way customers want to buy. To survive, they have had to develop more empathy for people they wanted as customers.

In a book on survival, the famous historian Arnold Toynbee, at the age of 82, gave this response to a question asking him what advice he would give to the younger generation:

> Try, I would say, above all, to remain compassionate-minded and generous-minded; try to remain capable of entering into other people's states of mind…even when you strongly disagree with them. Try to put yourselves in the other people's place and see why they hold these opinions or do these things with which you so strongly disagree.

> **TRY THIS:** To run an empathy check on yourself, imagine that you are someone who works or lives with you. See how accurately you can describe that person's experience of working or living with you. If you are willing to take a risk, try asking the person you have in mind to listen to your impressions. Ask for feedback on how accurate you are.

Empathy Increases Learning

The ability to absorb what another person thinks and feels lets you benefit from their learning experiences. Studying successful people lets their learning become your learning. Most people who master their profession start with a strong motivation to learn from the best. Companies wanting to succeed with a new product study other successful companies to avoid having "to reinvent the wheel."

Pattern Empathy

Playful curiosity and experimenting with life gradually lead to a practical understanding of the relationships between cause and effect, and to a sense of patterns, a recognition of what "goes with" what. This in turn leads to a comprehension of the effects of little things, and the ability to predict what will get the best results in the time available.

Pattern empathy—the comprehension of a complex pattern of dynamic relationships—is well developed in people who are excellent at what they do. A person with pattern empathy can walk through a building and immediately sense how well everything is going.

A good football quarterback must have pattern empathy. The quarterback must be able to read the movements of all other players on the field, and have a sense of what they will do. Such instantaneous comprehension requires taking into account both the present play as well as all the previous plays.

To be successful, an orchestra conductor, must have pattern empathy. He or she must detect among dozens of instruments the one player who is a little slow, soft, or off-key and bring that person into line with the entire group.

Playwrights, too, must have excellent pattern empathy. In his plays, William Shakespeare demonstrated an astonishing understanding of the differences among individual personality patterns as well as how different personalities interact with various situations and in combination.

Good Timing

The best indicator that a person is fully in touch with a situation, is aware of all the little things that count, and has a feeling for the rhythm and movement of the patterns, is a good sense of timing. The best musicians, lovers, comedians, therapists, public speakers, teachers, group leaders, parents, stage performers, salespeople, and military leaders all have good timing. They know what to do and when to do it.

Less Information is Needed

With experience, one is able to sense certain patterns from only a few bits of information. For example, a woman asking for my opinion about her husband said that he drank quite a bit, but she felt she could live with that. Her real concern, she admitted, hesitantly, was that she feared her husband was homosexual.

I asked "why do you think he might be homosexual?" She said he never enjoyed spending time alone with her. Almost every evening and weekend he would find an excuse to go off with his male friends. She had listened to his phone calls on the extension phone, and had asked around about his activities, so she was sure there was not another woman in his life. She was bewildered and wanted to understand her husband better.

I asked, "Is he the youngest brother from a family of brothers?" Her eyes widened. "Yes," she said.

"And you probably grew up without any brothers," I said.

She was dumbfounded. She stammered, "How did you know?"

"Because you've been describing the actions of a younger brother from a family of brothers," I said, "and are bewildered about this male in a way that is typical of a woman who grew up without brothers. Not only that, but you grew up being the center of attention."

She smiled and said, "I was an only child. My parents called me 'little princess.'"

We talked about various things she might do to help save their marriage, but when I later heard that she filed for divorce, I was not surprised. A younger brother from a family of brothers marrying an only daughter or a youngest daughter from a family of sisters is a very difficult match to make work. According to research done by Walter Toman, both are used to being "the baby" and neither has much understanding of what it is like to live with the opposite sex. Because I knew the pattern, it was not difficult to spot it from the little information she gave me.

Spotting Early Clues

People with pattern empathy have a better chance of being survivors because they do not need many clues to see what is coming. With minimal clues, they can spot a pattern and pick up on "hidden agendas."

Norman Locke, a friend of mine who owns a coin company, has done very well over the years because he is "street-smart." His survival in business comes in part from his talent for quickly knowing which people are honest and which ones are trying to cheat him with a confidence game.

Norm says con artists often make a comment or joke about what they are up to because they feel contempt for their "pigeons." When you ignore that clue, the con artists feel justified in taking you for all they can get.

"Another clue to a con," he says, "is when I feel confused about the deal they offer me. I'm an intelligent person, and if I can't understand what they're talking about, I know they're trying to hide something. Most people want to look smart, and won't admit they don't understand. I admit I can't follow the scheme and say, 'I must be too dumb.'"

A third clue, he says, "is when someone uses the technique of getting lots of 'yesses' from you. They ask questions that have you saying 'yes" and then they try to rush you into saying 'yes' to a deal before you feel ready." Once Norm has spotted a con game, he usually toys with the person and rates him or her on how good he or she is at trying to pull it off.

TRY THIS: To develop your skill at spotting early clues, think back to a situation in your life that turned out poorly. Think of a job, a relationship with someone, or a business deal that went sour. It is quite likely that you had early clues or warnings about this eventual development, but you chose to ignore the clues. You did not want to believe the early indications about what might eventually happen. Follow the steps for self-managed learning and decide what you will do "the next time."

Experience with life helps you learn the difference between imaginary fears and early clues that are legitimate warnings of eventual developments. Experience helps you develop a keen eye for the details that make you a competent professional.

As with other survivor qualities, empathy is a useful ability to acquire but it can also cause problems. At times there is a price to be paid.

A Disadvantage to Empathy

Women taking action to divorce physically abusive husbands often need lots of emotional help because they know their husbands will feel extreme distress. Compassionate executives forced by economic conditions to discharge workers and close plants often experience great emotional turmoil.

An empathic person needs courage when taking an action that others will be very upset about. Empathy for other people's feelings requires a counter-balancing quality of toughness to not be controlled by their pain. The same sensitivity that leads to having things working well, also exposes one to distress in others.

Empathy in Deadly Situations

Having empathy does not necessarily mean being nice. Rather, empathy enhances the ability to survive and to survive well in deadly situations. The United States military forces have prevailed in most wars because our commanders have understood the enemy better than their commanders have understood us. During World War II, General Eisenhower knew that Adolph Hitler followed the advice of astrologers. Eisenhower had astrologers work up charts to see what advice Hitler would be getting from his astrologers, and used that information advantageously in timing the invasion at Normandy.

General Douglas MacArthur was commander of operations in the Pacific Theater in WW II. From the time he was a cadet at West Point, he had recognized the Japanese threat, and had studied the way they thought and worked. MacArthur knew that the Japanese were superior at organizing thousands of trained followers to succeed in predictable situations. MacArthur knew that he had fewer troops, less well trained, and they were fighting with old equipment. Yet he was able to defeat the Japanese because he understood them better than they understood Americans.

How so? MacArthur's winning strategy was to by-pass the Japanese strongholds and throw the troops on both sides into unexpected situations. He knew that in unexpected situations the "Yankee ingenuity" of our front line troops would prevail over the regimented Japanese way of thinking—and he was right.

After the Gulf War, General Schwartzkopf stated in his press briefing that during the early phases, "We let Saddam Hussein think we were going to fight the war he was prepared to fight." Our military leaders were extraordinarily successful because they understood Saddam Hussein's thinking better than he did theirs.

Playfulness, good synergy, and empathy all have emotional components. The emotional dimension is subtle, often irrational and defies logic. The next survival components are elusive, yet important to understand, because intuition, creativity, and imagination often play a role in survival and in the ability to convert misfortune into good luck.

CHAPTER 7

THE SURVIVOR'S EDGE: INTUITION, CREATIVITY, IMAGINATION

What is Intuition?

Row Rowan, author of *The Intuitive Manager*, says "Intuition is knowledge gained without rational thought." Some people have unexpected intuitive flashes, others develop intuition by practicing. In either case, intuition is the ability to be receptive to information coming from one's subconscious mind.

The vice-president of a chain of theaters told me about an experience he had while having dinner at the home of one of his newer theater managers. The manager was in his mid-twenties, married, and had two children. He was a charming, talkative host.

The vice-president said that part way through the evening he got an emotional flash, "This guy is ripping me off!" He continued to be a pleasant guest for the rest of the evening, but the next day he had the corporate controller search through all the theater's records for signs of embezzlement. "Sure enough," he said, "we found it. The manager had discovered a way to skim money out of snack bar sales."

Intuition is a Survival Skill

Feelings are the most frequent source of information from the subconscious mind. People who consciously monitor their feelings have a more accurate comprehension of what is happening than people who specialize in being only logical or rational. Psychologist Weston Agor, founder of the Global Intuition Network, says that intuitive managers "function best in crises or situations of rapid change." He reports that "Without exception, top managers in every organization differ significantly in their ability to use intuition to make decisions on the job."

De-mystifying Intuition

Your brain has much more subconscious information swirling through it than can ever be grasped by your conscious mind. Did you know that one of the main functions of the nervous system is to block conscious awareness of all the stimulations hitting our sense receptors? A stimulus must reach a certain level of intensity before you become conscious of it. Notice in the illustration how conscious awareness remains at zero until a stimulus builds up to an intensity strong enough to reach the threshold level, called the "limen," by psychologists.

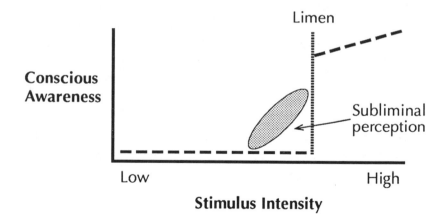

STIMULUS AWARENESS

Limen is the Latin word for threshold. Research into the way thresholds work has revealed that the body begins to respond in detectable ways when stimulation is at a level just below this threshold or *sub*-limen." Instruments like the ones used in "lie detector" tests show that the person's body is registering awareness of the stimulus input even when the person has no conscious awareness if it. The facts are indisputable, *every person is physiologically equipped for subliminal perception.*

Subliminal research included the famous experiment in which a message to buy popcorn was flashed on a motion picture screen during the movie. To the dismay of the theater owner, what was subliminal for the average person was *above* the threshold for the more sensitive person. Some people complained and demanded their money back. But when the message was speeded up to make it undetectable to the most sensitive people, it was below the subliminal level for most the audience. The small increase in popcorn sales did not cover the cost of the equipment.

This research revealed that people have different threshold levels; that a person's sensitivity can change depending on their alertness and physical condition. *Some people are better survivors than others in part because their perceptual thresholds are lower.* Awareness of subtle changes in their bodies gives them useful information from subliminal perceptions.

With practice anyone can improve their ability to consciously access subliminal information. For example, when someone is talking to you, his or her tone of voice and body language may be out of harmony with the words they say. Once you notice your body is responding to something, even though you are not consciously aware of what that something is, you can lower your threshold of consciousness by relaxing and being curious about what is happening. Part of the survivor orientation is to be sensitive to subtle inner feelings.

TRY THIS: The next time you are in a meeting or are discussing an important matter with someone you do not know well, scan your body once in awhile. A tight stomach, breathing fast, a hand clenched into a fist under the table, a bouncing foot, or a slight feeling of agitation may be clues that something is not quite right. These signals can be set off by anything—a person's tone of voice, something not said, a group's quietness, a forced laugh, someone's quick glance—anything that does not fit.

Once alerted, the survivor orientation is to remain focused on discovering what is up. The person attentive to subliminal cues may continue on as though unsuspecting, like the vice-president of the theater chain, or may stop and ask questions about what is going on. In either case, the person remains alert and curious about what is really occurring.

Letting Your Body Protect You

Many survivors report taking action without understanding why, or having logical reasons for what they do. For example, a student nurse told me about the following incident:

> Last spring, I was sitting at the bus stop down on Sixth Avenue, waiting for the 3:40 bus. It is the one I usually take up the hill to school. The sun was shining for a change, and I sat on the bench enjoying it. The warmth felt good after days of cold, wet rain.
>
> I still do not know why, but I stood up and walked back to stand near the wall of the store on the corner. I didn't want to be in the shade, I wanted to be in the sun, but I stood there anyway. Something was holding me there, it felt weird.
>
> A few seconds later, a car came racing up the hill. It was a teenage boy in a souped-up car with big tires. When he came around the corner, he lost control and skidded across the street. The car bounced up over the curb and smashed into the bench right where I had been sitting. I couldn't believe it! I still do not know why I got up and moved.

Is this an example of ESP (Extra Sensory Perception)? Probably not. At some level of consciousness her past observations would have taught her that cars coming up the hill around that corner often have difficulty making the turn. Since she moved only a few seconds before the car hit, it is possible that in her relaxed state she subliminally detected the sound of the speeding car when it was several blocks away.

Many people are survivors because they have acted on hunches even though the actions didn't make sense. Also, when no logical solution is apparent, an individual with the survivor orientation can operate on the basis of feeling alone.

People with intuitive abilities allow themselves to feel whatever they feel. They let themselves react to people and situations as children do. They do not apologize for their feelings. They may decide, for practical reasons, not to *reveal* a feeling, but that is different from allowing rational thinking to squelch intuitive impressions.

Led By an Inner Guide

Some people survive because of an exceptional ability to trust subconscious directions. Winston Churchill, a former Prime Minister of England, was a war correspondent when he was a young man. While in South Africa covering the Boer War, the war between South Africa and England, he was captured and sent to prison in Pretoria. One night he managed to escape. Emerging from the prison, though, his problems were far from over. As he describes it, he walked out alone into the night and assessed his situation. Three hundred miles stretched between him and safety. He could not speak Dutch or Kaffir, the two languages of the region. The town was picketed, the country patrolled, the trains searched, and the roads guarded. He wondered, "How am I to get food or direction?"

Winston managed to get aboard a train car carrying empty coal sacks and rode most of the night. Before dawn he jumped out of the train and hid. During that day, he says, "I prayed long and earnestly for help and guidance." When night came, he struggled on foot over rough country, through scrub bushes, bogs, swamps, and streams. Drenched, exhausted, weak from hunger, and almost drained of hope, he saw some distant lights and struggled toward them. He approached but then hesitated. What to do?

"Suddenly, without the slightest reason," he said, "all my doubts disappeared. It was certainly by no process of logic that they were dispelled. I just felt quite clear that I would go. I had sometimes, in former years, held a 'Planchette' pencil and written while others touched my wrist or hand. I acted in exactly the same unconscious manner now."

He walked to the distant fires and came to a coal mine with some houses grouped around it. He had heard that a few English residents were still in the country to keep the mines working. Had he been led to one of these?

He approached a two-story stone house and knocked on the door. The man who answered was English. Winston identified himself and told of his escape. The man said, "Thank God you have come here! It is the only house for 20 miles where you would not have been handed over. But we are all British here, and we will see you through."

Winston was kept in a chamber at the bottom of the mine for several days. An escape route was arranged and he eventually made it to freedom.

People with a survivor style follow hunches and use intuition as a natural part of their lives. Here's how Robert Godfrey describes Outward Bound program instructors:

> The best Outward Bound instructors are those who have the ability to trust their own intuitive responses most faithfully and to act on the basis of those intuitions. It is a real act of personal faith for the instructor to respond to his or her own convictions in the Outward Bound situation, where both the physical and psychological welfare of the participants are at stake.

Godfrey says that when he watched one particular instructor, Anne, deal with a challenge:

> She doesn't mentally reach for the instructor's handbook. She doesn't flip through the rules and regulations and guidelines to find what somebody else says she should do to deal with the situation. What she does do—and you can literally see her do it—is first and foremost *compose herself*. Her eyes just ever so slightly glaze over, not the glaze of a daydreamer, but the intent expression of a person looking inward, a deliberate closing out of peripheral and distracting stimuli....It is clear that her attention is temporarily inward, checking out her internal response to what is happening.

Developing Intuition

Developing intuition as a reliable, trustworthy skill is a matter of practice. First, begin with deciding to be more receptive to subconscious, irrational information even if it is contrary to what seems logical.

Second, plan ahead. The next time you are in a situation where there is some confusion or you have to make a decision without all the facts, detach your conscious mind from the external action. Relax. Stop inner conversations. Scan internally for answers to the silent questions "What am I feeling? How am I reacting? What is happening? What would be the best action to take?"

Third, keep a record. Whether you acted on your impression or not, write down what thoughts, impressions, or feelings you got from your subconscious. Then check later to see how accurate you were.

Just observe your results. Do not try too hard, and avoid criticizing yourself if you are off target or make an inaccurate call. Critical, judgemental thinking *suppresses intuition*.

Programming Intuitive Actions

Some people program their subconscious minds to provide guidance for survival. Harold Sherman, author of *How to Make E.S.P. Work for You* and other similar books, relates this personal account. He states that after several close calls in New York traffic, he decided to instruct his mind to always give him guidance. He says he put himself into a relaxed, meditative state and instructed his subconscious "In the event I should be faced with an accident, to instantly, by impulse, do the right thing to protect myself."

Some months later he was riding in a cab when he said he received a strong urge to move immediately to the other side: "I had no sooner done this than the cab driver shot across Fifth Avenue going against the lights! In that instant, I saw we were going to be hit by an old sedan, which subsequently was found to have been filled with lead pipes."

"My first impulse," Sherman says, "was to grab the strap which hung beside the car door and to brace myself for the coming impact, but as I took hold of it an inner voice commanded, *'Let go of that strap!'* From that moment on, something inside me took over, causing me to put my arms across my face and head and double up my knees to protect my body."

The cab was hit broadside with such force that it was hurled through the air, landed on its roof and turned over twice before coming to rest. Sherman says that when he was lifted from the cab, spectators were amazed that anyone could have come out of that taxi alive. Later, when interviewed by an insurance adjuster, Sherman learned that he had instinctively done the right thing. The adjuster explained that most passengers in accidents grab for the straps. This makes their bodies rigid, and, as a result, they suffer broken bones, head and internal injuries.

Many such examples make it clear that intuition is not a random, mysterious human experience. It is a useful ability that can be developed and cultivated like any other.

What Did That Dream Mean?

The most direct access to the subconscious mind is through dreams. When we fall asleep all rational, logical, orderly thinking is relaxed. Our brains take a break from doing what we want and do what *they* want. Research has proven that every person dreams at night and that dreaming is essential to maintaining an integrated personality.

Our dreams contain information about what is happening in our lives, our bodies, and the world around us. The problem is that the language of dreams takes time to learn and understand. Still, for the person who is receptive to subconscious information, curiosity about what a dream might have meant often leads to fascinating insights.

Some dreams are so strong and so obvious it takes no special effort to understand what they mean. Others take some work. The starting point is to develop the habit of asking, during the first moments of awakening, what did I dream last night? Then observe what you recall. For remembering later, it can be useful to tag the dream with a key word or phrase that identifies the dream.

If you want to examine it for it's meaning, write the dream down as soon as you get a chance . Then ask "What did this dream mean? Why this dream rather than another?" To make sense of what seems to be non-sense ask "What is my feeling about this? Is this feeling similar to any situation in my life?"

When you practice remembering dreams you improve your intuition skills and your ability to catch creative solutions that swim by in your thinking like fish in a river.

Creativity is a Survival Skill

Creativity comes from the skillful use of sub-conscious processes. Intuition is a matter of listening to the subconscious; creativity is a matter of putting the subconscious to work.

A practical definition of creativity is that it is an unusual idea or action that works right. In difficult or dangerous situations, survival solutions and actions must often be creative.

E. James Anthony, the psychiatrist known for his studies of "invulnerable" children, reports that all resilient children show a high degree of either "constructive competence or creative competence." He says that constructive competence "is a fairly practical, concrete, down-to-earth approach to tasks and problem solving." On the other hand, a child with "creative competence may take flight from reality and investigate in novel ways, the less tangible but no less important facets of a problem."

Marcia Sinetar believes that "creative problem solving is the prerequisite skill for successful 21st century living." She says that because our world is now "characterized by constant, major, simultaneous change," the most important, essential ability for humans to develop is that of "creative adaptation."

Here is an example of a creative way of adapting to a difficult situation that includes playfulness, empathy for others, and being oriented to having things work out well. A specialist with a large electronics company told me that one year the company had a serious loss of revenue. The executives sent orders to all departments to lay off 20 percent of their employees. His job was put on the list.

Most of the long time employees felt outraged. Severance pay and outplacement help did not keep morale from dropping. He sat back and looked at the situation from the company's point of view. He saw that he had specialized skills essential to the completion of an important new product. He heard that a few consultants would be hired for essential work. He went to the company's employment office, presented them with his qualifications for being a consultant to his old department and was given the contract to replace himself.

He said that after a year the company determined it would save money by hiring him instead of paying his consultant's fees. He laughed and said, "I went from being an employee to consultant to employee and stayed at the same desk the entire time!"

TRY THIS: Creativity comes from an ability to see unusual connections, find unusual ways to combine things, and make remote associations. The following items are patterned after a test of creativity developed by psychologist Sarnoff Mednick:

Find a word that these three words have in common:

stool   powder   ball

The answer is "foot"—foot stool, foot powder, football. Now find the connecting word for each set of these three words (the answers are in the Chapter Notes and References):

blue	cake	cottage
made	cuff	left
motion	poke	down
wood	liquor	luck
key	wall	precious

The ability to invent a workable solution to a problem comes from wanting to find a good solution, thinking independently, and stepping outside the boundaries of old perceptions, explanations, and responses. Creativity comes from being able to imagine something that is new and different and yet has the right ingredients. It means being able to allow one's subconscious mind to come up with an unusual solution to the challenge at hand.

Research by psychologists shows that creative people, original thinkers, have what is called a "perceptual" or observing way of looking at the world around them. In contrast, people lowest in creativity have what is called a "judgmental" or dogmatic style of contact with the world.

The observing, perceptual person experiences the world with a mind that is silent. He or she is open-minded or, if you will, "open-brained." This person absorbs information about how things work just for the sake of knowing. Then, if a problem develops and a solution is called for, the person has a wide range of information to draw upon.

The judgmental style is revealed in such statements as, "Don't bother me with facts, my mind is already made up." People with this style react emotionally and judge people and situations quickly. They label others as "perverts," "weirdos," and such.

Fast judgements shut the mind to information that could contradict prejudices. Psychologists describe this mental reaction as "premature perceptual closure." It's a kind of thinking incompatible with creativity. One cannot be creative if facts, details, and information have never been absorbed in the first place.

Try to imagine the world as experienced by people who differ this much in how they react to what their minds are exposed to:

Observing Person:

accepts	neutral	rejects

Judgmental Person:

accepts	neutral	rejects

The person who has a wide zone of acceptance and a wide neutral zone is an observing person. This individual is curious about the world, learns about people, and enjoys exploring and bumping into new things. There is not much that this person encounters that leads to a negative opinion or a judgment.

An observing person may read a book or see a thought-provoking film and then, when asked for an opinion, state "I don't have any opinion, I'm still thinking about it." When asked, "Was it a good book or a bad book?" the observing person might say something like, "I'm just trying to absorb it."

How to Brainstorm

Brainstorming is a way to speed up creative thinking about a specific challenge or problem. Alex Osborne, originator of this famous technique, emphasized that critical evaluation of ideas must be suspended during the idea gathering phase. Judgemental thinking inhibits the expression or even the thinking of delightful new ideas. The brainstorming process is to pick a problem to be solved or a challenge to be handled well. Then...

- Take time away from other distractions to make a long list of wild, playful, weird, crazy, uncensored ideas. A good indicator that this is going well—bursts of laughter, groans, and an excited, rapid flow of ideas.
- A rule to be enforced is that during the idea gathering phase there is to be no criticizing, ruling out, or declaring an idea to be impossible or impractical.
- Ideally, no evaluation of ideas or suggestions should take place the same day. More ideas will come along during the evening and the next morning.
- After the list is finished, then use critical reasoning to select the two or three of the best possibilities to evaluate.

Studies of the brainstorming process show that great ideas often come after a period of wild, outrageous, funny suggestions. In other words, a terrific new idea cannot be reached by going in a logical, straight-line way from where you are to where it is.

Imagination is a Survival Skill

A retired friend of mine, professor Howard Stephenson, wrote a book many years ago about people who were successful at finding employment during the devastating economic depression in the 1930s. He said that the successful job seekers, the ones who did not have a brother-in-law who could hire them to sweep out the storeroom, "all had imagination."

The imagination of most survivors is well developed. When asked, "Would you say you have an active imagination?" Those who identify themselves as having survivor personalities say "yes" or "very." On my survey questionnaire, some added such comments as:

- "Unbelievable, and daydream—have done so all my life—do it to the point of not hearing what is around me—it's deeper than daydream, though—it is beyond conscious thought and I did it even as a child."
- "Active is a conservative term."
- "Yes, a dreamer—love to arrange and set up for work and play in my mind."
- "Some days too active."

Imagination has many dimensions. It is a bridge between the conscious and the subconscious mind. It may be a fantasy place to go to have fun. It may be passive daydreaming. It may be an active and purposeful mental activity in which you brainstorm or interview yourself using a question-and-answer dialogue.

Active Imagining

There is another aspect to imagination that often plays a role in having things turn out well. It is the ability to consciously hold an image in mind, repeat it over and over, and have things to turn out as imagined. This practice is emphasized by all teachers of the power of prayer and the power of positive thinking. For example, Emile Coué, originator of the saying "Day by day, in every way, I am getting better and better," explained that it is "the *education of the imagination* that must be sought for."

Maxwell Maltz, a plastic surgeon, discovered that the expectations his patients repeated in their imaginations about the effects of the surgery, had a far more powerful effect on their lives afterward than the surgery itself. The principle here is consistent with an observation made to me by a minister. He said "I wish I could make several members of my congregation understand that constantly worrying about something that might happen is the same as praying for it to happen."

What this all means is that your imagination and expectations can work for you or against you. Some people are so creative with their fears about horrible things that might happen, they become paranoid.

Intuition, creativity, and imagination are abilities developed and used by life's best survivors. These abilities give a person an advantage in new, challenging, or dangerous situations. The starting point is counting on the subconscious mind to help out by providing useful information, signaling alerts to problems, and offering creative solutions. Having a paradoxical nature allows almost any thought, feeling or action to be available and gives a person exceptional flexibility. Playfulness and self-confidence lead to risk taking, experimenting, rapid learning, and making quick corrections. Empathy lets a person comprehend what others think and feel, and adapt to their needs. And all of this is organized and directed by the commitment to find a way to have things work well for everyone .

Interfering With Nature's Plan

Unfortunately, many children are not allowed to develop a survivor style. When I am asked what can be done to teach children how to be survivors, my answer is to point out that most children are born with the inner potentials but that these potentials seldom fully develop because of interference from adults. Children are trained to stop asking questions and learn what they are told. They are taught to have some feelings and not others. Many times their intuitions are negated or invalidated.

It is as if the original equipment comes from the manufacturer with a factory installed software program designed to constantly upgrade itself as it is used. But well-intentioned parents and teachers who believe they have to train children to feel, think, and act in certain ways, interfere with the installed program. They freeze it up so it never develops beyond a primitive level.

As a result, many adults live their entire lives trying to act like "good" boys and girls. What they were taught to be like *decreases* their survivor chances in today's world. The next chapter shows how and why.

CHAPTER EIGHT

THE "GOOD CHILD" HANDICAP

A man wearing a dark blue suit walked up to me during the social hour before his professional group's dinner meeting. He introduced himself and said "You're a psychologist, what can I do to stop my three-year-old daughter from being selfish?"

"In what way is she selfish?" I asked.

"Last Saturday," he said, "some friends came over to our home for the afternoon. They brought their little boy. She didn't want him to play with some of her toys. We told her to share the toys and not be selfish but she still tried to hold on to her favorites. She cried and got upset when we made her hand them to him."

"What's wrong," I asked, "with her not wanting to let another child play with her favorite toys?"

"That's selfish!" He said. "We don't want her to be selfish when she grows up."

Most parents want their children to grow up to be decent, well-liked, and responsible. They do not want their children to turn out "bad." But efforts that create a "good child," unfortunately, often produce in an adult who is not able cope well with life. Further, such a person is usually an energy draining "pain" for others to live and work with.

The biggest barrier to developing a survivor personality comes from having been raised to be a "good" person. For example, in my workshops when I describe the benefits of paradoxical traits such as selfish-unselfishness or pessimistic-optimism, some people shake their heads and say they can be one way but not the opposite. They resist the idea that being paradoxical might be a source of strength for them. Why? Their resistance stems from inner prohibitions that their well-intentioned parents trained into them when they were children.

TRY THIS: Before reading about inner prohibitions that become emotional handicaps in adulthood, take time to list specific statements a child hears when parents give it "good" boy or girl instructions....

The basis for most "good child" messages comes from what parents do *not* want their children to become. Everyone knows about people who cause problems and drain energy from others by:

- complaining all the time
- hurting others
- acting in highly selfish way
- lying, cheating, and stealing
- feeling and acting superior to everyone else
- refusing to cooperate

Parents who raise children to not be "bad," erroneously think they must prohibit all traces of bad ways of feeling, thinking, and acting. They use "bad" people as anti-models and try to raise their children to be the opposite.

Parents such as the man who asked me how to stop his daughter from being selfish, are using prohibitionist logic. During the prohibitionist era in the United States in the 1920s, people wanting to eliminate the evils of alcohol from society succeeded in getting laws passed that prohibited the production, sale, and consumption of alcohol. Their reasoning was that prohibiting alcohol would eliminate all the problems it causes. In a similar fashion, parents believe that a good child is one who is:

- not negative
- not angry
- not selfish
- not rebellious
- not self-centered or prideful
- not dishonest

When parents and other adults raising a child dwell on what a good child *is not*, these are the sorts of "good boy/good girl" messages a child hears:

- Don't talk back.
- Be good.
- Hang up your clothes.
- Don't hit.
- Share with others.
- Stop complaining.
- Don't cry.
- Don't be stuck-up.
- Don't be selfish.
- Don't pick your nose.
- Be polite.
- Stop pouting.
- Don't whine.
- Don't fight.
- Tell the truth.
- Smile.
- Stop asking questions.
- Don't be angry.
- Don't chew with your mouth open.

The prohibitions appear as "don'ts." The don'ts are often accompanied by statements of what a good child *should* feel, think, and do. It is as though there is rule book for thoughts and feelings that each generation feels compelled to pass on to the next.

Because perception always requires contrasts, most parents point out to their children what bad boys and girls are like. The following list is typical of the "bad child" messages a child hears. "Bad kids":

- fight
- are dirty
- cheat
- skip school
- cause trouble
- argue
- wet their pants
- smoke
- break things
- are noisy
- swear
- sass back
- lie
- steal
- are selfish
- do not obey their parents
- play doctor and nurse
- drink, do drugs

Children hear these statements about what a "good" boy or girl shouldn't do, and learn that it is extremely important to cooperate in trying to be good and not to be bad. To be "good" means to receive love, hugs, acceptance, and candy from others. To be "bad" means to be punished, spanked, rejected, scolded, and sent to your room without dessert. Thus, in order to please their parents and receive much needed love and acceptance, most children try very hard to be good and not bad. But there is a serious flaw in the outcome. *The person raised to be good and not bad is emotionally handicapped outside of a structured, unchanging environment.*

A Testimonial from a Former P.O.W.

The "good child" syndrome is so pervasive in our society that it prevents most people from coping well with rapid change, unexpected difficulties, and extreme crises. When Bill Garleb, an ex-prisoner-of-war, read an early description of the "good-child" pattern, he immediately wrote me:

> My need to comment is so strong I could not pass it up. When I went to parochial school, as a child, if you changed your mind and could see the other side of something, they accused you of being inconsistent, or "thinking like a woman." In other words, they programmed you to be polarized and one-sided, the opposite of what a survivor personality needs to be to cope. I am overjoyed that I have learned that being biphasic is good. I like myself better now. It is important to note that, although I was trained and programmed as a child not to use biphasic traits, when my survival was threatened, I relied on basic, inborn traits and ignored conditioning.

To survive as an adult, Garleb had to go against how he was raised. His experience is not unusual among survivors.

A Child's Personality Theory

Hearing adults talk about "bad" boys and girls and "good" boys and girls fits with a child's way of thinking. It is a personality theory a child can relate to because children's emotional reactions control how they perceive others. Children usually view people in a global way, as being *all good* and someone to be trusted, or *all bad* and someone to be feared.

One Halloween I went over to my sister's house to take my four-year-old niece, Cheryl, trick-or-treating. Cheryl wore a witch's costume with a black, pointed hat and an ugly mask on her face that kept slipping down. We started down the block with Cheryl dragging her shopping bag behind her on the cement. She seemed to know exactly where she wanted to go, so I followed behind. She went to one house with the porch light on, then she went across the street to a large house. From there she went about four houses down the street, and after that around the corner to another house.

I stopped her and asked, "Why are you only going to a few houses? Why aren't you stopping at all of the houses with their lights on?" She said, in a matter-of-fact way, "I go where the nice ladies live." I crouched down on my heels and said to her, "On Halloween you can go up to any house that has a porch light on and they will give you candy or other good things."

At first she wasn't convinced it was a good idea to go up to just any house. But when I talked to her some more, and since it was her uncle urging her to go ahead and she would get much more candy that way, she agreed to do as I urged.

As we continued up the street, she stopped at most of the houses with lights on. But here and there she would scurry past a well-lit porch and head for the next house. The third time this happened I motioned to her back to me and said, "Cheryl, come here." I crouched down near the front walk of the house she had just gone by and waited for her as she walked slowly back to me.

I patted her on the back and asked, "Why didn't you go to this house?"

Her eyes grew big and with an impish smile she stated what should have been obvious to her uncle. She declared, "A witch lives there!" Then she turned and walked rapidly to the next house—with one glance over her shoulder to see if I was going to let her get away with that.

In some cases beliefs about people being either "good" or "bad" become so deeply ingrained during childhood, the person continues thinking the same way in adult life. Many adults live their entire lives attempting to behave like a "good child." And, just as Prohibition created serious social problems in the 1920s, children raised with inner prohibitions cause many problems for others.

Even at the age of 43 they still think and act like the child they were conditioned to be at age 5.

Still Behaving

In their relationships they give lots of clues about how good they are. Some typical actions of a "good" child trying to function in an adult body are as follows. They:

- smile when upset.
- rarely let you know they are angry at you.
- seldom make selfish requests.
- point out your faults, saying "I'm only telling you for your own good."
- give "should" instructions to others.
- get upset with you and then say "You really hurt me."
- smile and compliment people to their faces but say critical things behind their backs.
- alert and warn others about "bad" people.
- cannot accept compliments easily or agree they are good at something.
- when confronted about something hurtful they said, they emphasize their good intentions by saying, "But I meant well."
- fear being regarded as hurtful, tough, selfish, insensitive, or uncaring.

The irony is that they were raised from childhood to be emotional liars. They had to lie about their emotions; it was what their parents demanded of them. Rather than being allowed to be emotionally honest, they had to learn to present the "right" emotions and not the "wrong" ones.

As a result, they come across as two-faced. Such a person can be sitting in the lunch room at work gossiping about you to several co-workers. The person will be extremely critical of your character and your motives. If you should walk in, however, this person will turn to you, smile, and perhaps compliment you on the sweater you are wearing. Their conversation will be polite and sweet—until you leave, that is.

The "good child" will not express criticism directly. In group meetings they will smile and agree with the boss. When asked to express a contrary opinion, they are unable to do so. As soon as the meeting is over, however, they let loose.

For example, a friend told me about a woman in her church who, over a period of months, called up members of the congregation, asking them to agree with her that the minister was incompetent and not capable of doing his job. She stirred up unrest and oriented people toward fault-finding. If someone said, "Perhaps you're right," she took that as strong support for her position. Finally, the responsible members of the church held a meeting with her and the minister present. They asked her to tell the minister what her complaints were. She smiled and said he was doing a fine job. She would not speak out or state in a face-to-face meeting what she had been telling everybody on the phone. Later, after the meeting was over, she resumed her old habits.

Self-Deceptive Selfishness

Instead of making open requests, a person with the "good child" syndrome hints at what they want, hoping you will volunteer to do what they have in mind. At work a conversation with them might go something like this:

The person notices you are leaving for another part of the building and says, "If you feel like it, would you bring me the envelope from accounting, if you go by there?"

You say: *"I wasn't going that way, but I'll get it if you want me to."*

"Oh, no, I wouldn't want you to go out of your way for me."

"I will if you want me to. It wouldn't be any trouble."

"Not if you have to go out of your way. I can walk over on my break."

"Look, I'll go by accounting and get the envelope for you, all right?"

"Only if you feel like it."

Appeals to get them to ask for what they want, or to admit to selfish desires will have very little effect. Although they act in selfish ways, they cannot allow awareness of their selfishness into their consciousness. This helps explain why they must reassure themselves that you do not think they are selfish and why they feel the need to explain their motives to you even when you have not asked.

"Good children" must make sure you do not have the wrong impression about them. To admit to selfish or angry feelings would be to act like their anti-model—a "bad" person. The "good" person fears being seen as a selfish, angry, insensitive, rebellious, tough, negative, stuck-up, talking-back "bad" person. The frame of reference for being a good person is to avoid doing what bad people do.

The Energy Draining Effect

Here is why these "good" people drain energy out of others and are such a "pain" to live and work with:

- **They do not give you useful feedback.** Even when you ask them to express their feelings directly to you instead of talking behind your back, they won't. While it may be obvious to you that they feel angry or upset, they often cannot admit that they are. If they do admit to being upset, they have a victim reaction. They blame you for causing them to have the unhappy feelings they experience. If you were supposed to telephone and did not, you may be told, "You really hurt me when you didn't call."

- **They are self-deceptive.** They believe their efforts to help others are completely unselfish. For example, when a woman asked me for advice on how to get her husband to stop being so negative, I asked, "Why are you working so hard to change him?"

  "It's for his own good," she said. "He would be so much happier."

  The nature of the "good" person's self-deception is such that they can act in ways harmful to you, while truly believing they are doing so for your own good. The combination of sweetness in your presence, destructive criticism behind your back, and a belief that their actions are for your own good is behind the statement, "With friends like these, who needs enemies?"

- **Their efforts to make others have only good feelings about them, often cause the opposite reaction to occur**—such as when they try to force you to eat some candy or cake. Then, when they sense some irritation or dislike, they work even harder to get the reassurances from others that they need. Their efforts then cause stronger negative reactions, which leads to them trying harder—and so on. Instead of doing something different when their actions do not work, they do more of what elicited the negative reaction in the first place. The pity of it all is that they have not learned they would be more likeable if they stopped trying so hard to be liked.

- **There is a hidden threat under their efforts to make you see them as "good."** If you react negatively to their ways of trying to control what others think and feel about them, they may decide you are a "bad" person and punish you. The dynamic is this: *Victims need victimizers; victimizers deserve to be punished.* This is why you run the risk of becoming a target for their destructive gossip and emotional abuse if you do not let them coerce you into expressing only those feelings for them that they need to hear.

- **They avoid empathy.** They become slippery when you try to discuss an upsetting incident with them. In their way of thinking, some things they say don't count. They may send you reeling with a sudden accusation. After thinking about the incident you see how much they misunderstood. You may bring up the incident, ready to discuss it, but they say "I don't remember saying that" or they give themselves a quick excuse. They judge themselves by their intentions, not by how they affect others.

- **They have mastered the art of being emotionally fragile.** No matter how carefully you try to find a way to get them to listen, have empathy, or observe themselves, they will find a way to become upset. Then they try to make you feel guilty for upsetting them.

  In work settings this individual is very difficult to give a performance evaluation to. Almost any effort to talk about doing better work, or getting along better with others, or being more direct in making requests triggers a defensive reaction. A "good" person may say, "Why are you picking on me? I'm not a bad person. Why don't you criticize Sheila? She's worse than I am." Their reaction to your effort to make things better is to make you feel guilty for bringing up the subject of how they might improve.

- **The "good person" cannot distinguish between constructive and destructive criticism.** They react to unpleasant feedback as though it is destructive and has a harmful intent. They believe that if you really care for them you *will not confront them* about their upsetting actions. That is much different from a person with a survivor style who believes that if you care for them you *will confront them* about their upsetting actions. The consequence is that they learn very little from experience. That is why a "good" person remains at the emotional level of a child throughout life.
- **They feel unloved and unappreciated.** Even though you give them lots of love and attention, they experience very little. They are like a person standing under a waterfall yelling "I am thirsty!" Some typical statements: "After all I've done for them..." and "They'll feel sorry when I'm gone."
- **They are self-made martyrs.** First they blame you for their suffering, then they forgive you for all the hurt and pain you have caused them. As incredible as it may seem, the "good child" feels emotionally and morally superior to you.
- **Confronting them makes things worse.** If you get fed up and confront them about their victim style they will have a victim reaction much worse than you've seen before. They cannot handle a confrontation about what they do because *the victim style is the best that they can manage.* As with any child, they have almost no capacity for self-observation or for conscious choices about thinking, feeling, or acting in different ways.

Thus it is that the "good child" syndrome is antithetical to the survivor style. Such a person does not learn from experience, suppresses paradoxical traits, avoids empathy, and has a desynergistic effect on others. Although they mean well, this not a person you want to have in charge of something important.

Protecting Yourself

There is nothing "bad," of course, about a person who tries to control others by getting upset. The question is, what can one do to be less vulnerable and less drained by someone who does this?

One possibility is to accept the situation as it is. Decide to play "Let's Pretend" and just do it.

Another option is to view the situation as a learning opportunity for yourself. What is to be learned? For one thing, you can stop allowing yourself to feel victimized by their victim style. Do you keep thinking to yourself that things would be so much better if only this person would change? If so, you are reacting to their victim/blaming style with a victim/blaming reaction instead of a learning/coping reaction.

How can you react differently? Stop trying to get them to have empathy or observe themselves. Stop spending hours trying to think up ways to get them to understand. Simply tell the person how you feel at each moment in response to what they have just said or done.

When you are accused of not caring or wanting to hurt them, try saying "You're wrong," "It's too bad you let your mind think that way," or "You have it backwards." Then be quiet. Do not explain your statement. Stop letting them avoid responsibility for the energy draining effects of what they do and say.

Try shifting to a different level of communication. Realize that *words* will not work with such a person, any more than words can get a person addicted to drugs, alcohol, or gambling to change. Experiment with actions that will make them aware of the consequences of their behavior.

Be quick to praise improvement or any change for the better. Giving up an old way of doing things is easier when there are immediate benefits.

Uncovering Hidden Barriers to Change:
The Co-Dependency Hang-Up

Whenever a person repeats the same behavior pattern over and over, you can be certain that the person derives many emotional benefits from it. "Co-dependency," for example, has been identified in recent years as an undesirable behavior pattern. Yet it has been very difficult to change. Why? Because of the emotional payoffs a person gains from co-dependency. That, and an inability to deal with the many fears stirred up by thoughts of changing.

Co-dependency is a term that came out of research attempting to understand why treatment efforts with persons dependent on alcohol were seldom successful. The research discovered that alcohol dependency often occurs in a relationship in which a non-user gains many emotional benefits from rescuing and forgiving the user. The non-user, being indirectly dependent on the alcohol, is thus "co-dependent" on it.

Perception is based on contrast. Those who want to be seen as "good," need to create a contrast for themselves by portraying others as "bad" or defective in some way. The husband or wife who constantly cares for, covers up for, and forgives their alcoholic spouse, is often seen by close friends as "a saint." This forgiving and loving person receives admiration and respect for bearing such a huge burden in life with unselfish dedication.

A less extreme but similar pattern is found in the way that some women get together and complain "ain't men awful." It is a sort of bragging about how much they suffer because of the men in their lives. As with all repeated actions, there are benefits to the shared suffering. They experience close emotional intimacy with each other, closer often than with their partners. This activity helps explain why many men keep getting bad performance evaluations from their partners and cannot get an accurate job description. Their partners need fresh material for the next meeting.

There are many hidden barriers working against those changing from being co-dependent or feeling like victims. To change would mean to:

- give up the negative frame of reference upon which their identity is based;
- lose a main source of esteem and appreciation from others; and
- appear to be tough, insensitive, and uncaring if they take a stand against the addicted person—that is, to seem like what children are told are signs of a "bad" person.

What may seem to be simple or easy changes for a person with survivor personality qualities, feels emotionally insurmountable to the "good" person because this person has a constructed personality, not a discovered personality. Unfortunately for them, the first attempts to help "good" people break out of their dissatisfying patterns of co-dependency were seriously flawed.

How Co-Dependency Therapists Fostered a New Form of Co-Dependency

Labelling someone "a co-dependent" is not useful. Labelling of any kind, including referring to someone as "a co-dependent," is a co-dependent thought system. The therapist is seen as a caring, enlightened, wonderful person surrounded by others portrayed as trapped for life in an emotionally unhealthy state.

Urging a person to declare, "I am a co-dependent" pressures him or her to accept a negative identity. This is abusive to someone who already has weak self-esteem. It helps maintain the co-dependent pattern of letting others define one's identity.

Calling someone a negative name because of an undesirable behavior pattern doesn't help that person to give it up. On the contrary, the effort to change is made more difficult by well-intentioned rescuers who ask the person to first accept a negative identity ("I am a co-dependent"), and then try to help the person to *not be* what he or she has just confessed to being.

A better approach is simply to work toward replacing a dissatisfying, ineffective pattern of behavior from childhood with one that is more healthy, synergistic, and satisfying. It is important to recognize that the "good child" co-dependent pattern was functional during childhood. It was a way of surviving. It was the best the child could do in a very difficult situation, and it worked.

Breaking Free from Prohibitions: Difficult but Possible

The challenge for someone raised to be a "good" boy or girl is to develop new, *additional* ways of thinking, feeling, and acting. To do so requires *courage* because it means stepping outside the artificial shell of "goodness" into risky, even frightening territory.

Anyone trying to act like a good child is vulnerable to be overwhelmed when faced with challenges beyond the capacities of the act they were trained to perform. This is why "good," well-behaved, white, middle-class young people, when faced with real world problems, are so vulnerable to cults. After years of being praised for good conduct in school, it feels familiar to once again sit for many hours in uncomfortable chairs without being allowed to go to the bathroom or get a drink of water until given permission. It feels familiar to passively sit and listen to an authoritative person tell them how to think, feel, and act.

The survivor personality, in contrast, is not a way of being that can be learned from someone else. It is not a consciously constructed new act designed to replace an old one. Rather, it is the emergence of innate abilities made possible by learning from experience. It is self-discovered, not taught. It unfolds from within as emotionally constricting prohibitions are loosened. The good child syndrome is to act as one *should*, while the survivor style is to act according to the effects of what one does.

The chapters ahead show how real life difficulties create better opportunities for uncovering new strengths, and developing healthy emotional flexibility than taking workshops or reading self-help books. The lessons are not easy, however, because to be more flexible often requires counter-balancing a "good" feeling or action with one that may have been labelled as "bad." For people raised to be "good," developing a survivor style usually requires learning to be more negative, selfish, angry, and self-appreciating.

The sequence of the following chapters is a progression. They show how disruptive change, distressing situations, negative people, angry people, and job loss can be converted into opportunities for overcoming the good child handicap and becoming better at handling difficult situations.

Learning how to gain strength from these everyday experiences, in turn, helps prepare a person for handling more extreme situations such as crises, serious illness, disasters, and torturous experiences, should they occur. Real life challenges are the best opportunities you will ever have for learning how to cope, thrive, and develop a survivor style.

CHAPTER NINE

THRIVING

Adversity comes in many forms. It may be a major, life-disrupting change, many constant changes, one major life challenge, or dozens of small pressures. Life's best survivors do more than cope with such adversities—they gain strength from them, they thrive.

Thriving During a Major, Life-Disruptive Change

What would you do if your government seized your bank accounts, took possession of your business, physically removed you and your family from your home, and trucked you all to another part of the country—with orders to stay there?

This happened to many Japanese-Americans in 1941. Shortly after the Japanese attacked Pearl Harbor and invaded the Philippines, Japanese-Americans living on the Pacific coast were quickly rounded up. Many were taken to internment camps. Others were taken inland and, while allowed to occupy private residences, were restricted to the local area.

The Naito family was taken to the outskirts of Salt Lake City, Utah. The father, Hide Naito, was despondent. He had been a good citizen. He had worked for years to build up his Norcrest China importing company. The family was very upset. How could the U.S. government get away with taking away everything they owned? It was un-American.

The oldest son, 16 year-old Bill Naito, looked at their situation. He knew they had to find a way to support themselves. He asked "What can we do?" They needed a business that required very little capital, something the whole family could work at together.

Bill says that he and his younger brother, Sam, "came up with the idea of raising chickens and selling eggs. We obtained some chickens, carefully washed and packaged the eggs and sold them to neighbors. We hatched more chickens, and produced more eggs. As the business grew the whole family got involved, my mother, father, and sisters. We supported ourselves for four years selling eggs," Bill says, "and we had lots of chicken manure so we traded it to a Japanese farmer for fresh vegetables." Smiling, Bill adds, "Our business grew so big we built two large chicken coops—with concrete floors! The farming people around there had never heard of a chicken coop with concrete floors. They were amazed at us."

Now, some fifty years later, the Naito brothers have a reputation for succeeding with major redevelopment projects that other developers won't touch. The owners of over a dozen businesses and many commercial buildings, they have won many awards for reshaping the downtown area of Portland, Oregon, with their daring ventures.

Bill Naito says "Dreams come from difficulties. The question 'What can we do?' leads to imagination, to exploring possible solutions. I *like* it when someone says that what we have in mind is impossible."

Gaining Strength from Adversity

In comments about psychologically healthy people, Abraham Maslow referred to what he called his "continental divide" principle. He said "I use this principle to describe the fact that stress will either break people altogether if they are in the beginning too weak to stand distress, or else, if they are already strong enough to take the stress in the first place, that same stress, if they come through it, will strengthen them, temper them, and make them stronger."

How are some people able to thrive and get stronger while others in the same circumstances get weaker? What makes the difference?

People who thrive follow a similar pattern of actions and reactions after being knocked off track by disruptive change. They:

- regain emotional balance;
- cope during the transition;
- adapt to the new reality;
- recover to a stable condition; and
- thrive by learning to be better and stronger than before.

Here is a diagram that shows the thriving sequence and different ways people react to disruptive life changes:

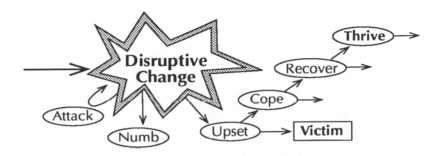

Some attack those they blame for upsetting their lives. Some feel overwhelmed, they go numb. Those who become victims feel ruined for life. Some people learn how to cope but never fully recover. For people who thrive, the way of reacting to disruptive change is to *get upset* and then *expect things to turn out well*. With an optimistic spirit they *ask all sorts of questions*: "What is happening? What is the new reality? What can I do? *Why is it good that this happened?*" Often they *notice something amusing* or funny in the midst of the drama. They use *empathy* and creative thinking to *imagine* an outcome they believe could work. They act with *self-confidence* when they experiment with *learning* a better way doing things and *remain flexible* about unexpected developments.

The Sequence: Handle Feelings First

To regain emotional balance from such major, disruptive life change as job loss or divorce, the important first steps are to express feelings and join together with others for mutual support.

Psychologist James Pennebaker and his associates used an emotions writing technique with a group of professionally skilled workers who had lost their jobs because of downsizing. They had been laid off by a major corporation and had not been successful in finding new employment. Eight months after writing about their emotions for twenty minutes a day for five days, 68 percent of the participants had full-time or satisfactory part-time employment; 48 percent of a matched group that wrote about their time-management plans had employment; only 27 percent of a third, non-participating group had found work.

Pennebaker reports that during their interviews, all of the people in the group that wrote about feelings said *they wished they would have written about their feelings sooner.* By not handling their feelings well they did not do well when they had job interviews.

NOTE: If you or someone you know has been laid off and is searching for employment, "Appendix B" provides practical guidelines for coping and thriving.

Why a Support Group is Helpful

During a disruptive life change, it is extremely helpful to spend time with others who will listen while you talk. A support group helps a person get through the "crazy" period when one's mind is obsessed with negative thoughts and feelings about ex-bosses or the soon to be ex-spouse.

When managers reduce the size of the work force, there is no way to do it "right." Workers have an endless litany of all the ways the executives and managers are doing it wrong and how their incompetence created the situation in the first place.

The same is true during a divorce. One's mind can repeat over and over what the other person is not doing it right and what they should be doing differently. Past experiences come welling up and get added in to long internal conversations. One rehearses all the things the other person should know about themselves— while feeling frustrated because the other person doesn't want to hear it. A support group helps a person get through all that and refocus in a positive direction.

The Cumulative Effects: Some get Bitter, Some Get Better

People stuck in the victim pattern, as illustrated below, accumulate negative experiences.

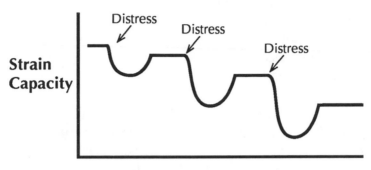

People who thrive become stronger and more capable. Their self-confidence increases as each disruptive experience is surmounted:

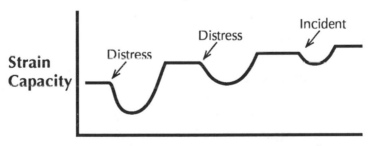

The effect here is similar to what the Outward Bound programs purposefully arrange for their participants. Henry W. Taft, Outward Bound President, said that the program experiences "teach you to survive in the wilderness of life." They give a person the feeling "If I can do this, I can do anything."

Experiences with disruptive changes teach a person how to go through the thriving sequence in days or hours rather than months. Each challenge is quickly processed as another incident and converted into a new adventure. One feels the distress, takes steps to cope with the transition, asks for help from family and friends, locates useful resources, develops "Plan A" and "Plan B" and "hits the ground running," feeling enthusiasm about having a new life direction. Movement, rather than helplessness, is what makes the difference.

Here is an example. I was involved at a chemical fertilizer plant during a time when it was undergoing a 70 per cent reduction in the work force. When I did a workshop on handling the emotional side of the job loss, many employees were feeling shocked, bewildered, and glum about the future. Four months later, after the RIF was over, I was back at the plant to conduct a workshop with the employees that had been retained. As I was walking across the parking lot with one of the few remaining supervisors, I asked him "How does it feel to be one of the survivors?"

He looked around as though to make sure we wouldn't be overheard and said "Frankly Al, I'm kind of disappointed."

"You are?"

"When corporate headquarters announced the layoffs I assumed I'd get the ax. I always wanted to get a college education so I wrote for catalogs. I talked to several advisors, picked my courses, and had my application forms all filled out. I was ready to send in my check the day my layoff letter arrived." He smiled and said, "I'm glad to have a job, but disappointed about having to postpone college."

I could understand why the plant managers had decided to keep him and let most of the others go. Whatever life threw at him, he was ready with a positive new plan.

Who is Responsible?

How well or how poorly a person reacts to disruptive change boils down to an important difference in people. That difference is one's answer to the question *"Who is basically responsible for the way my life goes?"*

Years ago psychologist Julian Rotter found that some people believe that the primary point of control in their lives is *inside* themselves. He described them as people with an "internal locus of control." Other people believe that the primary point of control in their lives is *outside* themselves. He described them as people with an "external locus of control."

People who thrive in difficult situations reflect "internal" attitudes and beliefs. People who go numb, feel victimized, or who lash out angrily, reflect "external" beliefs.

A Demonstration Test

The following statements demonstrate some differences between "internal" and "external" feelings of control. For each of the pairs of statements, check the one you believe is more true than the other.

Which statement do you agree with the most, the one on the left or the right?

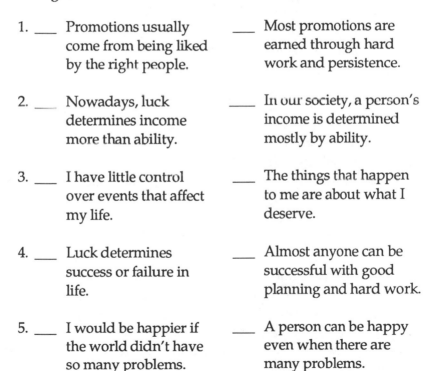

1. ___ Promotions usually come from being liked by the right people.
   ___ Most promotions are earned through hard work and persistence.

2. ___ Nowadays, luck determines income more than ability.
   ___ In our society, a person's income is determined mostly by ability.

3. ___ I have little control over events that affect my life.
   ___ The things that happen to me are about what I deserve.

4. ___ Luck determines success or failure in life.
   ___ Almost anyone can be successful with good planning and hard work.

5. ___ I would be happier if the world didn't have so many problems.
   ___ A person can be happy even when there are many problems.

Scoring: The statements on the left side reflect external locus of control beliefs. The statements on the right side reflect internal locus of control beliefs.

A fascinating finding in this research is that *both sets of beliefs are self-validating*. The person who believes his or her fate is under the control of outside forces acts in a way that confirms that belief. The person who knows he or she can do things to make life better acts in a way that confirms that belief.

Thriving During Constant Change

The more internally directed person is also best at thriving in conditions of many smaller, constant changes. The unrecognized problem with lots of smaller changes is that they can sneak up on you and accumulate, one-by-one, without being fully noticed. You adjust to this, adapt to that, and keep on going.

In today's world, where *change has become constant*, new skills are needed. In the past one could expect that a change was a one-time event to be "gotten through" until things settled down again. In the past a person could settle into a job, and keep it until he or she became old enough to retire. Now people are being prepared for four, five, or six careers.

In the past, a company might change hands once in a worker's lifetime. A relative getting divorced was a rare occurrence. It was rare to receive a notice from your bank informing you that it has a new name because your old bank has been purchased by a larger one. Now such changes are frequent.

After awhile you notice that you feel emotionally tired. Your energy is stretched thin. You feel irritated when your favorite store moves to a different location or goes out of business. You may feel a bit lost, as if the world you are living in isn't the world you knew.

To handle constant change effectively requires, first of all, that you be conscious of the changes. Take some time to look at the following list of ways that "Now" is different from the "Past." Add from your own experience more ways that now is different from the past. It would be very helpful to get together with others to talk about these changes.

PAST:	NOW:
future certain	future uncertain
plan long-term	plan temporary
resist change	manage change
reliance on leaders	reliance on self
trained to fit into stable organization	coached to change with organizational change
trained for existing job	learn to create job
know the answers	know the questions
seek safety, avoid risk	manage risk
eliminate stress	handle stress
loyalty to organization	loyalty to profession
job focus on the product	job focus on service
avoid mistakes, errors	learn from errors
trained to be "good"	learn effective habits
disagreement suppressed	disagreement encouraged
safe conditions at work, home	unsafe at work, home
two parent families	single parent families
children watched by older adults	children watch television
rigid male and female roles	male and female roles unclear
long-term goals	instant gratification
invent games to play	sold games to play
common moral values	moral values unclear
infrequent bad news	frequent bad news
earth absorbed human activities	human activities overwhelming earth
die earlier	live longer

All this change requires learning throughout one's life. Change also means letting the past go. The "good old days" will never return. That is why transitioning from the past is helped by spending some time remembering and talking about the past.

To facilitate the emotional side of the changes, get together with a few others and interview each other about your best memories. What are you proud of? What do you feel sad about losing? What do you feel glad to get away from?

Then ask what is better now than before? What is good about all the changes taking place?

Thriving During a Major, On-Going Challenge

To thrive means to find value and opportunity in events outside one's control. Jim Dyer had worked as a state employee for over 20 years when a new director was appointed to run his agency. At a meeting with the agency managers, the director announced a reorganization plan that would ruin years of good work by field office managers. Jim says, "When I spoke up and asked a question about implementing the plan, the director got very angry at me. He glared at me and said my problem was that I wasn't a team player."

Three weeks later the administrator reassigned Jim to a different position. A month after that his position was transferred to a different agency. A few months later he was reassigned to yet another office. A year after that he was switched to another position, then to another agency section, and so on.

What was Jim's reaction to each transfer? He said: "I like people. I like doing things for people. Each morning I'd say to myself 'this is a fresh chance to do something for people.' Plus I had interests outside my job. I did not depend on my work for feelings of importance to others."

Jim learned each new position quickly and made himself as useful as possible. He enjoyed the challenge and liked having a chance to learn about different offices and units. He said that after six years of being bounced from position to position, "a deputy director confided to me that the director of the agency had tried to get section heads to reduce me in grade or force me to quit. But they had not complied because they could not find grounds. I was always too capable and useful."

Jim's status began to increase. Because of the knowledge he had gained about the inner workings of many state agencies, he became a special trouble-shooter handling citizen's complaints. Then, two years before he retired, he got an unexpected reward. He says, "When the job classifiers looked at what I was doing, they jumped me *three* pay grades, from a 24 to a 27! And I didn't even give them all the documentation they usually need. I retired at a much higher grade than I expected!"

Overcoming the Illusion of Stress

Jim Dyer's ability to effectively handle a situation at work that would have "stressed out" most people, is typical of life's best survivors. Instead of reacting like a victim and eventually filing a stress disability claim, he thrived.

Stress has gotten a bad name in recent years, in part because of a mistake made by Hans Selye, the physician who did the pioneering research on "stress." After retiring, Selye apologized for choosing the word "stress" to describe his findings, but it was too late. His writings had spawned a mob of stress management "experts" who were ringing the "stress" alarm and running around trying to rescue people from attacks by invisible stressors.

Born in Europe, Selye obtained an M.D. and then a Ph.D. in organic chemistry. In 1934, after several trips to North America, he accepted a position as a lecturer in biochemistry at McGill University in Canada. At McGill, he conducted research to learn why the body's glands and organs react in a similar way to many different diseases, illnesses, and toxins (poisons). He wanted to understand the physiology of "being sick."

His research led him to discover what he called the "general adaptation syndrome." The G.A.S. showed how illness and death can occur when constant alarm reactions (sometimes called the "fight or flight" response) exhaust the body's response capacities. High blood pressure, heart attacks, ulcers, decreased immune system resistance, and physiological exhaustion are not the result of specific diseases. They are "diseases of adaptation." That is, they occur when body's ability to respond to constant demands becomes exhausted.

For many years, Selye wrote and spoke about what he called "biological stress." After he retired, however, Selye confessed in his memoirs that he had used the wrong word to describe how the body's adaptive resources become exhausted. He wrote:

> In seeking a name for my theory, I borrowed [a] term
> from English physics, where "stress" refers to the inter-

action between a force and the resistance to it. I merely added an adjective to emphasize that I was using the term in a special sense, and baptized my child "biological stress." But frankly, when I made this choice I did not speak English well enough to know the difference between "stress" and "strain." In physics, "stress" refers to an agent which acts upon a resistant body attempting to deform it, whereas "strain" indicates the changes that are induced in the affected object. Consequently I should have called my syndrome the "strain syndrome...." I did not distinguish between the causative agent and its effect upon the body.

In other words, the challenge for each of us is strain, not stress. The world is not filled with stressors darting around like invisible piranha eating away at you. There is no stress in any situation until a you feel *strain*.

Surveys identifying "job stresses" and workshops on job stress reduction are often more harmful than helpful in that they mislead people, and have spawned an explosion in stress disability claims. For example, whether or not a person experiences stress at work depends upon the person's perception of what is going on and the person's coping skills. It is not the circumstance, it is your reaction to it that counts.

What is stressful for one person is not stressful for another. This means that job stress cannot be objectively defined. The *distress* a person may feel is not a result of what actually *exists* objectively in the job. It is a result of how the person perceives what is happening.

Here is an example. If a weightlifter loses control of a 100 pound barbell held overhead and drops it toward another athlete, will it be stressful for this person to try to catch the barbell? Yes, if she is a slender teen-age girl, even if she is a medal winning gymnast. It is very likely she would be hurt trying to catch the barbell. But if the other athlete is a professional football lineman, he might catch the barbell in one hand and hold it out saying, "Did you drop this?" For him, a 100 pound barbell is not enough weight to give him a good workout.

The point is that a 100 pound barbell is just a 100 pound barbell. It is not a harmful stressor until a person trying to lift it feels *strained* beyond her or his strength level.

If you had a job where you had to handle three hundred telephone calls a day from people wanting some sort of action from your company, would that be stressful? For most of us it would. But if you worked in customer service at an insurance company, three hundred calls might be an easy day. In one office I visited, the customer service representatives average over four hundred calls a day. A work load experienced as a source of severe strain for one person is easy for another.

Many people have also missed the point that a strain can be beneficial. Selye coined the term "eustress" to emphasize that a certain amount of strain is necessary for life. A moderate level is desirable. Athletes build up their physical strength through frequent workouts. Professional schools build competence by pushing people to their limits and slightly beyond. Distressing experiences can motivate people to learn new coping skills.

For these reasons, then, books, articles, and workshops on job stress reduction are often more harmful than helpful because they create the illusion that something called stress is "out there," constantly assaulting each of us. In truth, what most people call *stress* is really an internal feeling of *strain* that they don't like.

Why "Stress" is an Important Concern

No matter what term is used, if one wants a long and healthy life, it is important to understand the many ways that stress and strain affect the human body. Humans with bodies like ours first appeared on the planet about 100,000 years ago. For most of that time, the average length of life was about 35 years. In the last 100 years as humans identified and controlled contagious diseases and infections through sanitary practices, personal hygiene, vaccinations, and antibiotics, the average life expectancy climbed to 50 and then to 60 years. Then, with increased longevity, *life-style* was discovered to be a significant cause of death. People were shortening their lives through smoking, unhealthy eating, drinking, reckless living, and lack of exercise. New knowledge about the importance of physical fitness, nutrition, and safe living led to an increased average life expectancy to nearly 70 years.

HUMAN LIFE SPAN

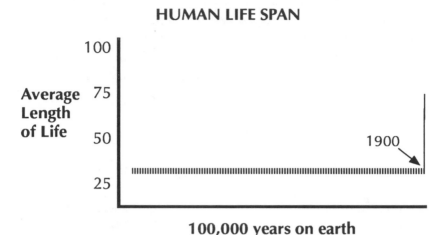

100,000 years on earth

Then heart attacks, tumors, cancer, high blood pressure, and ulcers emerged as the main causes of death. Even people with good physical and nutritional habits were dying from what Dr. Selye identified decades previously as "diseases of adaptation."

But is stress the problem? No. The problem is that some people react to circumstances and events in their lives in ways that lead to illness and early death. The real killer is too much constant *strain* and the victims are often it's accomplices.

Many people are self-frazzling. They bring on diseases of adaptation through poor self-management. Evidence that humans in general do not know how to handle emotional strain very well is found in the widespread use of tranquilizers, drugs, and alcohol. According to the National Institute on Drug Abuse, Americans obtain millions of prescriptions for Valium, Librium, Prosac, and other tranquilizers every year. *Millions* of people use alcohol, drugs and other substances to reduce tension and feel better.

Illness Susceptible vs. Illness Resistant Behaviors

A great deal of research has been conducted to determine the possible relationships between illness and human behavior. This research indicates that persons *more likely* to develop illnesses related to the strain syndrome:

- experience distress in routine activities.
- feel vulnerable, helpless, and without choices.
- have limited internal and external resources upon which to draw.
- are not sure what they feel, and can't express feelings easily.
- blame others for their unpleasant feelings ("You upset me").
- feel socially isolated, not accepted.
- have little capacity for self-change.
- accumulate negative experiences.

In contrast, persons *less likely* to develop illnesses related to the strain syndrome:

- seldom experience distress in routine activities.
- feel capable of taking effective action about upsetting events.
- draw action choices from a wide range of inner and external resources.
- experience family and friends as caring and supportive.
- know how they feel and can express feelings.
- separate their reactions from the cause ("I feel upset about what you did").
- manage self-change well.
- convert negative experiences into beneficial learning.
- actively pursue positive, enjoyable experiences.

There is a pattern here that is similar to how our cells react to a foreign substance. Allergic reactions occur when our cells mistakenly interpret food or benign substances as toxic. When a person has an allergic reaction to wheat or dairy products, for example, the person's cells react as though the substance is a poison. Selye explained that if a cell interprets a substance as toxic, it has a "catatoxic" reaction. That is, its reaction is to destroy the toxin. If the cell interprets the substance as not harmful, it has a "syntoxic" reaction. It puts up with it.

Some people appear to have allergic minds. They feel alarmed and distressed about many ordinary events. Conversely, some people develop strong mental and emotional immunities to circumstances and events that upset others. They convert what others experience as toxic into something nutritious.

The situation is similar to how people react to bee stings. A few people are so allergic that they are at risk of dying if stung by one or two bees. Most people have a "normal" catatoxic reaction to a bee sting. The spot swells up as the body's defenses isolate the bee venom and work to destroy it. Beekeepers, however, have a syntoxic reaction to bee stings. They have such an immunity to the toxin they have little reaction to many stings. Emotional immunity is like that. It can be acquired by learning from experience.

Overcoming Inner Restrictions

People raised to be good children often have difficulty dealing with life's various strains because they were raised to not complain or be unhappy, and to not be selfish. Yet to avoid developing diseases of adaptation *one must be able to express unhappiness* and *act in ways that may seem selfish.*

To feel unhappy and negative for a few hours is like letting yourself fall down when you've lost your balance. You do it and then get up. A person who sometimes expresses negative thinking is not the same as a person who is negative all the time.

One day I telephoned my friend Joanne Hazel, the psychiatric nurse. We hadn't talked in over a year, and I wanted to chat for awhile and find out what was happening in her life. When she heard it was me on the phone she said, "Oh Al! You would call *today* of all days! I feel miserable! My mother is visiting and yesterday she had several of her friends over for breakfast. They got so busy talking they forgot they had a skillet with sausage on the stove. It caught fire and set fire to my kitchen cabinets. Now my kitchen will have to be torn apart to replace the cabinets....

"I got a call from my daughter's school. They're having a problem with her so I have to go see the school counselor. I feel very upset about that....

"Yesterday I said something very stupid during a meeting. I feel really embarrassed....

"This morning I decided to paint an old bookcase. I spilled the paint and have paint splattered on me...."

She paused for a moment and then said, "You know, Al, it's too bad that more people don't know how to enjoy feeling depressed."

I laughed. Here is the best psychiatric nurse I know, one of the most durable, hardy, synergistic people I've ever met, having a good time feeling miserable.

She went on to say, "I'm giving myself until 4 PM to enjoy this. Then I have to clean up and go to a dinner meeting."

Joanne knows that letting yourself feel really negative about things once-in-awhile does not make you a negative person. Just the opposite. It is a sign of excellent mental health. People who try to program themselves to have *only positive feelings* are fragile. They need a protective environment because they don't handle pressure or conflict well.

Thriving Under Life's Strains

One way guaranteed to increase your distressing experiences is to not want to be where you are. Your emotional distress decreases by deciding, like a flower seed, to bloom where you are planted. If you want to handle your life situation better, here is a simple, effective method for decreasing strain, avoiding feeling helpless and hopeless, and maintaining vitality:

- *First* make a list of everything you find irritating and upsetting. Ask "What upsets me? Makes me feel unhappy? Feels stressful?" Take your time. Play it up.
- Wait awhile and then go through the list of negative experiences, item by item, asking questions such as:
    - What if I ignored this? What if I avoided contact?
    - Could I do something about this? What could I do to change what bothers me?
    - Can I make it go away? Get it out of my life?
    - If I can't avoid it, change it, or make it go away, what if I changed my reaction to it? What if I decided to stop letting it bother me?
    - What can I learn from this? Why is it *good* that this happens?
- Select one or two items on the list and develop a plan of action for making some changes.
- *Next*, make a list of what revitalizes you. List what you find invigorating and fun. Ask:

- What do I have fun doing? Get enthusiastic about?
- What would I like to do that I keep putting off?
- With whom do I enjoy sharing good experiences?
- Am I ignoring or taking for granted some positive aspects of my life?

- Then ask questions about how to repeat, increase, or have new positive experiences.
- Develop a plan of action for increasing positive, revitalizing experiences.

This personally created plan that you develop by asking and answering questions, is an effective way to *decrease* distressing experiences and *increase* revitalizing ones. The result is that you avoid feeling helpless and hopeless; you continuously learn new ways of making your life better.

Keep in mind that time plays a part in this. Certain pressures can be changed today, others will take a year or so, and still others may take longer. Some pleasant activities may take awhile to bring about. In the long run, however, this is a very practical way to lessen "overload" sensations, and replace them with positive anticipations about your future.

In fact so much good information exists on how to make your life less stressful and more positive, if you feel constant stress, and are not taking action to improve your situation, ask yourself: What prevents me from handling my situation better and finding ways to enjoy my life and work? What benefits do I derive from having things as they are? What are some payoffs I don't want to give up?

It may be that you derive so many indirect benefits from being harried and overworked, you can't imagine life without them.

In *The Road Less Travelled*, M. Scott Peck says "Wise people learn not to dread but actually to welcome problems." The chapters ahead show how to learn and thrive in situations that other people react to by feeling frustrated or victimized. The school of life arranges for some wonderful learning opportunities for people who react to difficulties by learning new skills. And, by practicing thriving skills with everyday adversities, one is better prepared for handling even more difficult challenges if they occur.

CHAPTER TEN

HOW TO BE POSITIVE
ABOUT NEGATIVE PEOPLE

"I hate negative people!" The balding businessman fumed. He looked at the other participants in the seminar room and said, "I own a real estate company. Negative sales associates pull the whole office down." His face got red as he continued, "They suck me dry! They sit around at *my* desks in *my* office space waiting for *my* ads to make the phone ring while they complain about how bad the market is!" Most of the people in the room nodded agreement.

One of life's great irritations is having to associate with people who complain all the time. It wears on your nerves to be around a constantly negative co-worker or family member. It hurts when they criticize your suggestions and see nothing good in your plans. It might not be so bad if the person considered your suggestion carefully, evaluated its merits, and then pointed out deficiencies. What is irritating is that people with negative attitudes react with an unthinking, pessimistic reflex.

Does it work to try to make them change their attitude? No. Trying to get them to see things in your more positive way is rejected. Your efforts to perform an "attitude transplant" have no chance of success if the recipient is unreceptive.

Can anything be done? Yes, once we understand the source of the problem, a solution emerges.

Learning About Positive and Negative Attitudes

About twenty years ago, the first time I gave a workshop on "How to Keep a Positive Attitude in Negative Situations," I decided to find out what the people in the workshop thought about the differences between someone with a positive attitude and someone with a negative attitude. I put them into small groups and had them list the differences.

TRY THIS: Before reading further, make up two lists. In one, describe people with negative attitudes. In the other, describe people with positive attitudes. Do that now.

Results

The following lists are typical of what most people come up with:

Positive Attitude	Negative Attitude
friendly	unpleasant
cheerful, smiling	frowns, sulks
open-minded	closed minded
accepts others	blames others
makes best of bad situations	finds worst in good situations
optimistic	pessimistic
good outlook	constantly gripes
sees glass ½ full	sees glass ½ empty
helpful	makes excuses
humor	whines
good listener	uncommunicative
concern for others	insensitive
supportive	critical
looks at both sides	inflexible, rigid
cooperative	uncooperative
tolerant	hostile
constructive	finds faults
respects others	defensive
enjoys work	complains
persistent	gives up easily
loves life	unhappy about life

Who is Negative?

There was something about the two lists that puzzled me. Something seemed out of balance in the descriptions. Take a moment to see if you can spot what it is. Reflect especially on the emotional tone of each list.

Notice that the description of the positive attitude includes being "tolerant," "open-minded," "supportive," "constructive," "friendly," "understanding," and "accepts others." With that in mind, look at the descriptions of people with negative attitudes. How much tolerance, open-mindedness, understanding, and so forth are demonstrated in the way negative people are described?

Do you see the problem?

The descriptions in the two lists express a belief that being positive is much more desirable than being negative. The positive list reads almost like a funeral eulogy. It includes statements that people identify with and often use to describe themselves. The negative list contains words we use for people who irritate us.

What the two lists show is that most *people with positive attitudes have a negative attitude about people with negative attitudes!*

An Emotional Handicap

The belief that positive thinking is desirable and negative thinking is undesirable is a version of the child's good person/bad person personality theory. If your way of thinking about positive and negative people is similar to the two lists, you know that your belief feels right. But the drawback is that reacting to a disliked opposite in negative ways renders you helpless with such a person. It is emotionally handicapping.

Why so? For a combination of reasons. First, since perception is based on contrasts, you are using the negative ("bad") person as a frame of reference for your positive ("good") person identity. Second, you believe that for things to improve, the negative person should change. Third, you spend lots of time and energy in unsuccessful efforts to try to make him or her *not* be the person your good person identity needs for them to be.

These reasons help explain why in most families, organizations, and work groups, a person with a negative attitude has the most power. In your mind you have it set up that unless the other person changes, the situation will never improve. You have placed your fate in the hands of others and then blame them for not being willing to change.

A person who identifies with being positive and who uses negative thinking as an anti-model, expends emotional energy trying to suppress negative thinking. Then, to make matters worse, the laws of nature make the situation *even more difficult!*

If you work at being positive and not negative you create a vacuum for negative thinking. Nature will not let you get away with that. It fills the vacuum by pairing you up with someone who is negative and not positive. Nature reestablishes a counter-balance between opposing forces and the two of you drive each other crazy. Both of you go around protesting, "If only this other person would change, things would be much better for me."

Time and time again, someone walks up to me at a workshop, smiles nervously, and says, "I came to your workshop because I've always been such a positive person, but my...." At this point I can usually predict the rest of the person's statement. This individual's husband or wife or child or co-worker is someone they experience as always negative.

When a positive attitude person has a negative attitude about negative attitudes, somewhere in that person's world there is a negative person who makes life difficult for them. It's a sure bet, because that is how the laws of nature function. (The clincher that they are operating from a "good child" identity is when they claim that they are acting only for the other person's own good.)

If your lists describing positive and negative attitudes are similar to the two lists above, it shows that you were taught a way of thinking that is emotionally handicapping. Your attitude toward negative people makes it possible for negative people to have much more control over situations than you do. By being negative they can upset you, cause you to spend time and energy trying to cope with their negativism, and frustrate your efforts.

What can be done? *First,* recognize that your distress, frustration, and lack of success are signs that you do not understand what is going on. *Second,* stop your victim/blaming thinking: "If only they would change, my life would be much better." *Third,* shift to the curious, empathic mode of thinking that makes a person a survivor. Find out what is valid about a person repeating a negative mental/emotional pattern over and over.

Martin Seligman says that optimism and pessimism are determined by a person's explanatory style and that both styles are *learned*. Thus the way to handle a person with a negative attitude is to change how *you* think, by shifting from a pessimistic to an optimistic style. To change means to realize that:

- You are *not helpless*. You can learn effective ways for handling yourself with negative people.
- As frustrating as it feels, *the situation can be improved* by changing how you view it and how you interact with negative people.
- The situation with negative people is not entirely negative. People you have labelled as "pessimists" are only negative *part of the time* in *specific situations*, and it can be *to your advantage* to have them voice their negative views.

A Positive Way Out: Observe, Empathize, Validate

There is nothing wrong with having negative reactions to people with negative attitudes. But when you get tired of being stuck in a polarized, good-bad pattern with a negative person, the way to break free is to challenge yourself to put into practice the qualities of a positive person. *Challenge yourself to develop a positive attitude about negative attitudes.* If you believe a person with a positive attitude is someone who can find some good in anything, is open-minded, likes people, is understanding, and so forth, then challenge yourself to be that way with negative, pessimistic people.

To gain mastery over your mind and stop reacting in a "knee jerk" way to people with negative attitudes, take some time to answer this question:

What are the benefits, payoffs, and advantages gained from having a chronic negative attitude?

Many people find this question one of the most difficult they have ever tried to answer. If your reaction to the question is,

"There can't be any benefits!" or if you find it very difficult to think of any payoffs or advantages, this indicates your need to have someone to dislike is stronger than your need to have things work well.

Keep in mind that looking for answers to questions about the benefits and payoffs of negative thinking does not mean you approve. Maintaining a one-sided, negative view of negative or pessimistic thinking, however, is a handicap. It is a barrier to understanding and effectiveness.

Benefits of a Negative Attitude

A fundamental principle of psychology is that anytime a person repeats the same behavioral pattern over and over the person is receiving payoffs for that behavior. People in my workshops have identified over a dozen benefits for a person with a negative attitude:

- **Attention.** One of the primary payoffs of a negative attitude is it can make the person the center of attention. People determined to have everything positive will try hard to get the negative person to cheer up and stop being pessimistic.
- **Express feelings honestly.** A negative person is being emotionally honest. They don't try to hide their feelings. They may avoid ulcers or other problems that come from suppressing anger or irritation.
- **It takes less energy.** It is easier to be negative. It takes less energy than trying to solve problems or improve things.
- **Avoid failure.** You do not experience failure if you do not try.
- **Prepared for the worst.** The person is emotionally ready for bad developments. They are not surprised when things to go wrong. They knew it would happen.
- **Enjoy being right.** It can be satisfying to say, "I told you so, I knew that would not work."
- **Left alone.** Some people need to be left alone. Being negative may be the best way to get privacy. They are seldom asked to join groups. (The exception is when a negative, outspoken worker is selected to be the bargaining group negotiator.)

- **Not burdened by other's problems.** People seldom turn to a negative person for help and support.
- **Feel independent.** The negative person does not try to get along with others or live up to people's expectations. The ability to resist efforts by others to change their attitudes, feelings and thinking reinforces feelings of autonomy and self-determination.
- **Avoid responsibility for bad outcomes.** When things go poorly, the negative person avoids feelings of guilt, responsibility, or blame. "It's not my fault. I tried to warn you."
- **Avoid difficulties.** By being vigilant about the negative outcomes of efforts, this person may be more likely to see possible difficulties than others. They often can anticipate problems better even though they may not be good at developing solutions to the problems.
- **Draw positive talk from others.** A person who complains receives lots of praise and encouragement. Other people say "Cheer up, things will be all right," "You're doing fine," "Everything will work out well," or "We're going to succeed at this."

Perhaps now, as a result of curious observing, empathizing, and validating people with negative attitudes, you can understand why a person with a negative attitude is not easily changed. There are too many benefits to give up!

Guidelines for Handling Yourself With Negative People

The primary challenge, therefore, is not the negative person's attitude, it is *your reaction* to his or her attitude. The synergistic response, when you feel frustrated or feel an energy drain, is a learning/coping reaction. You treat the difficulty as an opportunity to learn about yourself and others and look for new, better ways of handling what others do.

Negative people give you an opportunity to practice being flexible, playful, empathic, and synergistic. The list of benefits and payoffs for people with negative, pessimistic attitudes opens up many possible ways of responding. You can:

- **Withhold attention.** Since attention is a big payoff for people with pessimistic, negative attitudes, stop responding to their negative statements. Sometimes the best way to get a person to stop complaining and wasting your time is to become "selectively impolite." For example, a computer operator in a state agency said her biggest problem at work was a co-worker, an older woman, who constantly talked and complained about problems at home. When I asked if she had been raised to be polite and to listen when spoken to, she said, "Yes."

  "So when this complaining co-worker is talking to you," I asked, "you sit and smile and listen attentively while quietly wishing she would shut up?"

  She nodded vigorously and said, "Yes!"

  "What would happen if you ignored her and went right on working?"

  Her eyes opened wide. "That would be rude!" she said.

  Being what others might think is rude is, of course, not consistent with the self-image of someone raised to be a good person. Such a person usually gets no improvement from others because they rely on the victim response, "If only others would change, my world would be a better place." In this case, however, the computer operator was bothered enough by the co-worker to attempt to change things. With the help of several friends, she developed a plan for being "selectively impolite." It took courage for her to go against her up-bringing but she did it, and it worked. She ignored the co-worker when she complained, showed interest when her co-worker did not complain, and the complaining decreased.
- **Say to them, "You may be right," then change the subject.** You were not given a personal assignment at birth to invalidate and eliminate negative thinking. The universe created this individual, so why not let his or her negative talk drift into outer space?

  Often the best way to handle something is not to oppose it, but to align yourself with it. If *you* do not serve as an opposing force, negative individuals must set up some internal balances to control it themselves. An employment agency counselor had a client who complained about being inadequate, incompetent, incapable, and worthless. The counselor listened for awhile, felt that the words were not sincere, and said, "You know, after observing you carefully, I guess I have to agree with you." The client was shocked and became irritated at the counselor for not behaving like a counselor. This led to progress in the session.

- **Ask them to be considerate.** Say, "I can't handle that kind of talk right now. Please hold off." You may be surprised at how sensitive and cooperative the complaining person will be.
- **Tell them to shut up tactfully.** Say, "Your complaining bothers me. I don't need that. Please don't talk that way around me."
- **Tell them your mind is your territory and ask them to stop broadcasting their complaints into your territory.** A nurse working nights said this is how she got an aide to stop his constant griping. She asked him to turn down the volume on his personal "boombox" because she needed her mind to do her work.
- **Be playful. Beat them in their own territory.** Listen for awhile and then say, "It's much worse than you know." Then describe more things to be upset about than they have mentioned.
- **Give them honest feedback.** Say, "What you're telling me is not useful to me and it bothers me to have you only talk about the negative side of things."
- **Say "You're wrong," then be quiet.** It's sometimes useful to merely state in a matter-of-fact way, "You're wrong. It's too bad you let your mind think that way." Do not explain why they are wrong. Merely state that they are wrong, then wait to see if they ask why you have said that. You still may get into an argument, but you'll have a much better audience if you first state *that* they are wrong rather than explain *why* they are wrong.
- **Beat them to it.** An office manager and I devised a plan for dealing with a woman who complained about her husband all the time. Monday mornings were especially bad. Her co-

workers would sit and wait for her to initiate what they knew was coming, and be upset even before she started talking.

The plan called for the office manager to walk up to her the next Monday morning, as soon as she walked in the door, and say, "Well, what did the S.O.B. do to you this weekend?"

When the moment arrived, he did exactly what we planned. As predicted, she was startled. He told me later that her reaction was to say, "Why are you saying that about my husband?"

He exclaimed, "You've convinced me! I've listened to you talk about him for three years and I agree with you. He is the most rotten S.O.B. who has ever existed. He married you for the sole purpose of making your life miserable. He is a horrible man."

When she said, "He's not that bad," the manager challenged her to prove him wrong. Anything she said good about her husband, he said, "That doesn't count." Then he went back to his office, shaking his head.

Months later he told me she never again complained about her husband at work!

- **Make the complaint more extreme.** Some high-powered sales courses teach the salesperson to handle complaints this way. For example, suppose you have a problem with your copy machine. When the company representative comes around you say, "Sometimes little black spots get on the paper and about once a day paper jams up in the machine."

  The rep is trained to respond by saying, "That's horrible! The machine splatters over the pages so badly you can not read them and it ruins most of the paper you put into it. We'll pull that machine out of here this afternoon!"

  Most people respond by saying, "No, it's not that bad."

  You may have spent days rehearsing your complaint, but within seconds the sales rep has you turned around, defending the equipment.

  Try it. Take the negative person's complaint and magnify it into a horror story.

- **It may be useful to view negative complaining as the adult version of crying.** Children cry when they are upset. They cry to gain attention and to express their feelings about the world they are in. It is not usually okay for adults to do that; it is not all right for a person at work to burst into loud crying. What adults can get away with is expressing their unhappiness. Sometimes complaining is a form of crying.

NOTE: If a normally pleasant friend, relative, or co-worker becomes negative in a way that seems out of character, that person probably deserves a lot of your time and attention. The suggestions in this list are for use with a person who is habitually negative.

- **Put their negative predictions on the record.** Sometimes negative people want it known that they are predicting failure. Then if things fall through they are not to blame. This way they can participate in the credit if things work out well and avoid responsibility if things do not work out well. It is a political move of sorts.

  The supervisor in a printing shop said he had an old-time printer who was always pessimistic about special printing jobs. The printer would explain why it could not be done and all the problems that would probably cause things to go wrong. The supervisor would tell the printer to go ahead anyway. In almost every instance the printer would turn out a perfect job.

  The point: *Do not try to make negative talk go away if you're getting good results!*

  Sometimes when children are told to wash their hands or go to bed, they will moan and complain all the way to the bathroom or their bedroom. But the fact is, they get up and do what they were told.

- **Ask them not to complain in your presence.** A minister said he had a volunteer working in the church office who spent her entire time complaining about the awful things in her life. His solution was to take her out into the hallway and tell her there will be no complaining in the church office. He explained to her that if she wanted to talk about something bothering her, he would step out into the hallway and talk with her, but the office was to be a pleasant, friendly, positive place.

During the first few days of his plan, he went to her every once in awhile, patted her on the shoulder, and complemented her for the wonderful improvement. He told me the change she made in the church office carried over into other parts of her life as well. Her relationships with her neighbors and relatives improved.

- **See the benefit in their negative thinking.** Compliment negative people on how much creativity and intelligence they show in seeing risks, barriers, and problems in every situation.
- **Ask them to put their complaints in writing.** A manager of a motorcycle shop had a young mechanic do this. Then the manager read the list of complaints back to the mechanic. It had a useful effect. Some people do not know how negative they sound.
- **Ask what they want.** Say that describing a problem is step one. Step two is to clarify what outcome they want. Do not do their work for them. Make them describe the goal. Ask what their plan is for handling the situation.
- **Ask them to also see something positive.** Tell them you will not listen to the negative side unless they also talk about some positives.
- **Give rewards when they are quiet or positive.** If a negative person works quietly for awhile or says something pleasant, immediately give him or her your pleasant attention. This does not mean you need to stick candy in his or her mouth, although that might not be a bad idea.
- **Ask the negative person to tell you what could go wrong.** Make them a resource. Ask them to be negative about a plan or program to help you anticipate difficulties. Praise them for being experts at predicting what will not work. Take advantage of this ability. In group meetings you can say, "It's useful when you tell us about problems we've overlooked. What might go wrong with this plan?"

The last item is essential for executives, managers, and committee heads to learn to do. Psychologist Irving Janis found that groups make poor decisions when they get into a condition he called "groupthink." One of the main symptoms of groupthink is that *disagreement is suppressed*. The leader squelches contrary opinions, dismisses negative predictions, downplays problems, and portrays opposing groups as having bad motives.

In the Pacific Northwest, the loggers and forest industry companies are paying the price for having a groupthink reaction to people wanting to protect spotted owl habitat. The loggers' reaction was to ridicule and disparage the wildlife conservationists. Now, because they refused to listen, many forests are unavailable for timber sales, hundreds of logging operations have been shut down, and thousands of people are out of work. I feel sorry about their circumstances, but I also see that their closed-mindedness helped create the situation that is now devastating their lives.

Response Flexibility

An electrician, plumber, or maintenance worker who shows up to repair something brings along a kit with lots of tools. The list above is like a tool kit for dealing with negative people. It shows that you have many ways of reacting to pessimism, complaining, and negativity. You have many choices other than feeling helpless and victimized by another person's negative attitude.

How to Change An Attitude

If you believe it would be useful to change your attitude about negative attitudes, you can. Changing your attitude will not be easy, however. Attitudes are habits. Like all habits, they develop slowly and change slowly.

Social psychologists have identified three basic components in attitudes: cognitive, affective, and motor. What this means that attitudes are not just mental. They are a function of your *mind*, your *feelings*, and your *muscles* combined into a unified response.

For example, Leslie is sent to the vice-principal's office for hitting a boy in her class. The vice-principal asks, "Do you know why you were sent to my office?" Leslie shifts in her chair, clenches her jaw, sighs deeply, looks out the window, and nods disgustedly. Her body language communicates that she has a negative attitude about the topic of the discussion—namely, that she hits boys she does not like. Her attitude about the pending conversation is expressed in her muscles and feelings as well as her thoughts.

Work at changing an attitude the way you would work to change any habit. It requires desire and consistent effort over a period of time. To succeed in changing your attitude toward negative people:

- Make it a self-chosen project.
- Work at the new attitude the way you would develop a new habit: be consistent and give it time.
- Focus on developing a new way of reacting rather than merely getting rid of an old one.
- Consciously practice new reactions until they begin to occur automatically.
- Review your progress after each incident. Look for small improvements over the past.
- Compliment yourself when you see progress. Do not criticize yourself if you revert back to your former attitude. That happens, and is to be expected. With time it will happen less often.

The key to making your life better is to focus on changing yourself more than changing others, especially when you find yourself irritated by someone who is not going to change how they act or talk.

The Benefit: Both Positive and Negative Thinking

Life's best survivors can be both positive and negative, both optimistic and pessimistic *at the same time*. The ability to think negatively helps minimize the disadvantages of being overly optimistic. The ability to think positively helps to overcome discouragement and generate renewed energy. Each benefits the other.

In contrast, many people expend a lot of energy trying to think and feel as trained by their patents. They try to think only in positive ways and work to avoid negative thoughts and feelings.

When it comes to positive and negative thinking, most people fit into one of three patterns.

LEVELS OF POSITIVE AND NEGATIVE THINKING

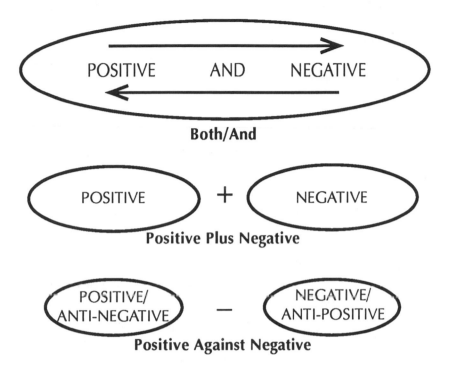

Both/And

Positive Plus Negative

Positive Against Negative

At the bottom level, people who work at being positive and not-negative have a strong, negative reaction toward people with negative attitudes. They feel stuck in frustrating conflict with their upsetting opposite, unaware that both the cause of their difficulty, *and the solution to it*, is within themselves. This emotional life-style is the most primitive and inflexible of the three.

The guidelines we just covered show how to move from this tight, restricted, emotionally helpless level to a position where there is more emotional freedom. A person in the middle state is more tolerant and open to others who may be different from him or herself. At this level, each person can specialize in what he or she does best and appreciate differences in others. A woman told me that she and her husband are a good team because she appreciates his ability to warn her of potential problems, and he, in turn, appreciates her optimism, enthusiasm, and cheery nature. Together, the two of them share counter-balancing traits, and their relationship is much better than relationships in which people become upset with a partner who thinks and feels in opposite ways.

The benefits of developing an ability to be both optimistic and pessimistic are many. Harvard psychologist David McClelland found that people who achieve the most career success show a sort of "pessimistic optimism" when choosing goals. He found that when looking at a proposed project, the person with the highest probability of success can seem as negative as any person who is negative all the time. Before making a commitment to a goal, the successful person will explore and examine everything that could go wrong. Successful people know that anticipating barriers to goals increases the likelihood of success.

Overcoming a Hidden Inner Barrier

The most challenging inner barrier against accepting people with negative attitudes is to become conscious of all the psychological benefits you derive from having someone around who makes you look good when you compare yourself to that person. To break free from energy draining conflict with negative people, a key question to ask is this: "Are the advantages I gain from having a negative attitude toward negative people greater than the benefits I stand to gain by changing myself?"

Just as there are advantages to being negative, there are advantages to being negative about negative people. You have someone to blame when your ideas do not get approved. You get attention when you go home with the latest story about how difficult your job is because of this difficult person. You know you have some flaws, but compared to a negative person you look pretty good.

To be more accepting of people with negative attitudes means you have to give up the emotional benefits you gain from using them as anti-models. You have to give up using them as scapegoats you can blame. A good indicator that you have developed mental and emotional freedom is when you emotionally accept that a negative person has the right to be here on the planet exactly the way they are. This is not easy to accomplish, but is a challenge worth undertaking.

CHAPTER ELEVEN

HOW TO HANDLE YOURSELF WITH ANGRY PEOPLE

Encounters with angry people are high on the list of dislikes for anyone who deals with the public. A young woman who worked at the city hall window where people pay their traffic fines told me, "I don't know why people yell and scream at us. They're the ones who broke the law. The judge is the one who fined them. It isn't fair."

I nodded.

"They hired a consultant to help us," she said, "and she had them paint the walls in the waiting area pink. It's supposed to calm people down, but it hasn't helped. People still yell at us. It isn't fair."

She is right, of course. It isn't fair. And, like many other city employees, she was not warned during her job interview that an unpleasant part of her job would be having to deal with angry people.

Angry people are an unexpected problem in many jobs. No one working in law enforcement, customer complaints, collections, or tax assessment has ever said to me that when they were doing career planning they hoped to find employment where they would be forced to deal with angry people.

What do you do when faced with this kind of unpleasant situation? As with other difficulties, you can have a victim/blaming reaction or a learning/coping reaction.

The following guidelines will walk you through the steps of how to have a learning/coping reaction to angry people.

Observing

The first step is to take a look at what you have learned from personal experience that does not work with angry people. Here is what a number of people say doesn't work. Do you recognize any of these reactions as applying to you?

- Get angry. Argue back.
- Shake head "no," cross arms, refuse to listen.
- Say, "Don't feel that way."
- Tell the person to be quiet and listen to you.
- Ridicule or criticize the other person's statements.
- Deny what they say could have happened.
- Dismiss the person's complaint as not important.
- Say, "Yes, but ...." (The "yes, but" game was the first game analyzed by psychiatrist Eric Berne. It is a subtle way of saying, "I let you talk first, but now I'm going to explain reality to you.")

When you act in the ways listed above, the odds are very good that you will maintain the conflict, if not escalate it. If you think to yourself that your job would be less difficult and more pleasant if only they would change, you are correct. But, as in other situations with difficult people, the chances that angry people will transform themselves for your benefit are pretty slim.

There is a solution, however. Because you are human, you can learn skills for handling yourself well with angry people just as others, for example, learn martial arts skills for handling physical attacks.

Guidelines for Getting
Win/Win Outcomes with Angry People

Life's best survivors rely on curiosity and empathy when looking for a way to handle an adversary. Their synergistic motivation has them expecting and looking for an outcome that works well for everyone.

Here is a well tested, useful sequence of steps for converting angry conflict into a good outcome:

- **Ask.** Immediately ask the person to tell you what is wrong. Interrupt if necessary. Humans can hear while they talk. The first step is *not* to listen quietly. Avoid remaining silent while the person rants and raves. The angry person may suspect you are silently defensive or are discounting what he or she says.

  Use your own words, but find some way to develop a reflexive response in which you reach out and pull the person's anger toward you. When you ask, "What's wrong?" you communicate that you are someone who sincerely wants to listen to what is upsetting him or her. You also communicate that you expect to handle the problem.

  At this time *do not* attempt to explain your side or your position. When an individual is angry and upset, a jumbled brain is in control of the person's mouth. The cerebral cortex is unavailable for input. This is the worst possible time to attempt to get the angry person to listen to your explanations.

  If possible, have the person sit down. It is harder for a person to remain angry when sitting. Then sit near, with no desk or barrier between you, and lean forward slightly.

  Remember, the first step toward converting an angry attack into a good outcome is to ask questions. The aim is to divert the anger past you while drawing into your brain an accurate understanding of the other person's case.

- **Listen.** As the angry person talks, listen carefully to what he or she says. Challenge yourself to listen so well you will be able to repeat back exactly what the person says to you. It may be useful to write down what is said on a pad of paper. Writing down his or her complaint shows this person you are listening. To listen well does not mean that you agree with what is said. People with self-confidence can listen to an angry attack with understanding. It is often a sign of emotional weakness when people refuse to listen to views or perspectives contrary to their own. As you listen, notice your body language. Do you sit or stand upright? Look at the person in an attentive way? Sincerely attempt to understand the upsetting predicament? Or do you slouch with a scowl on your face, tap your fingers, fidget around, and look out the window, obviously irritated with the person? Body language affects angry people.

What if the person is swearing? A supervisor in the collections department for a city water bureau said that when she has an angry, swearing customer on the phone she says, "Please slow down. I have to write all this down for my manager." She said in most cases the swearing quickly stops.

- **Don't take it personally.** In many cases the angry person is angry at someone else, not you. The anger may come from news he or she doesn't want, an organization's policies, or a mistake made someplace. You just happen to be the human toward which the angry feelings are vented. Take a deep breath, relax, and maintain your composure.

- **Ask clarifying questions.** Ask questions that help the person communicate. Imagine how you would react if you met a good friend after work who was angry about something. You'd ask lots of questions. "When did this happen?" "Was this the first time?" "Who else have you talked to?" In fact, by acting like a friend you are acting in ways contrary to assumptions the angry person may have made about you.

- **Repeat back.** The one time an angry person will pause and be quiet is to listen when you try to verify that you've heard him or her correctly. Do not let the person go on and on. If you were to take martial arts training, you would not be told to let an attacker beat you until he or she collapses from exhaustion.

Interrupt the person and say, "Let me see if I understand what you're angry about. You are angry because...," and then repeat back to the person what has been said.

The quickest way to get a person calmed down and less angry is to listen, ask clarifying questions, and repeat back what you know of the upsetting situation.

Repeating back can be useful in other circumstances as well. Sometimes people don't know you have really heard them. Have you ever had a person repeat something to you again and again and again? He or she doesn't know you've heard them. If you want the repeating to stop, take time to repeat back to the person what has been said. Now the person will learn that you have heard what he or she had to say, and the reason you're not responding is because you choose not to.

- **Validate the other person's feelings.** If the person is angry about something that is basically a misunderstanding, you can find a way to validate the person's feelings even though you disagree with his or her assertions. You might say, for example, "If I thought that was going on, I'd be upset too." The aim, here, is to find tactful ways of saying to the person, "It's understandable for you to be upset, and now let's take a look at the facts of the situation to see what we can do."

  Learn the difference between validating feelings and validating facts. Saying to someone, "Don't feel that way," has an alienating effect. Supervisors sometimes tell subordinates not to feel what they feel and then wonder why the workers become less motivated, and lose confidence in management.

  Think back to a time when you told someone about something that was upsetting you and the person said, "Don't feel that way," or, "You shouldn't feel upset." How did you respond to that kind of reaction? You probably ended up feeling doubly upset—upset about the original problem and then upset about being told not to feel what you were feeling. It can be distressing to have someone tell you that your feelings are not acceptable, or that you should make those feelings go away. Keep this in mind as you legitimize the person's anger without necessarily agreeing with the complaint.

- **Find areas of agreement.** Let the person know about those aspects of the complaint or irritation you can agree with. If there is justification for the complaint, then of course acknowledge that, and ask the person what remedy they would like to have.

- **Thank them.** It is a sign of emotional strength to be able to thank people who give you unpleasant information. Thanking people for expressing their anger directly to you is also practical. I saw a card on a restaurant table that read, "If you like our food, tell others. If you dislike our food, tell us." The restaurant manager understood a simple principle. The less you listen when people have something unpleasant to tell you, the more they will go around telling their story to others. The corollary is, the more you can listen accurately to unpleasant messages, the more quickly you defuse the other peoples' anger, and the less likely it is people will be saying negative things about you behind your back. You may also find that you have learned information that proves useful.

- **Add more.** After you learn how to do the above fairly well, an advanced level skill is to add more arguments in favor of the person's case against you. One of the most effective ways to demonstrate to the individual that you truly understand what he or she is going through, is to help make the person aware of a supporting argument, viewpoint, or fact which hasn't yet been considered. You might say, "And beside that, you're a busy person; you don't have time to come down here to try to straighten out a mess like this."

An excellent example of an effective use of these steps is in Shakespeare's play, *Julius Cæsar*. After Brutus and the other conspirators stab Cæsar to death, they bring his friend Mark Anthony in to see what they had done. They don't kill him because they hope he will strengthen their hand by supporting them. They stand with their hands on their daggers and present him with a choice, "Are you for us or against us?"

Mark Anthony sees that if he sides with his friend Cæsar against the conspirators, he will be stabbed to death. Yet, if he sides with the conspirators, he knows that everyone will see him as a weak, cowardly, unreliable friend.

His response is to not accept either of these two choices. He says he wishes to speak to the crowd at Cæsar's burial, and he promises to say nothing against the conspirators. The conspirators need his support, so they agree to his request.

When Mark Anthony steps before the crowd, he is facing an angry mob. The conspirators have inflamed the crowd by convincing the Roman citizens that Cæsar had to be killed because he was such a great danger to the country. Mark Anthony is known to have been Cæsar's best friend, so the anger the people are feeling toward Cæsar is now directed toward him. With vigilant conspirators standing behind him, and an angry mob in front of him, Mark Anthony begins his famous speech, "Friends, Romans, countrymen, lend me your ears. I come not to praise Cæsar, but to bury him."

In his speech, Mark Anthony states the case of the conspirators against Cæsar. He justifies their actions, supports the validity of their beliefs about Cæsar, and adds more arguments in support of what they had done.

But then he starts asking questions. By the time he is through, the mob has changed from being angry at him to being outraged at what the conspirators did to Cæsar. They chase Brutus and the others down and kill them.

When you have to handle an angry person or group, the suggested steps (in whatever combination you find practical for yourself) are very useful for reducing high conflict to a more moderate level. This does not mean that by doing the above you're going to end up agreeing with the other person. What you are doing is drawing off the strong negative emotional charge so that the person is more capable of discussing and talking with you about the situation.

People think and solve problems most effectively when they are in a state of moderate emotional arousal. By going through the steps above, you can bring people from a state of extreme anger to a more moderate emotional level. You may also find that after having demonstrated good listening, the other person will be influenced to imitate your example.

- **Describe the problem or goal.** If your aim is to reach an agreeable resolution with an angry person or someone opposing you, and you have followed the steps that are useful in resolving conflict, what next? Where do you go from there?

At this point, describe to the person the problem or goal behind the procedure or incident. Then ask for suggestions about a better way to handle the problem. Almost everything you do that has an effect on other people can be described in terms of either being an effort to solve a problem or reach a goal. Keep in mind this principle: *People are seldom influenced by the answers unless they experience the problem.*

This means that after the person has calmed down and is in a more receptive mood, you can state, "This is the problem we have if we don't do things this way. Do you know of a better solution?" Or, "Here's the improvement we hope to make with the new procedure. Do you have any suggestions as to how we could improve our procedures without causing this particular difficulty?"

Results

This series of steps won't always work, of course. But it gives you a much better chance than you might have had previously. In most instances, people will respond more positively than you might imagine. That's what happened to a dental hygienist who followed the above-listed steps for resolving conflict. She wrote me saying:

> Yesterday I got a very hostile patient to (1) sit down; (2) I established eye contact and gave her my complete high-quality attention; (3) I rephrased her complaints (which took a little doing when she said the doctor's attitude was "shitty and he was a pain in the ass"). I suggested that although she felt he projected a crappy attitude, he was caring. I let her know I was interested. She was in a less hostile mood and more receptive when the dentist came in. She left happier and we weren't emotionally exhausted the way we usually were. These suggestions really worked!

Here is the result obtained by a school principal:

> I reported to work early Monday morning, charged up with the information I learned about dealing with conflict. It wasn't ten minutes before the phone rang. An irate parent called using the same old, run-of-the-mill obscenities that are continually overworked. She told me she had sent her eldest son and daughter to school to "get me."
>
> The young people entered my office, likewise vocalizing obscenities. They threatened my body with harm,

etc. I listened and said to myself, "This won't get me down, this won't get me down," and then began following the steps on how to handle conflict.

When the young people left, they were apologetic, asking what they could do to assist in remedying the problem. They were willing to explain to their mother what had occurred, and they agreed not to come back in such a manner again. It was great! I feel that as a result, the process is now firmly imbedded in my mind and will be used as often as necessary.

Increasing Your Chances of Success

When you use the recommended steps, many times the angry person ends up apologizing. There will be times, of course, when the approach will not work. It won't work when you have an individual who has a consciously planned strategy worked up around being very angry.

People responsible for collections, for example, find that when a person owes money, sometimes the underlying purpose behind an angry complaint is to get the amount reduced. Some people have found that it is worth money to yell and scream as though greatly offended.

When looking for a way to resolve a conflict, particularly with an angry client or customer, ask the person, "What would satisfy you? What do you want?" Don't make assumptions about what the person is after. Find out from the person. Let the person tell you. Better yet, *ask* the person to tell you.

Once both of you are clear that money is the issue, then you must decide whether or not you feel it would be useful to reduce the bill. As a practical matter, it may be less expensive than the cost of turning the account over to a collection agency.

It is very important in any such conflict to develop relaxed awareness and to achieve as much empathy as possible for the person you're dealing with. This gives you your best chance of coming up with a satisfactory solution. If you sense that a person is playing a game with you, then you are able to take a more firm position and insist on payment.

Other Benefits

If you try to resolve a conflict by seeking a win/win outcome—a positive outcome for *both* you *and* the other person—you will soon find out whether the person is basically reasonable or is someone who needs a target for his or her anger. In the presence of an active, empathic, question-asking listener, most people will calm down and be willing to work something out.

The average person has enough common sense to know that all organizations are run by human beings and that mistakes, difficulties, and errors occur from time to time. By being open to listen to people even when they are upset, you keep the main body of the community on your side. The vitriolic person who takes an extreme position against you, makes threats, and rages at you will not rally support for his or her vendetta. The chronically hostile person will end up isolated from community support.

Where to Draw the Line

When someone directs a derogatory, hateful attack towards you and refuses to listen to reason, there is a point at which you can call a halt to offensive language. A claims adjuster with an insurance company told me that when someone loses control he may say, "I don't have to listen to this. We'll talk later when you've calmed down." Then he hangs up or walks away.

An employee in the city water bureau was threatened and subjected to abusive language by a citizen who owed the bureau money. The incident was reported to the city attorney, who sent a letter to the angry person informing him that it is against the law to threaten a city employee with physical harm and that another incident could lead to prosecution. All people, even IRS auditors and county tax collectors, have the right to protection from threats.

Distinctions Lead to Choices

When someone is angry, there are at least three possibilities as to why: (1) you and/or your organization have made a mistake; (2) the person mistakenly thinks you made a mistake, and/or (3) the person needs a target for his or her wrath. When you ask, listen, repeat back, ask clarifying questions, validate feelings, and add other arguments in favor of what seems to be happening with this person, you can determine fairly quickly which of the three instances exists. In the first case, you have gotten information you immediately agree with. In the second instance, you can clear up a misunderstanding and perhaps turn an antagonist into an ally. In the third case, you are no fun to fight with.

Isn't This Manipulation?

Some people ask if using these steps for resolving conflict is manipulative. The answer depends on the intention of the person using the steps. Learning how to be more effective with people doesn't mean you are manipulating them. Manipulation usually implies that one person is taking advantage of another in an unethical way. The method outlined here is a way of influencing highly emotional situations so that everyone can benefit from the outcome. It is an ethical "win/win" strategy.

If you are unfamiliar with useful ways to handle conflict with people, then the steps can feel unfamiliar and artificial at first. But this is the case whenever you learn a new skill, procedure or concept. At first you will be self-conscious about trying to put the skill or idea into practice. Over time, however, you will learn to do so automatically. The same is true for handling conflict. You'll find with experience that following these steps works so well it becomes very natural and is simply a useful thing to do.

The concern about perhaps appearing to be false raises the issue of what it's like to have a survivor orientation. The question is: Just because some people use techniques to manipulate and deceive people, does that mean that you won't follow steps that can be extremely useful because you want to avoid appearing like a manipulative person? And does this mean you feel it is your responsibility for how others perceive you?

Perhaps the best way to resolve any doubts about the suggested steps for dealing with angry people is to ask how you would feel if handled in such a manner when you were angry at a person or a group? Would you want people to react by asking questions, by listening carefully, and by making every effort to see how your complaint is legitimate and reasonable?

Even if you are strongly motivated to resolve conflict in a mutually winning way, other people may not cooperate with you. When others act in ways to prevent things from working out well, you will not be as successful as you hoped.

For example, an office manager who had attended one of my workshops gave me some unexpected feedback when I ran into him at a basketball game one evening. He said, "Al, I had a chance to use that technique you taught us."

"What happened?" I asked.

"My boss wanted me to change several of the procedures in the office, but I refused to go along with him. I let him know I was in charge and I was going to run things my way. One day he called me into his office. The regional vice-president was there and they started asking me why I wanted to keep the procedures the way they are, so I told them. They listened to me and said everything back to me and told me what I was doing was reasonable."

His eyes got intense, he smiled, and said with pride, "I saw what they were doing. They were using your method on me, so I made sure it didn't work!"

"Thanks for the feedback," I said, "I like to hear how people have benefited from my workshops."

If you suspect someone is using these steps as a technique to get rid of you, or to trick you into thinking you've been heard, then decide for yourself what you want to do about it.

When you feel it would be useful to improve your awareness of what's happening with people who are angry and upset with you, then try the steps to see how well they work. If you feel that the results are not worth the effort and you like handling people in another way, you can always go back to your former method of reacting to people.

The suggestions made are not put forward in the sense of what anyone should do, but what one *might* do as a way of learning how an everyday difficulty can lead to becoming stronger and more skillful. Reacting to angry people with curiosity, empathy, self-managed learning, and synergistic intentions is a very powerful way not just of surviving, but of thriving, in life. With practice you no longer become distressed or experience emotional turmoil. Handling angry people feels more like a workout than a battle.

Psychological Self-Defense

Some people have a cutthroat attitude. Their only concern is for themselves. They are not motivated to achieve a win/win outcome. In dealing with them, you may need to use the method of empathic listening as a means of psychological self-defense. If you have any training in the martial arts or hand-to-hand combat, you may recognize the same principles. To do well in Karate, Judo, Aikido, or any other martial art, requires essentially the same orientation as used for handling an angry person. When an individual attacks you, you must remain relaxed and alert. When the person makes a move toward you, you must be active; it does no good to passively stand and let your opponent beat on you until he or she collapses from exhaustion. You must take positive action to move toward the energy coming your way, make contact with it, and then divert it. You make contact with your opponent's hand or weapon and deflect it away from you. Your aim is to divert the person's energy past you so that you don't take the force of it directly. When successful, you're standing next to your opponent with his energy moving away from you.

Empathic listening is a way of deflecting an angry person's verbal attack so that his or her hostility also moves away from you. When the person attacks, you respond by pulling the message toward you instead of freezing up or pushing back. When you ask questions, clarify, repeat back, validate, and demonstrate understanding, you end up standing together, shoulder-to-shoulder, looking with the person at the problem they are upset about. You are not the target.

Or You Can Call It a Friendship Response

If you look back at the sequence of responses for dealing with angry people, isn't it what you would do if a good friend were upset and wanted to talk with you? Your friend is upset and has asked you to come over right away. When you arrive, you quickly ask what happened. You listen intently and check to make certain you are getting it straight by repeating back certain portions. Your friend is so upset that the story is a bit disorganized, so you ask clarifying questions. You agree that your friend's distress is legitimate and even remind him or her of several other supporting facts. You go through the story several times and then, as things calm down, ask what he or she will do now.

That is why empathic listening works so well. The angry person expects you to act like the enemy. You throw the individual off balance by responding like a friend.

"Black Belt" Emotional Skills

When you develop the ability to remain relaxed and in control of your reactions with angry people, you may even look forward to encounters with them. You no longer feel helpless and react like a victim of emotional abuse. You experience handling angry people like an easy workout, in the same way that a martial arts master handles an unskilled attacker.

With experience, you can handle anger and threats quite easily. An inspector with over 20 years of service in the Army Corps of Engineers told me about going to inspect a section of river bank on some property owned by a small trucking company. He suspected the owner had been dumping fill along the river bank to increase the size of his property without having a permit to do so.

As the inspector walked up to the old mobile home used as an office, the owner happened to step out the door. The owner glared and yelled at the inspector, "If I'd seen you coming on my property without permission, I'd have shot you!"

The inspector didn't flinch. He said, "Who put a burr under your saddle?"

The owner shook his head and said he'd "had it" with government paperwork, all the tax payments, delays from job site inspections, idiotic fines—he was totally fed up.

The inspector listened and talked with the owner. Later they came to an understanding about the river bank.

Why is it So Difficult?

Learning how to handle angry people is not easy if you were raised to be a "good child." Why? First, you were raised to think that a good person does not get angry at others. You training was to invalidate angry feelings. That makes it very difficult to validate angry feelings in others.

Second, because you were not taught how to handle your own anger well, an angry encounter threatens to overwhelm poor inner controls.

Third, a good person reacts like a victim when upset by what another person does. It is an opportunity to use the incident as a chance to be a martyr.

It is not easy to learn how to handle anger in healthy ways, but it can be done. All human beings have the ability to overcome mistakes made with them as children.

How to Get Angry and Have Things Get Better

The person raised to be a "good child," men who batter their wives, and bosses who yell and scream at employees all have something in common. They have never learned how to express anger in words in a way that can lead to their relationships getting better. George Bach, a social worker by profession, found that when couples came to him for counseling on how to save their marriages, he had to teach them how to fight fair with each other. The following guidelines adapted from Bach's work show how to express anger and deal with conflict in a way that can make things *better* with others.

- First, appreciate that you can't get rid of an old, unproductive habit without attempting a new, more effective way of acting. To make things better, you must take risks.
- Make an appointment with the person. The skill to learn here is the ability to ask someone who has done something upsetting to speak face-to-face with you at a time when they are prepared to listen. It doesn't accomplish anything to talk behind his or her back, catch the person by surprise, communicate indirectly through actions, or send an angry letter.
- Meet in a place away from other people.
- Remind yourself that you do not want to mortally wound the person, you want only to express your feelings about an upsetting behavior.

- When the time is right, say to the person "I feel _____ because you _____ ." Do not start your statement with "You...." That puts most people on the on the defensive and makes it harder for them to listen. Rehearse saying "I feel _____ , because _____ " over and over.
- Ask the person if he or she realized that what they did or said upset you. Ask why they did it. Listen to their explanation.
- Limit your talking to only this one matter. Do not bring up the fifteen other things they've done in the past that you got upset about.
- Request what you would prefer that they do in the future. This is very hard for a person raised to be unselfish, but it is an essential step for working things out.
- Discuss the situation and what might be done to avoid it in the future.
- Regardless of the outcome, thank the person for taking time to talk with you. This keeps the door open for future times.

Models for Action

Human beings upset each other in many different ways. The guidelines for using a learning/coping response as an effective way to improve how you handle yourself with angry people and negative people show what you can do when you work to change yourself instead of others. The guidelines can be adapted to a variety of people that you find difficult to work or live with.

Whenever you get tired of feeling frustrated or vulnerable to what another person says or does, try thinking of them as a teacher assigned to you in the school of life. You can decide to not learn any lessons at this time, of course. That's OK because the school of life is so well organized, it will arrange for you to have many more opportunities to learn!

Having now covered some practical ways for learning how to handle difficult people and difficult situations, it is time to look at how our inner "selfs" play a role in determining how well or how poorly we deal with life's adversities and disruptive changes.

CHAPTER TWELVE

THE ROOTS OF RESILIENCY: YOUR INNER "SELFS"

A group of about 180 state managers sat talking with subdued voices. Their faces were strained. They had just learned that in the months ahead over 4000 state employees would be laid off and their departments would be reorganized. Many of these managers would be laid off as well. That, or demoted to their last clerical position. Never before, in their many decades of public service, had they ever faced such devastating changes.

Losing your job through no fault of your own can be extremely distressing. When an organization lays people off, it does not matter that you have worked hard and gotten excellent performance evaluations. Your job is eliminated; you are out of work.

People react to job loss in different ways. A few are resilient and cope well. They rebound quickly, orient to the new situation, and start dealing with it. For some the situation is so emotionally devastating they go into emotional shock. Others feel like victims. They blame management, politicians, foreign competition—anyone—for what has happened.

With thousands of people being laid off, it turns out that white males in mid-level management positions are the most emotionally devastated by job loss due to budget cuts, down-sizing, and reorganization. Many of them feel deeply distressed despite assistance with resume writing, out-placement services, and job interview coaching.

The unemployment crisis has uncovered a hidden weakness in many male managers. Their sense of identity and feelings of worth have been based not on an inner sense of who and what they are, but on external proofs of masculinity. The validation of being a man was derived from job title, office location, budget amount, number of people managed, and income level.

Many men taking college classes to prepare for new careers often report feeling diminished. Many men who have to sign up for unemployment benefits while their wives bring home a paycheck feel depressed. Their job loss is more than an unemployment crisis, it is also an identity crisis.*

Guidelines for overcoming the inner weaknesses that keep a person from coping well will be covered later in this chapter. First, however, it is important to examine and understand the roots of human resiliency. Crises that require you to manage your own survival force you to develop your inner resources. While there are many services and external resources available to you during such rough developments as job loss, divorce, bankruptcy, or disabling injury, you will not be able to utilize those resources effectively unless you also draw upon your *inner* resources.

Thriving In Adversity: Developing Stronger Inner "Selfs"

Our bodies have three major nervous systems, the autonomic, somatic, and central. The autonomic nervous system governs the state of our feelings. The somatic controls our physical actions. The central nervous system contains the cerebral cortex that makes possible our verbal, conceptual thinking and nonverbal, visual thinking.

As we grow up we develop a sense of ourselves linked to the three major nervous systems. We develop *feelings* about ourselves, we anticipate our ability to take effective *actions*, and we develop *thoughts* about ourselves. These internal experiences of one's self are referred to as *self-esteem*, *self-confidence*, and *self-concept*. When they are strong, positive, and healthy you can cope well with job loss, divorce, disabling injury and other life adversities. If your inner resources are not strong, you tend to suffer more and cope less well. Here is how they function, and affect you:

Self-esteem is your emotional opinion of yourself. It is how you feel about yourself as a person. A demotion, job loss, or divorce

---

* Men deriving feelings of masculinity from their jobs may help explain the "glass ceiling" that has kept women from promotions. If women can handle management positions as well as men, how can males prove they are men? See chapter 19 for more about this.

may uncover how your feelings of esteem were derived from your job title, paycheck and social role. But these external proofs of importance are not the real source of anyone's *self*-esteem. People with weak self-esteem often exaggerate or cling to those external proofs to compensate for a *lack* of self-esteem. The emotional benefit you can gain from losing your position or employment is to realize that positive regard for yourself is essential for coping with losing external proofs of how special you are.

People with strong self-esteem feel less vulnerable to the negative opinions of others. Their self-esteem acts like a thick energy blanket around them. It enables them to shrug off hurtful criticisms. It also lets them appreciate compliments. People with strong self-esteem neither play up nor play down their accomplishments. Surely you know someone who is a good example of this kind of high self-esteem. There is a kind of solidity, or stability to them, as if their *core* is not effected by the turbulence around them. If you are like most of us, you feel this way sometimes, and at other times feel a bit more wobbly. The good news though, is that strong self-esteem can be developed during challenging times. The more frequently you appreciate yourself, despite what goes on around you, the more you will feel *strong inside*.

Self-confidence refers to how well you expect to do in a new activity. It is an action predictor. Generally this confidence is based on your reliable abilities and strengths. People lacking self-confidence feel they cannot rely on themselves, and they avoid risky efforts. These people suffer a great deal of anxiety when unwillingly thrown into a situation that requires them to perform unfamiliar work, and navigate in unknown territory.

People with strong self-confidence know they can count on themselves *even more than they can count on anyone else*. People who exhibit impressive self-reliance have strong self-confidence. Such people expect to handle adversities and succeed in new activities.

Self-concept refers to your idea about who and what you are. Some of your self-concept may have been based upon your occupation or employment by an organization. Many out-of-work loggers and communications workers are having a difficult time retraining for new careers because their identities have been based on their work.

You may have noticed that some people go to great lengths to prop up their self-concept. The need for a positive self-concept is so strong that some people will lie about what they have accomplished and how much they earn. Others deny immoral or unethical actions when confronted because they cannot handle the truth that they acted as they did. Some try to compensate for a weak self-concept with impressive clothing, titles, high income, important friends, "the right address," outstanding children, and other external "proofs" of being successful. That is why they are so devastated when they lose those external proofs.

Why Strong Inner "Selfs" Are Essential

People coping with job loss need the inner strength that comes from healthy, positive, inner "selfs." A positive self-concept, strong self-confidence, and healthy self-esteem give one the ability to shrug off *almost* being hired and go into the next interview feeling positive. A person looking for a good position needs to demonstrate to prospective employers how well he or she can hold up under pressure, quickly grasp and empathize with the employer's needs, and accurately and confidently state his or her qualifications for the job.

A divorced person survives the emotional blow better when his or her inner "selfs" are strong. People who don't cope well may have been relying on their spouses to compensate for deficits in their self-esteem or self-concept. (Which may have contributed to the breakup of the marriage.)

Women and men who are raped, especially by acquaintances, often find emotional recovery very difficult. The process is made easier in a group with other survivors (not victims), especially when each person is encouraged to develop strong conscious feelings of positive self-regard, rebuild self-concept, and develop self-confidence.

People with head injuries or a disfigurement need strong inner selfs to act as buffers against the negative stares they get from insensitive people. People who find themselves a minority and people made the target of rumors also need a strong inner buffer between the self they know and the hostile talk.

Some people work in settings where they are subjected to intensely negative feelings from others. Dentists, for example, report that when socializing, it is not uncommon for them to meet someone who says, "I hate dentists!" It takes strong self-esteem and self-concept to survive being the focus of such insensitive hostility.

Public employees need strong self-esteem and a strong self-concept. It is common for them to meet someone in a social setting who asks what kind of work they do. When they say, "I'm a state employee," or, "I'm an accountant for the federal government," or, "I work for the city," they often get a negative reaction. The other person changes expression, draws back, and a cold look comes over his or her face, as if to say, "Oh, you're one of *those*." Then the person leaves as soon as possible.

It takes a strong, positive inner sense of self to deflect that kind of prejudice. Anyone whose work is in the public eye needs a strong inner identity. Public officials, editors, and school superintendents, for example, routinely receive many letters and phone calls telling them what they're doing wrong.

Your Inner "Selfs" Determine How Well Your Life Progresses

Strong self-esteem, solid self-confidence, and a positive self-concept, provide the inner foundation for:

- recovering from major setbacks such as unemployment, divorce, disfigurement, or loss of a loved one.
- setting challenging goals, imagining yourself as successful, and handling success when it occurs.
- accepting praise, recognition, and friendship as legitimate.
- learning from mistakes and failures.
- not being pressured into undesirable actions or situations out of fear of being disliked.
- resisting being manipulated by insincere flattery.
- rejecting undeserved criticism as something to ignore.
- admitting mistakes and apologizing to others for them.
- handling new, unexpected developments, knowing you can count on yourself.
- building your identity on being a unique, special human being.

A Self Strength Assessment

Interestingly, a person may be strong in one self dimension and weak in another. To determine how strong your different aspects of self are, ask yourself the following questions:

- Am I reluctant to engage in self-praise? Do I avoid thoughts and feelings of self-appreciation? What do I fear might happen if I think nice things about myself?
- How do I react when someone compliments me? Do I get nervous? Or quickly dismiss the compliment and escape from it?
- Do I like how I dress? What is the condition of my car? My bedroom? Does the place where I live and sleep show that I regard myself as a special person?
- When faced with a difficult challenge, do I know I can count on myself to handle it well? Am I pleased to have me on my side?
- What kind of self-talk do I engage in? Do I tear myself down? Scold myself? Call myself names? Try to beat people to the punch and criticize myself first?
- How do I describe myself? What is my identity?

Your ability to respond with resiliency to minor or major life adversities is strongly determined by these inner "selfs." If weak, they can handicap your efforts, and if strong, they can be an invaluable resource. The stronger all of them are, the more you have a personal advantage in difficult situations.

How to Build a Strong Team of "Selfs"

How to Develop Strong Self-Esteem

How do you develop stronger self-esteem if you desire it? The best way is to separate the way you feel about yourself from the way others seem to feel about you. This may sound difficult if you haven't done it before, but it is a mental habit that can be practiced and developed. Take time to make a list of all the ways you value yourself and feel good about yourself. Become aware of your self-talk. You may need to take a strong grip on your inner dialogue, and to repeat things like: "Despite what has happened, I like myself." Become a staunch supporter of your inner sense of your worth and value. Honor yourself, even if others don't. Now...

MAKE A LIST: *"What I Like and Appreciate About Myself"*

This self-appreciating activity buffers you against insensitive comments from others. If you have been laid off, acquaintances and neighbors may want to know why you. Even though you may be wondering the same thing, you need to have a comeback ready, almost like having a good return in a tennis match, so that you won't be thrown off balance by a sudden question. If someone says the downsizing is "to get rid of some of the dead wood," be ready to set them straight. You might say: "The layoffs are being handled on the basis of least seniority—not competence." If you have been through a divorce, have some sort of short statement ready for the times when someone asks "What went wrong?"

Every time you choose to have high self-esteem in the face of others' negativity, you become strengthened and inwardly freed from the ups and downs of circumstance. This kind of self-esteem makes up the difference between the feedback you receive from others, and what you need psychologically to sustain yourself.

How to Build Self-Confidence

Memories of past accomplishments and awareness of praise-worthy abilities are not usually uppermost in the mind of a person going through an unwanted, disruptive, change but they need to be! To get a handle on this, make a list of all the things you've done well, the things you know you're good at making happen. Ask yourself "What are my reliable strengths and abilities? What do I do well?" This activity will provide you with a list of skills you know you can perform well. Now...

MAKE A LIST: *"My Reliable Strengths"*

After you have created the list of your reliable strengths, practice talking about your strengths to another person! Choose a good friend to help you with this exercise and practice on him or her. A "thriving" benefit you gain from this activity is that it is a way to overcome the false modesty of the "good child" syndrome.

The thing about self-confidence is that most of us require some kind of evidence before we allow ourselves to feel confident. The list of all the things you've done well in the past is an excellent, visible way to increase your feelings of self-confidence.

Part of coping well is to remind yourself of past times when you have survived and surmounted bad situations. Employees who have been through layoffs with previous employers know that they will handle this as well. Most people with disabilities know that the road to a better future will be rough but that it can be managed.

How to Enhance Your Self-Concept

Many times when we try to think of "who we are" we come up with nouns for roles such as "I am a *manager*" or "I am Sally's *husband*." But what happens if the external frame of reference for the role disappears? Where is your identity now?

To help get away from roles as a source of identity, take a moment to check out who you would be if the external basis for your identity disappeared. For example, if you were shipwrecked on an island with several other people, what role would you play in the new community? Would you still be funny and compassionate? Brave about taking risks? Would you be a natural leader, or are you best at supporting someone who takes charge? Taking away the scenery from your current life can sometimes help you identify the real you, and thus get a more concrete self-concept in place.

What if you lived in another time in history, as in the wild west, or in an ancient civilization. What would you be like? Think about it. It's startling isn't it? You would still be you, the real you, wearing a toga perhaps, and doing different things, but your personal attributes would be the same. These qualities: your perseverance, quickness, gentleness or whatever you see—are the genuine components of your self-concept. If you would still be you in another century, you can rest assured that you will still be you in another setting or in another relationship.

Completing the statement "I am... " ten or more times will bring out your thoughts about yourself. These thoughts work like instructions that affect your beliefs about yourself, and therefore about your capabilities. Now...

MAKE A LIST: *"My Self-Concept: I am..."*

It could be helpful to talk about this list with a good friend or with a support group. It is not easy to learn how to base your identity on your personal qualities, abilities, and values instead of your roles, but the effort is worth it. The less your identity is dependent on a job title, social role or marital status, the more inner strength you have for coping with major life transitions when these external props are yanked out from under you. When your three main dimensions of "self" are strong, you believe in yourself, you like yourself and you cope well.

What to Expect

Strengthening and developing your inner dimensions of self can change your relationships, however, and the change may not be easy for others to handle. In 1991, some married men returning from the gulf war found that their wives had developed strong self-confidence as a result of being forced to make their own decisions, arrange for repairs, take care of finances, and deal with home emergencies. People who develop self-confidence seldom regress. Many wives were not willing to resume a dependent relationship and some marriages did not survive.

In some cases other people in your life may be greatly relieved. A person with strong inner selfs enjoys living and working with others who also have strong selfs. Trying to live and work with a person with weak selfs is usually an energy drain on everyone. Instead of reacting negatively to the stronger you, they may say "It's about time!"

A Paradoxical Balance

Just as life can seem unfair when people in powerful positions break the rules, there are no rules limiting what you can do to survive, cope, and thrive. Life's best survivors draw power from the laws and forces of nature and their paradoxical inner strengths. My research has taught me that the most resilient people in rough situations are those with a:

- balance between self-esteem and self-criticism.
- blend of self-confidence and self-doubt.
- positive self-concept open to accept the existence of flaws and weaknesses.

A person who is self-critical without self-appreciation seldom accomplishes much. Furthermore, the person who is constantly self-appreciating without self-criticism seldom admits to mistakes, weaknesses, and errors. This could lead to missing important chances for learning. In other words, the "selfs" in resilient people are paradoxical.

Review

Take some time now to look back through the guidelines and recommended steps for developing strong inner selfs. Keep in mind that none of this is a quick fix. Emotional work is not easy. It can be hard work and you may have relapses. The payoff is worthwhile, however. Strong inner selfs help you survive and surmount difficulties of all kinds. In the following chapters you will see how being forced to deal with illness, crisis, disaster, or even cruelty can result in discovering personal strengths you would never have believed possible.

CHAPTER THIRTEEN

SELF-MANAGED HEALING

The Dreaded Words

Joyce noticed a boil on the inside of her left arm as she got ready for bed, but she felt too tired to be concerned. She had just been through an emotionally exhausting divorce and custody fight for her two children. She was working long hours at the bank branch she managed. At home, she often stayed up late doing household chores after her children went to bed. She wasn't sleeping well at night because of a persistent cough that disturbed her. "I was thirty and had always been healthy," she says "I thought I just needed to take more vitamins."

In the morning she found two more boils on her arm. By noon more had spread up her arm and neck, so she went to an emergency medical clinic. From the clinic she was sent to a hospital for more testing.

The next day she returned to the hospital to learn the results. When she saw the grim look on the doctor's face, her heart pounded so hard she was sure he could hear it. "I'm sorry to have to tell you this, " he said, "but you have leukemia, a cancer of the blood. It is too advanced for us to cure. You have about six months to live, a year at most if you take radiation treatments and chemotherapy. You should get your affairs in order right away."

Every year thousands of patients hear their doctors give them the fateful prognosis and every year thousands of people die from fatal illnesses such as cancer and acquired immune system deficiency syndrome (AIDS). Some people diagnosed as terminally ill, however, do not die. Some live many years longer, some recover completely. Joyce Goetze is one of those. She regained her health and now, fourteen years later, her children are grown and she is continuing her career in banking.

Why Don't Some Terminally Ill Patients Die?

Bernie Siegel, the physician who wrote *Love, Medicine, and Miracles*, says when he first began to practice medicine he told patients the grim news about their terminal condition like doctors traditionally do. But every so often a person he had diagnosed as terminally ill would show up several years later. The person had fully recovered and was healthy. His prediction about this individual had been wrong.

Siegel began to wonder "Why do we doctors always study dead people to see why they died? Why don't we study people who are still alive when they should be dead?"

He set out to find answers to his questions. He tracked down patients who had not died when physicians had predicted they should. He interviewed them. He listened. He learned from them.

Siegel developed an understanding of survivors much like mine. He found that differences in the way people react to major life threats affect who will recover and who will not. The question is, why do some people recover from critical conditions when physicians believe there is no hope for recovery? What do survivors do that makes the difference?

Why is Good Information So Scarce?

Answers to these survival questions are not easy to find, however. The medical profession has devoted little attention to, and may even have avoided looking at, why some patients recover after physicians have decided they will die. Siegel came from an excellent medical school and was on staff at an excellent hospital. Yet when he became curious about people who didn't die as physicians expected them to, he realized he had to do his own research.

Physicians have a term for times when a person's illness disappears for no apparent reason. The term is "spontaneous remission." If you ask a physician to tell you why some people recover after they are beyond hope for a medical cure, the chances are you will not receive useful information. If you are seriously ill you are more likely to be told not to develop false hope.

The medical profession's lack of understanding about "spontaneous remission" is not because information about it does not exist, however. Researchers at the Institute of Noetic Sciences have assembled the largest data base on spontaneous remission in the world, but during the last seven years they have been unable to find a publisher willing to risk publishing their book.

Psychiatrist W.C. Ellerbroek tried unsuccessfully for seven years to get medical journals to publish his paper about "how to keep yourself from getting cancer, or, if you have it, how to contribute to your own recovery." It was not until he re-wrote his paper as though it was an article about acne that he was able to get it published in a minor journal.

The Learning Challenge

It is not the purpose here to explore why physicians have not wanted to study or try to understand spontaneous remission from cancer and other illnesses. The purpose is to alert the reader to the reality that part of the challenge of finding useful information includes overcoming a touchy subject with physicians, a sort of professional blind spot that they have about people who recover from supposedly terminal conditions.

Individuals wanting guidelines for survival when physicians are predicting they will die must develop their own survival strategy. How? Interview people who have survived. Read survival accounts that include the inner story of what the person felt, thought, and chose to do. Find a way to sidestep physicians' pessimism.

A Second Challenge

Another challenge in trying to understand what it takes to recover from a major illness or injury is that every individual's way of becoming a survivor is different from every other's. Thus there is no direct transfer of "how to do this" from one person to another. There are no rules, no formulas, no recipes. What one person says worked for them will not necessarily fit with what you need to do, but perhaps you will be inspired to keep on searching and experimenting to discover what *is* right for you.

Barbara Brewster's recovery from multiple sclerosis included ending a dissatisfying marriage, giving up the small business she owned, and discovering that she had a yeast infection and mild allergies to many common foods. She also had to "change at other levels," she says, "to release outmoded habits, establish more wholesome behavior patterns, reorder my beliefs, turn inward, trust, and surrender to a higher power." And she says, "I had no idea how to do this or where the process would take me."

Barbara's way of recovering cannot be successfully repeated by anyone else because her life circumstances, her ways of thinking, the illness she developed, and the nature of her path to recovery were unique to her. It must be for anyone.

A Wake-up Call

Siegel says that most patients who get better instead of dying react to their illness as a "wake-up call." By that he means they make major changes in how they live, talk, think, feel, eat, and spend their time. Television talk show host Larry King says, "Until I had my coronary...I really think I had thought I was immortal. The shocking realization that I was close to dying was a brutal awakening to me....A heart attack changes everything. You turn inward and think long and hard about what life means to you...."

Individuals who change how they live, eat, think, and feel sometimes accomplish what seem to be miraculous recoveries. In 1975, Australian Ian Gowler was training for the decathlon when he developed a swelling in his right leg. When the swelling did not go down he consulted a doctor. He was found to have virulent bone cancer and had to have his leg amputated. Medical treatment did not halt the condition, tumors were appearing all over his body. In 1976, the physicians told him he had from three to six months to live.

Ian, a veterinarian, says he searched for and began to practice "a whole range of things to stimulate the immune system." He meditated up to five hours a day. He went to healers. He went on an intensive dietary regimen. Fifteen months later, in 1978, the tumors had completely disappeared—confirmed by a thorough medical work-up.

"Hey! I Have a Human Body!"

Changes for someone who has almost died usually start with the realization that his or her body is not exempt from the laws of nature. Larry King says "You have a heart attack. First thing you think is, 'I gotta change my life'....If you smoke you give up smoking. If you're a couch potato, you start exercising. If you live on steak, you switch to fish and broiled chicken." King, like others who get the "wake-up call," stopped doing things that contribute to illness and started doing things that lead to improved health. The message here is that it is important to look at both sides of the recovery process because an understanding of self-managed healing is incomplete without an understanding of what humans do that is self-sickening.

Let's explore what you know about what predisposes a person to illness. Take a few moments to answer this question:

"If you wanted to develop a serious or fatal illness *on purpose*, what would you do?"

A Self-Sickening Plan of Action

Here is what most people put on lists of what a person could do to develop life threatening illnesses:

- Be self-frazzling. Live a fast-paced, hectic life. Don't rest. Stay up late, get up early. Keep energized with coffee.
- Eat lots of pastries. Eat fatty and salty foods. Drink beverages loaded with sugar. Avoid vegetables, fresh fruit, and breads.
- Smoke and drink frequently. Use tranquilizers and stimulants to control moods.
- Have sex with many partners without using condoms. Shoot drugs with others, all using the same needle.
- Get angry at others but hide your feelings. Worry constantly. Feel unhappy but pretend to be happy.

- Get deeply into debt. Max out credit cards and get new ones. Don't pay bills, become fearful whenever the phone rings or someone knocks on the door.
- Dislike your life and your relationships but do nothing to make any changes. Blame others for your unhappiness. Feel helpless and hopeless. Feel trapped. Count on winning the lottery as the solution to your difficulties.

This list of how to be self-sickening suggests that many people act as though they *want* to develop serious illnesses. They couldn't do a much better job of becoming sick if they tried on purpose.

Is it possible that excessive smoking, eating, drinking, and living a hectic, irritated life are a slow form of suicide? Possibly so, but there is another reason why people hang on to self-sickening actions and resist the efforts by others to get them to change. Information about how to live long, healthy lives is not part of our human knowledge base.

For thousands of years the saying of "Eat, drink, and be merry for tomorrow we shall die" was a valid philosophy of life. It fit with how things were. The discovery that we humans have bodies designed for living in good health for over 100 years is a very new development.

Now the life-style "Eat, drink, and be merry for tomorrow we shall die" leads to early death. To live long we have to create expectations different from our relatives and humans of the past. Family histories, stories in books and plays, movies and television programs show most humans dying of old age in their sixties and seventies, if not earlier, of heart attacks or other diseases and illnesses.

Such images influence personal expectations. The expectations then become self-fulfilling prophecies. You believe something will happen so you live and act in such a way to bring it about.

Here are several questions to reflect on:

- How long do you expect to live? Is there a belief in your family about when most of you die?
- Do you want to live to be 100 or more? What images come to mind if you imagine yourself being 100? Can you imagine yourself living an active, healthy, happy life at 100 or more?

- Have you had negative reactions to someone trying to get you to change a life-style habit such as smoking, drinking, eating, or over-working? How important is it to prove to them that they can't make you change? Is it worth dying for?

Inner Changes Require Feeling and Thinking Differently

A long-time acquaintance of mine died of uterine cancer awhile ago. She was a smiling, loving, "new age" metaphysical counselor who tried every cancer treatment available, both traditional and non-traditional, with no positive results. When I suggested to her that there could be a relationship between the location of her cancer and having never expressed anger about being sexually molested by her step-father when she was a girl, she explained that she felt only unqualified love for all humans, including her step-father.

Perhaps there was no relationship in her case, but it is a quirk of human nature that when people develop afflictions they often resist suggestions that they stop doing what apparently contributed to the affliction in the first place. The recovery challenge often boils down to whether or not the person will try doing the opposite of his or her well practiced habit.

For a person raised to be "good" the inner change may be to stop being so nice and start getting angry. Research in Europe indicates that people who suppress angry feelings are more likely to get cancer, while people frequently angry at others are more likely to get heart attacks. For one person the inner change is to be *less* tolerant and forgiving, to learn how to express angry feelings. For someone else the change is to become *more* tolerant and forgiving, to learn how to give up the anger habit.

The reason for doing the opposite is to establish inner emotional balance. Every time you have a feeling, there is a corresponding neuro-chemical activity in your body. It can't be otherwise. Thus the outcome is inevitable. Lopsided habits in feelings and thoughts create matching imbalances in physical systems which then make the body vulnerable to diseases and illnesses.

The inner changes can seem impossible when people mistakenly believe they are their thoughts and habits. They think they wouldn't be themselves if they gave up some mental and emotional habits they learned as children. For the person raised to be a "good child," for example, learning healthy self-love is difficult even though almost everyone working in the healing arts emphasizes the importance of self-love in people with serious problems or illnesses.

Self-love is essential for withstanding the fear of not being loved by others when you drop old, energy-draining habits. Self-love has to be strong enough to support the thinking that you deserve a happier, healthier life. It takes self-love to be motivated to work for a better life, one that supports your well-being.

Ed Roberts spends much of his time in an iron lung, but can do some traveling in a wheelchair. Ed played a major role in getting the State of California to create Centers of Independent Living for disabled persons. In an interview he said that the long, difficult struggle started when he was a student at the University of California at Berkeley in the 1960s. He said that the people involved in creating the first Independent Living Center on campus were "a whole bunch of people with progressive disabilities like multiple sclerosis, muscular dystrophy, people whose disability was terminal. They got involved in the politics of independent living and they lived longer—not one or two years, but fifteen or twenty."

Ed, who was appointed Director of the Department of Rehabilitation for the State of California in 1975, says, "People who are going, who are motivated, don't get sick as much."

Sometimes the internal shift that leads to recovery may be to become *less* dedicated to helping others. Anne Seitz was 39 years old, happily married, and the mother of four young sons when she went to her doctor for a routine physical checkup. She thought it was unusual to have to go for extra tests but assumed the doctor was just being thorough. When she went to his office to find out the results she became anxious when saw the grim look on his face. She says she had to grab the arms of her chair and hold on tight to keep from fainting when he said that she had ovarian cancer. He said that no operation or treatment could save her, that at most, she had a year to live and should get her affairs in order.

Outside in her car she broke down and sobbed. She loved her husband. She loved her sons. She didn't want to leave them. After awhile she sat up and took a deep breath. She said to herself, "If I have to die young, I'm going to enjoy what's left of my life while I'm here!" On the way home she stopped at a market and bought fresh lobster tails for dinner. She made her family their favorite dessert.

Anne decided, "If I have only one more year with my family, it is going to be the best year of our lives." She stopped going to meetings. She said "no" to invitations. She stopped all activities that were not something enjoyable to do with her husband and sons. That was in 1971. Twenty-one years later she says she is enjoying her three *grandchildren* and that her life "continues to improve, considerably, with age."

Anne did not devote herself to having happy times with her family for the purpose of getting rid of the cancer. Regaining her health was an unexpected outcome of having wonderful times with them every day.

For Anne getting rid of the illness was not the goal. Her recovery resulted from making positive changes in her life. To try to make your body not be sick is a negative goal. Any negative goal, such as trying to stop smoking, or to not be sick, is difficult to reach. A positive goal is learning to do what is good for your health and well-being.

Self-Managed Healing

It would be useful here to comment on the title chosen for this chapter. Even though "self-healing" is a more commonly used phrase, I disagree that anyone actually heals himself or herself. What a person does is make a change that facilitates healing. Anne Seitz did not intend to heal herself. What she did was change her life in a way that led to her tumors disappearing. The term "self-managed healing," thus, gives us a wider perspective. It can encompass any recovery occurring after deciding to live a better quality life and making the changes. The healing can occur whether intended or not, whether due to inner thoughts or outer life-style.

The Change May Be to Become Defiant

After Joyce Goetze learned that the boils breaking out on her body were symptoms of leukemia, she went into the hospital for chemotherapy. She stayed thirty-three days. After one week off she, went back for chemotherapy again. She says:

> I felt upset and angry. I was raised a Catholic. I wondered "What have I done? Why am I being punished by God?"
>
> My parents took me to the coast as often as I wanted. I felt tired but I wanted to walk on the beach with my children. Just walking was tiring, but I'd push myself. Sometimes I'd sit and watch the waves. I'd cry, cry until I was dry, no more tears. When I came home I'd sleep for many hours. My father kept saying to not tire myself.
>
> After a few weeks I could see how the doctors and my parents were limiting me, restricting me. The doctors were telling me when I would die, my parents were telling me that they would raise my children. I was raised to obey my father, he was strict with us. The doctors saw hundreds of patients, they were the experts. They had done this hundreds of times, but it was the first time for me. They were talking to me like I was a statistic. But they didn't see it was me with leukemia. I didn't like how they talked to me. I'm not a statistic. I'm me.
>
> I kept thinking of having only a year or less to live. I saw it was what the doctors believed. The doctors were restricting how long I could live. I decided to take a stand. I put my foot down. I decided I was going to be in control. I decided I was going to handle this. It was a long shot, but I was going to take it. I didn't have to let the doctors and my parents limit how long I could live.
>
> I went to the beach whenever I could. I really pushed myself emotionally. I felt like the rubber ball on a paddle ball. I told myself again and again I didn't want to die, didn't want someone else raising my children, I wanted to raise them myself. I pushed the limits. I turned everything inside out, upside down, backwards and reverse. I pushed myself to the limits to gain control over my emotions and my life.

I cried, and when I couldn't cry anymore, I'd roll in the sand laughing. I must have looked crazy to people walking by. I'm 5'3" and my weight was only 65 lbs. My clothes hung on me like robes. I lost all my hair. You couldn't tell if I was a man or a woman. I wore a scarf or a cap on my head. When the wind blew, it could almost blow me away. Here is this strange looking skinny person sitting by the ocean crying and laughing. I set no goals, just kept going one day at a time.

Then one day in the spring, about 8 or 9 months after I was first in the hospital, my father was bringing me home from chemotherapy. It was a sunny day, flowers were blooming. I suddenly knew I was in control of the leukemia; it was not in control of me. I knew I had control over it.

I kept on day after day, week after week, until the year was out. By the end of summer I was still alive and getting stronger. The chemotherapy upset me. I didn't like it. You can't eat—or if you do, you throw up. But I knew I had to do it and got used to it. My doctor was surprised. He scratched his head. He couldn't explain why I was still alive, but he said, "Go for it."

I went to chemotherapy for two years before I stopped. The oncology doctors told me the leukemia would be in remission for 1, 2, or 3 years and then come back. I told them to not restrict me with their talk of 3 years. I told them to never talk to me that way.

Survivors Are Not Good Patients

Bernie Siegel discovered that people who recover from advanced stages of cancer are often described by the hospital staff as difficult patients. He says that when he consults on a case he likes to see entries in the patient's hospital chart that the patient is "uncooperative," "questions why tests are ordered," "demands to be told about test results," and "insists on explanations about treatments."

These difficult patients ask why other treatments are not being used or may insist that the physician try something different. They are patients with "an attitude." It is an attitude that they are in charge of themselves, not the physician. This is not an attitude that many physicians handle well.

Who is to Say What is Impossible For You?

Moshe Feldenkrais had a knee badly damaged from years of playing soccer and competing in the martial arts. Physicians told him that his chances of saving his lower leg with surgery were about 50/50. He didn't like the odds. Moshe, a physicist, reasoned that because the human body can heal and repair itself, he would help his knee do that. He studied books on anatomy and physiology to learn the precise structure and function of every muscle in his leg and hip. He then created and practiced a series of small, pain free, frequently repeated movements designed to rebuild the neuro-muscular connections and patterns. He succeeded and went on to teach others how to use the methods he pioneered.

The Cure is More in Taking Responsibility
Than in the Specific Treatment

Most people have heard how Norman Cousins, the long-time editor of *Saturday Review*, used laughter to help himself recover from a fatal disease. When I ask people about the lesson to be learned from his story, they usually say "laughing is good for you." For me, however, the important lesson is in the way Cousins reacted when physicians told him he was dying.

In August, 1964, Cousins had become critically ill. He could move only with great difficulty. He underwent extensive medical tests. He reports there was:

> ...a consensus that I was suffering from a serious collagen illness—a disease of the connective tissue.... Collagen is the fibrous substance that binds cells together. In a sense, then, I was becoming unstuck. I had considerable difficulty in moving my limbs and even in turning over in bed. Nodules appeared on my body,

gravel-like substances under the skin, indicating the systemic nature of the disease. At the low point of my illness, my jaws were almost locked.

The pain in his body was so severe he was not able to sleep. Specialists called in on his case found that the connective tissue in his spine was disintegrating also. Cousins asked his doctor about his chances for full recovery. "He leveled with me, admitting that one of the specialists had told him I had one chance in five hundred. The specialist had also stated that he had not personally witnessed a recovery from this comprehensive condition."

How did Cousins react? He says, "All this gave me a great deal to think about. Up to that time, I had been more or less disposed to let the doctors worry about my condition. But now I felt a compulsion to get into the act. It seemed clear to me that if I was to be that one in five hundred, I had better be something more than a passive observer."

He started asking questions. His search for information about how people recover from terminal conditions led him to vitamin C and the laughing cure. He decided that the hospital was not a good place for getting well. He checked out and moved into a hotel room. He borrowed videotapes of Candid Camera programs and obtained old Charlie Chaplin films. He found that after an hour of hearty laughing he could fall asleep and get the rest he needed. He gradually recovered his health, and began to write and speak about the value of laughter.

The Doctor/Patient Puzzle

Differences in how patients and physicians react to each other is a thorny puzzle to unravel. Some physicians speak in ways that discourage patients and make them give up hope. Norman Cousins, on the other hand, in writing about his illness and his recovery, says, "If I had to guess, I would say that the principle contribution made by my doctor to the taming, and possibly the conquest of my illness was that he encouraged me to believe I was a respected partner with him in the total undertaking. He fully engaged my subjective energies."

On the other hand, when Bernie Siegel announced the beginning of a support group where people with cancer could learn how to live better and longer he got a big surprise. He says he sent out a hundred letters. He assumed people with cancer would tell others and word would spread. He says "I began to get nervous about how to handle the crowd that would appear."

How many showed up? Twelve.

Siegel says it was then that he started to learn there are three kinds of patients. He estimates that about 15 to 20 percent at some level of consciousness wish to die and will do so no matter how excellent their treatment. About 60 to 70 percent passively cooperate with whatever the physicians say. They want an authority to tell them what to do and they cooperate fully, including dying when the physicians predict. About 15 to 20 percent are the exceptional patients. They refuse to be cancer victims or let their physicians discourage them. (It was for this latter kind of person that Siegel founded the national network of groups for Exceptional Cancer Patients (ECaP) because most hospitals and physicians did not support the spirit of uncooperative patients.)

Who is in Control?

The puzzle begins to unravel as we explore two significant ways in which physicians and patients differ from each other. Sometimes the differences in physicians and patients are beneficial, sometimes they are an upsetting mismatch.

Many physicians become irritated with patients who won't obediently follow instructions and who won't accept that the doctor's prognosis is accurate *for them*. Such physicians are not usually open to consider information about alternative treatments brought to them by patients or relatives. Other physicians, however, appreciate having a patient who asks questions, wants explanations, suggests treatment changes, and is active in creating a recovery plan.

On the patient's side, the majority want to be told what to do by "A Doctor." They do not seek, nor want to hear advice about what they can do on their own. Other patients, however, become defiant with physicians who expect patients to do as they are told.

The differences in patients stem from differences people experience about how much or how little control they have over their lives. Some people believe they are controlled by outside forces, that they are pawns of fate. Others feel responsible for whatever happens in their lives—their health or sickness, their successes or failures.

Psychologists refer to this personality variable as the "internal-external locus of control." Bonnie Strickland, in her presidential address to the American Psychological Association, said that people with a high *external* locus of control respond well to placebos. When the physician says the medicine or treatment will work, even if it is a sugar pill, the person usually gets better. On the other hand, people with a high *internal* locus of control do not respond to placebos. They ask for proof. They do not respond well to a physician saying, "Take this" without explaining how and why it will work or why this medicine is better than another.

So we have a situation where the very same words and attitude emotionally supportive for one patient prove alienating to another. As shown in the diagram, a physician with an authoritarian

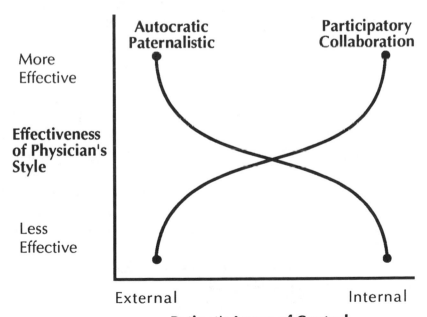

or paternalistic style is a poor match with an internal locus of control individual who may be infuriated by a doctor who gives "Simon Says" commands to patients. But the same physician is a good match for an external locus of control patient who needs to have an authority in control of what is done.

In contrast, a physician with a participative, open-minded style is a good match for someone similar to Norman Cousins who had a strong internal locus of control. Yet this same physician may be a poor match with an external locus of control patient.

High external patients do not want to be given choices, told about probabilities, asked questions about why the illness developed at this time, or made to feel guilty because they do not have the desire to transform their lives. They want a "Doctor" to tell them what medicine and treatments to take. One day, for example, I saw a secretary from the college limping across the street. When I inquired about what had happened she said she had developed a nerve disease in her legs and arms. As we talked I asked if she was doing anything on her own to recover her health. I said, "I know of some resources, if you are interested."

"No," she said, "my doctor told me that lots of people will give me advise but I'm not to listen. He is in charge of my treatment. I'll do what he says."

Being Both Internal and External

The paradoxical tendencies found in survivors holds true with the internal-external locus of control as well. Joy Blitch knew that the large masses growing in her chest were not normal. A religious woman, she prayed for good health but the masses kept growing. When she finally agreed to let her husband take her for a medical examination, the doctors said the masses were too large and that her condition was inoperable. They told her she had only a few days to live.

"I cried my eyes out for a week," she said, "and cried myself to sleep because I believed the specialist who said I had one week to live. I even made all the arrangements for my funeral!"

Joy stayed in the hospital, but even though she refused chemotherapy and radiation treatments, she did not die as expected. The doctors told her not to walk around because that would spread the cancer cells in her body. They advised her against talking much and told her that visitors would upset her.

"I prayed to God for guidance," she said, I somehow knew there were too many things unfinished in my life, that I had important work to do. I wanted to raise my son and see him grow up. I wanted to continue working with my husband in our Amway business. I had important Christian work to do.

"After five months of lying in bed, not being around people, not walking, and all the other things the doctors had me not doing, I decided if I acted as though I were well, instead of sick, I just might get well. Then I programmed myself constantly, 'It is not what the doctors believe, it is what *I believe* that counts!'

"One by one, the things they had told me started not counting in my mind." The change was not instantaneous. "I had to work at each thing by itself," she said. "First I ignored the 'don't talk out loud' instruction. Then 'don't be around any people,' 'stay in bed' and, finally, 'don't walk much'."

A year later she was back home. She went walking everyday and talked with people as much as she wished. Joy still had the tumors but she believed from reading the Bible that if she could find a minister to perform the healing ritual that God would heal her completely. She said, "My own minister wouldn't do it. I showed him the passage in the Bible but he turned me down. I went to other ministers but they wouldn't do the ritual. I telephoned many churches. I finally found a minister in Chicago who knew about the ritual and said he would perform it for me over the telephone."

Joy said that immediately after the ritual the tumors started to shrink. Several months later they were completely gone. "My doctor was amazed," she said, "he checked his records but found he hadn't made a mistake. I kept telling him it was God's will for me not to die."

Joy started telling her story to friends. She spoke about her recovery at Amway conferences. People from all over the country would telephone her late at night and early in the morning to ask her for help. She lost sleep. She tried to help everyone who contacted her. She wrote letters. She prayed for a long list of people. She talked on the phone for hours.

Then her tumors reappeared. She prayed for health but they got larger. She went to the doctor again. He said her condition was incurable. She had the minister in Chicago do another healing ritual and again the tumors disappeared.

This time she started saying "no" to most people requesting help. She no longer answered her phone during the night. She spent more time with her son and husband. About five years later the tumors reappeared but they did not respond to her prayers or the healing ritual this time.

Joy's way of reacting to the physicians' beliefs about her was to use an "internal" style to transfer control over her recovery from one "external" authority to another. She replaced her acceptance of the physicians' authority in such matters with her belief in God's superior power.

Spiritual Healing and Non-spiritual Healing

Keep in mind that Joy Blitch had been expected to die at the end of the week—yet she confounded the experts by living for many more years. Such astonishing cases are that rare. The Christian Science Church has thousands of testimonials from people healed through "spiritual-mindedness," a healing method "based solely on the healing power of God, not of the human mind."

At Lourdes, in France, at the sight where an apparition of the Virgin Mary appeared in 1858, there have been over 6000 miraculous healings registered. (Sixty-four of these have passed the stringent scrutiny of the International Medical Commission and have been officially declared miracles.)

Yet while many people are healed through a spiritual experience, there are many non-believers who experience healings. A man I know, an outspoken agnostic, has healed himself twice of cancer. Both times he used meditation and imagination in ways taught by Carl Simonton and Stephanie Matthews Simonton.

Healing: Can You Imagine That?

Carl, an oncologist, and Stephanie, a psychologist, have developed imaging techniques with impressive results even for cancer patents diagnosed as having medically incurable malignancies. As reported in their book *Getting Well Again*, about 9 percent of the patients using imaginative processes got rid of their cancer completely, 8 percent had the cancer regressing, and 11 percent had stabilized the disease. Altogether, the 159 patients in their first program lived roughly twice as long as other patients with similar conditions.

In 1974, the tumor in the center of John Evans' back was diagnosed as a malignant melanoma. The cancer was also found in his lymph nodes. John was told that even with extensive surgery the odds were ten to one against his surviving even for five years.

John's reaction was "I am not a statistic. I am a living, breathing, thinking, human organism. And as a unique individual, despite any highly abstract odds against me, I have at any given moment at least a fifty-fifty chance. My choice is that my life is to 'go' rather than 'no-go!'" He then contacted Carl Simonton by phone. John says Simonton encouraged him to develop his own imaging technique while following his physician's orders, and to use creative mental imaging as an adjunct to medical treatment, not a substitute for it.

The mental imagery that John used while undergoing the surgeries was to imagine "my white blood cells were huge white hunting dogs, with an uncanny sense of smell. My hunting dogs would sniff around and flush out cancer cells that might be hiding. The cancer cells were small, nuisance rodents which, when flushed, would be attacked by the dogs. A dog would grab and break its neck. I could then picture the dead and dying cells being sloughed off."

For each person the image has to be one he or she subjectively feels is powerful and effective. For this reason, it may not work well to be told *what* to imagine. It works best for each person to invent what he or she feels could be an effective cancer destroyer.

Healing By Changing Self-Talk

One difficulty with recommending images is that approximately one out of every two people cannot consciously create mental pictures. Telling them to create mental images only frustrates them. Fortunately, changing one's way of thinking about the illness and one's self-talk can also have a healing effect.

John Evans overcame his cancer, earned a Ph.D. in general semantics and counseling, and now teaches people how to think and talk about their illnesses in ways that promote healing. He teaches people with illnesses to stop asking "why did this happen to me?" and just look at *what* is happening. He teaches them to replace the question "why do I have this illness?" with the statement "I have this illness." He says "once clients can throw away the 'why' part of the question they are on the road to self-help."

On the other hand, Louise Hay finds that it can be very useful for a person to find answers to questions such as:

- Why this illness at this time?
- Who do you need to forgive?
- What is the truth that needs to be told?
- What is happening in your life at this time?
- Are you happy?
- What is your body telling you?
- What problem does this illness resolve?

Hay, a social worker by training, teaches that "the only thing we are ever dealing with is a thought, and a thought can be changed." As an example, the support group she started years ago for people with AIDS has changed its name to the "PLWA group"—"People Living With AIDS." Their way of viewing their condition is to see that having the HIV virus is like having a chronic infection, and an infection can be treated and lived with. And this is proving to be the case. Many people in her support group have become long-term AIDS survivors.

Information about the connection between thoughts, words, and illness have been around for some time although they received little popular attention until recently. Many years ago psychiatrist W.C. Ellerbroek discovered that "a 'disease' is managed by all the specific psycholinguistic and behavioral events in the life history" of a person and the entire field of the person's life experiences. Ellerbroek argued that "since postures, voices, behaviors, words, and thoughts are all modifiable behaviors—there is therefore no such thing as an untreatable disease."

His way of working with patients included teaching them, first, to describe their disease or illness as a *behavior*. For example, he taught them to replace saying "I have the measles" with "I am measling." Second, he taught his patients to accept whatever was happening as being exactly the way things should be. Any illness or condition, he emphasizes, is the effect of everything that has happened in a person's life and in the world.

There is much more to Ellerbroek's way of teaching how to regain health than can be included here. The point is that changing one's words, thoughts, and self-talk can have an amazingly positive effect.

ALERT: Self-Talk Can be Overdone

While many of the current teachings about self-healing emphasize the power of prayer, positive self-talk, and imagination, none of them indicate that trying too hard can be self-defeating. Early in the 1900s Emile Coué, a Frenchman, discovered that the frequently-repeated phrase, "day by day, in every way, I am getting better and better," can have very positive effects on health, finances, and relationships. Coué opened a free clinic and through his teachings helped thousands of people regain health and improve their lives. "Couéism" spread to the United States and became a popular movement in the 1920s.

The effect of his incantation/mantra/affirmation worked best when it was *repeated passively and casually*—without thinking about it much. Why so? To avoid *the law of reversed effort*. Coué discovered that strong conscious effort, what is called "will power," can trigger an opposite effect. Conscious, forceful, willing can create a reverse thought in imagination. Declaring "I *will* get well!" may be followed by a tiny voice in imagination that says "Are you sure?" or "What if you don't?" According to Coué, "when the will and the imagination are at war, the imagination invariably gains the day."

There is No Right Way, Just the Best Way for You

If you expect that you can get better, then doing *anything you feel will be helpful* will probably get better results than doing something you *hope* might be helpful just because others have said is. The power seems to be more in doing what *you* feel and believe is right for you, than in the specific method itself.

Some individuals who develop severe cancerous conditions, such as Paul Pearsall, author of books on joyous living, devote themselves completely to the treatments. They combine the best that medical science has to offer with prayer and family support. Others, such as a professional gardener seen by Bernie Siegel, walk away saying, "I don't have time to go into the hospital," and they recover.

The Medical Profession is Learning

If you are ill the most important step for survival may be to find a physician who supports your survival spirit. Your chances of finding such a physician are greater than in the past because the medical profession is giving more attention to what health and regaining health are all about. Here are some reasons why:

- The medical profession has become more willing to study the relationship between feelings, thinking, and health because they finally have a term for the subject that laymen can hardly pronounce. The term is psychoneuroimmunology (PNI).
- Norman Cousins was appointed to the Medical School faculty at UCLA and organized conferences on PNI. His book, *Head First: The Biology of Hope*, provided an easily accessible account of the many new ways that physicians and hospitals are giving patients emotional support and creating better healing environments. In it, for example, he reported that many hospitals now have "laughing rooms" that play comedy videotapes on television.
- The increasing number of scientific studies into the relationship between the mind and disease has made the mind-body connection an important part of modern medical education.
- More physicians are recognizing the role that an individual's survival spirit plays. A woman told me recently that when she was diagnosed with cancer, her physician said "Whether you live or die is up to you. I can treat the cancer, but you will determine if the treatment is successful or not."

- Physicians who want to treat the whole person, not just the illness, have formed a national network of physicians practicing holistic medicine. At their conferences they include sessions for learning how to set an example by living more healthy life-styles themselves.
- A few programs now exist that create conditions conducive to spontaneous remission. The non-profit Getting Well program in Florida, for example, is a support community focused entirely on learning to live and feel better by "laughing, juggling, playing, meditating, painting, journaling, exercising, and eating nutritiously." Deirdre Brigham, founder and director, says, "It is uncanny. When you see someone come in you may think 'no way' can this person recover, yet many terminally ill people in our program become healthier and go into spontaneous remission. And the ones who don't recover, do get healthier and die more quickly and peacefully."

The point here is that if you don't like the way one physician or therapist talks to you, ask for another—just as you would with any person providing a service you are paying for. Most importantly, it is vital to associate with people who help you maintain your spirit and help you feel loved.

The Power of Love

Actor Burt Reynolds had his jaw broken and suffered inner ear damage during a movie stunt. He suddenly discovered that he couldn't stand up without getting dizzy. He couldn't tolerate light or sound. He couldn't eat or chew.

He remained immobilized at home in a quiet, darkened room for two years. He lost over 50 pounds. "I was lying down, vegetating," he says, "while jokes and rumors circulated." False rumors spread about his having AIDS. People he had thought were his friends did not call or inquire. They "declared me 'graveyard dead,' as my father used to say."

"You can't get your health back," he says, "unless you make up your mind you want it." One day he said to his wife, actress Loni

Anderson, "I'm choosing to get well." He got in their swimming pool and swam a little. He "felt sick as a dog," he says, but he forced himself to travel from doctor to doctor until he found one who was able to correct the damage to his inner ears.

After Burt recovered, he found it difficult to get motion picture roles because of the rumors. "I was written off, washed up, finished, through," he says. He persisted in rebuilding his career, however, and came back to win many awards for his acting on television.

Burt credits his survival and recovery to the constant love of his wife. At one point he had encouraged her to leave. He told her he would probably be an invalid all his life, his career was over, and all the money would go. She refused to listen to him, however. Loni says none of that would have mattered, she would still be at his side. "You don't need love when times are good," she says, "you most need it when times are bad."

Do You Support the Spirit of People with Physical Afflictions?

To follow Loni's lead, have you thought about how much people with physical afflictions need love and friendship? People with head injuries, for example, must not only cope with having a body and a brain no longer easy to control, they must also deal with negative reactions and stares from others. When they go into public places they must endure the emotional abuse of insensitive remarks and unfriendly stares from others. If they seek employment they encounter irrational prejudice. Their previous friends may no longer want to associate with them.

When you see someone with a head injury, cerebral palsy, multiple sclerosis, spinal injury, polio, or muscular dystrophy can you look into the person's eyes and smile? Make a friendly comment? Can you look past the body of a person in a wheelchair to see the person's spirit?

If not, consider making the effort the next time you have a chance. If necessary, remind yourself that what they have is not catching, and that you might discover a very special friendship.

Guidance and Inspiration From Survivors

Individuals who have survived and overcome extreme physical difficulties often become a source of encouragement for others. Dorothy Woods Smith had polio as a child. She worked for years to strengthen her legs. She learned to walk without braces.

Many years later, after becoming a nurse, educator, and consultant, she developed "post polio" problems. She had muscle spasms in her back, pains in her lower back and legs. She had to draw on her years of experience to recover.

She now writes articles about recovery from what health care professionals may inaccurately believe is a hopeless, debilitating condition. She talks to physically challenged people about "giving up the false comfort of magical thinking, no longer empowering the doctor, nurse, and therapist to make our choices for us, and learning instead to join with health care professionals as partners."

Jeanette Hafford had to drop out of school when she was a girl because of a rare, very painful, genetic bone disease that was to fuse almost every joint in her body. Jeanette kept her spirit alive, however, through years of pain and struggle. She says "When a home burns down you grieve the loss. You feel the pain of disaster. Then you dig around in the ashes and find smouldering shreds of dreams that can, with a little fanning, come alive. And, as the flames of these dreams burn brighter than ever before, it's surprising what a person can find...."

At the age of 29, Jeanette returned to high school. She obtained her diploma and went on to take college courses. She has won awards as a singer, song-writer, and poet. Still restricted to crutches, even though most of her frozen joints have been surgically replaced with artificial joints, Jeanette has founded a successful publishing company named "Tiny's Books For Children." She says when things go wrong she reminds herself, "Hope is the rope that swings you to the other side of despair....I allow that rope to swing me to the other side."

Creating Serendipity: Ending Up Lucky

While the original goal of self-managed healing may be to get over an illness or injury, something else often happens.

One's life spirit emerges stronger than before and usually in a new direction. Life's best survivors often report finding a gift in their tragedy.

Donna Cline was an attractive, 20 year old college student majoring in theater arts when she went off for a week-end trip with a girl friend. Their car was involved in a serious accident, and Donna's back was broken. The injury changed her life irrevocably for she was paralyzed from the waist down, and would never walk again.

After months of denial and depression, Donna accepted the reality of what had happened. Her hopes for an acting career were over, but communications still drew her, so she decided to train for a career in radio broadcasting. She obtained radio work, and although she did well, she found it dissatisfying. Her success in radio led her to pursue a career in television broadcasting. Television broadcasters are only seen from the waist up anyway, she reasoned, and she could sit and present television news as well as anyone else.

She obtained a television position at a TV station in Arizona, and did very well. From there she went to a station in Nevada. After a few months at her new position, she was asked by a group of community leaders to participate in the "Ms. Wheelchair Nevada" contest. Amused and intrigued, she entered the contest and won. From there, she went on to participate in the "Ms. Wheelchair USA" contest. And again, she won. As the contest winner, she was invited to the White House to meet President Ronald Reagan. She spoke with him about the need for the removal of barriers for people in wheelchairs, and was so persuasive that he later involved her in efforts to pass legislation to remove barriers and improve physical access.

Eventually, Donna moved on to a larger television station in the Midwest where she continues her work on behalf of people who are physically challenged. When interviewed about her experiences, Donna said, "If it hadn't been for the accident I wouldn't be doing the work I'm doing or be the person I am today. I feel chosen and lucky to know why I'm here."

CHAPTER FOURTEEN

SURVIVING EMERGENCIES AND CRISES

Facing emergencies can be especially challenging because of the shock—the unexpectedness involved. Often survival may hinge upon taking certain actions, adapting, before one has fully absorbed what is happening.

A Dream Becomes a Nightmare

After dinner Paul and Kathy Plunk touched their coffee cups together and toasted the end of their first day as the new owners of the Yachats Inn. Paul, 41, knew that buying the rustic old inn, a small, deteriorated place on the Oregon coast, was a financial risk. The down payment had taken most of their savings. He had been a mortgage broker in Arizona and was worried about how they would make the mortgage payments.

They had come to the Yachats Inn for their honeymoon three years before. Kathy, 33, had stayed at the inn almost every year since childhood. To own it and be able to raise their daughter Katie in this community was a dream come true.

It was a Thursday in January, and even though the motel business on the coast is very slow at this time of year, they had taken in their first dollar. Two men in their early twenties had registered and paid cash for a room. Paul felt reluctant about leaving that evening to attend a planning meeting, but Kathy encouraged him to go, saying it was a good opportunity for him to meet community leaders.

Soon after Paul left the two men came into the office. Kathy saw that they were nervous. They paced around and looked out the window. They demanded more fire wood. They demanded more towels. Kathy, smiling, told them where the wood and towels were.

Suddenly, both men pulled out handguns and demanded all the money. They searched the cash drawer but found less than $100. They were angry. They knew there had to be more. Pressing the barrels of their guns to each side of Kathy's head, they marched her up the stairs to the manager's apartment.

Once upstairs the leader, RK, waved his gun at Kathy and ordered her to undress. "Oh dear," she thought to herself, "this really is going to happen."

RK raped Kathy, his face distorted with anger and rage. Afterward he made her take a shower "to wash away the evidence." While she was drying off he sniffed some white powder he carried in a small plastic sack. He raped her again, so brutally that she bled.

The two men started searching through the apartment for money. Kathy saw a chance to escape. Wearing only a towel she scooped Katie up and ran down the stairs. RK was fast behind her, however. Kathy tripped and fell. RK put his gun to her head and said if she didn't cooperate he would kill her, her husband, and her daughter.

Paul Plunk returned about 9:30 PM When he walked up the stairs into the apartment he was shocked to see JF holding a gun to Kathy's temple. She said, "Don't do anything. Just walk in calmly."

RK jumped Paul from behind and wrestled him onto the other bed. The men tied Paul's hands and feet behind him and warned him not to cause any trouble.

RK searched through the apartment and found a bank book with a large balance. He decided to keep the Plunks hostage and force them to drive up the coast in the morning to withdraw money from their bank in Lincoln City.

During the long night of terror, RK kept snorting the white powder and raping Kathy, sometimes forcing Paul to watch. In between times, to amuse himself, RK played "Russian roulette" with Paul. He would put one bullet in his revolver, spin the chamber, put the gun to Paul's head and pull the trigger. Paul, expecting to die at any moment, thought to himself "Well, I won't have any more mortgage payments to make."

Paul and Kathy learned from the men that they were wanted by the police in Wisconsin and had been on a week long, cross country spree hijacking cars and robbing the drivers. Kathy saw that JF, the younger of the two men, was more decent and gentle than RK. When JF saw that Kathy was chilly he gave her a blanket to cover herself. Kathy decided to cooperate when he asked for oral sex. She says she hoped she "could develop some kind of connection or something that might help our cause."

Friday morning the two men drove the Plunk's van up to Lincoln City and rented a motel room. RK stayed with Paul and Katie in a motel while JF took Kathy to the bank. Following Paul's suggestion, they withdrew only $2500 to avoid arousing suspicion.

Back in the motel, the two men heard a radio bulletin giving an accurate, detailed description of them. They became panicky even though no one in Yachats had discovered yet that the Plunks were missing. The men decided to drive north into the state of Washington keeping Paul, Kathy and Katie as hostages.

What followed for the Plunks were many more hours of threats of death at any moment. To make the situation even worse, their risk of dying was increased by the two men speeding recklessly up the highway while drinking beer and taking drugs.

Throughout the entire time, Paul and Kathy were careful not to do anything that would put either man over the edge. Paul looked for openings to grab a gun or spot a chance for them to escape but he restrained himself because of the threat to his wife and daughter. He felt *very* frustrated. A voice in his head screamed "We never have an opportunity to do anything!" Outwardly he managed to stay calm. He and Kathy asked the men questions, tried to understand them, and attempted to show personal interest.

Kathy's plan was to do anything she had to do to avoid having her family get caught up in what she saw as RK's "death wish." Her efforts to develop a connection with JF succeeded. Late Friday night, in a motel near Mt. Rainier, RK and JF had an argument. RK wanted to kill the Plunks "and get it over with." JF disagreed. He said, "They're a nice family with a baby. They've done exactly what we asked. Let's go drop the husband in the woods like we talked about." JF convinced RK to settle for abandoning Paul up on the mountain.

About 2 AM Saturday morning, RK made everyone get into the van. He drove up an isolated mountain road. When the snow became too deep for the van, RK ordered Paul and JF to get out to put on the tire chains. When they finished, RK gave Paul a blanket and, at Kathy's urging, a stocking cap. Then he drove off, leaving Paul behind.

Paul struggled through the deep winter snow for five hours before finding an occupied mountain home. He called the police and gave them a description of the van.

After leaving Paul, the men took Kathy and Katie back to the motel for a few hours sleep. Back on the road again on Saturday morning, the two men heard a police bulletin describing the van. They pulled into a state park. RK jumped out of the van and strode across a field to search for a way to escape. Kathy and JF got out of the van and stood watching him.

A woman stepped out of a mobile home parked nearby and asked if anything was wrong. JF, keeping his gun concealed, whispered to Kathy to stay by his side. But Kathy decided to take a chance. Summoning her courage, she clutched Katie tightly in her arms and walked to over the woman. JF followed, not knowing what to do. When Kathy stood next to the woman and wouldn't move, JF turned around and followed after RK. Kathy said to the woman, "I need to get to the Police Department."

In another area of the park, RK and JF walked up to a parked tow truck. They pointed their guns at the man and woman sitting inside and got in with them. RK drove the truck out of the park. When they tried to shoot their way through a police blockade, JF and the woman were killed. RK was shot in the neck but survived, stood trial, and received a life sentence.

The Survivor Style

Throughout their ordeal both Kathy and Paul had the self-control to not do anything that would get any of them killed. They succeeded and survived because they focused on survival. They chose to remain calm and do whatever they had to do, to give all of them a chance to get out alive. This required them to adapt and develop new survival strategies many times, under the worst of conditions. Their intention to survive, and their willingness to do whatever it took never wavered.

It is common for people to think of Kathy and Paul as extraordinary people, that the average person would not have done so well. But Paul and Kathy, as do most survivors, know that they are ordinary people who were forced to cope with an extreme situation.

The question is, what make it possible for an ordinary person to survive an extraordinary life crisis?

The answer, I believe, is that *a survivor style results from interacting with everyday life in ways that increase the probability of survival when survival is necessary.*

In other words, your habitual way of reacting to everyday events influences a your chances of being a survivor in a crisis or an emergency. It is an interaction style based on using inborn potentials rather than acting as taught. The style includes three basic elements:

- Quickly absorb information about what is happening.
- Expect that something can be done to influence events in a way that leads to a good outcome.
- Be willing to consider using *any* possible action or reaction.

Because of their life-long curiosity, people with survivor personalities react to a surprising incident or unexpected development by wondering what is going on: "What is this?" "What's happening?" Their automatic openness to absorb new information epitomizes the survivor orientation. It characterizes their response to the world under normal circumstances as well as unusual ones. Whether going for a walk or reacting to an emergency, they are alert to external circumstances, events, facts, or developments.

As a consequence, in a crisis, the survivor style enables a person to *rapidly read reality*. Survivors are those who comprehend and adapt quickly just as Paul and Kathy Plunk had to do again and again.

Faster Than Words

It is difficult to write about how to rapidly question, assess, decide, and act, because the sequence happens faster than words. The questions remain unverbalized. Possible outcomes of several alternatives are weighed against each other and action is taken so quickly that the whole sequence seems to be a reflex. This can occur in fractions of a second.

Let's examine the following scenario. You receive a telephone call from a hospital late at night. A loved one has been admitted with a serious injury. You run to your car and race toward the hospital driving very fast. Ahead is a stop sign. As you come to the intersection, you slow down. You glance right, left, front and back, looking for cars. There are none. You scan for pedestrians, children, cyclists, and police cars. There are none. In a split second you absorb all this information, decide it is safe, step on the gas, and speed through the intersection.

A workshop participant once related the following incident to me. He said: "I was driving out of the city one afternoon thinking about my work. I was at a place where the highway goes under an overpass. Off to my left I noticed a man racing down the embankment on the other side of the road.

He looked desperate. He was looking back over his shoulder behind him. He ran straight across the traffic lanes between the cars and I knew he wasn't going to stop at the median barrier. I knew he didn't see me and that I couldn't avoid hitting him even if I stepped on the brakes.

"I stepped on the gas and swerved onto the emergency lane. He jumped the median barrier the way I knew he would and, still looking back over his shoulder, came across the lanes running at full speed. I don't know how I got past him, but I did, and I swear he didn't miss my left rear fender by more than a foot and a half. I stopped the car when I could and walked back. By that time, the police had him in custody. They told me he had just robbed a store."

This driver was amazed at how rapidly and how accurately he had read the situation. He took the right action without thinking about what he was doing. He had reacted automatically and did the right thing.

His experience was not that unusual, however. Athletes in competitive sports such as football, soccer, and basketball do the same thing all the time. The best athletes "read" the play, process the information, and take effective action in a fraction of a second.

Fast Questioning Expands Awareness and Develops Action Choices

The quick scan of a critical situation usually includes a fast reading of what other people are perceiving, feeling, and doing. The ability to take in information rapidly might be called accelerated learning or high-speed curiosity.

This quick grasp of the total circumstance is a "pattern empathy." The survivor style is to quickly read reality and simultaneously reach for the best action or reaction from one's reservoir of paradoxical resources. This automatic and sometimes unconscious process can cause the individual to later be astonished by what they've done, and to wonder just how he or she accomplished it.

In a crisis, the survivor reflex is to rapidly "ask" unverbalized clusters of questions, such as:

- What is happening? Not happening?
- Should I jump, duck, grab, yell, freeze, or what?
- How much time do I have? How little?

- Must I do anything? Nothing?
- What are others doing? Not doing? Why?
- Where do I fit in the scene?
- Have I been noticed? How do I appear in their eyes?
- How are others reacting? What are their feelings?
- How serious is this?
- How much danger exists now? Is it over?
- Does anyone need help? Who doesn't?

The more quickly a person grasps the total picture of what is happening, the better his or her chance for survival. Anger, fear, and panic narrow what a person sees and reduces awareness.

Truck drivers, for example, know that they are more likely to have an accident when they are angry at an automobile driver. When they get angry at a driver for squeezing in front of them, they lose awareness of what is happening in traffic farther up ahead.

Insurance company records show that people going through separations and divorces are high accident risks. A driver who is angry, upset, or preoccupied loses awareness of the highway and other drivers. The evidence is clear on this point. Being alert and aware decreases accidents; strong emotions inhibit that awareness.

Alertness, pattern recognition, empathy, and awareness can be viewed as a sort of "open-brainedness." This open-brainedness is a mental orientation that does not impose pre-existing patterns on new information, but rather allows new information to reshape the person's mental maps. The person who has the best chance of handling a situation well is usually the one with the best mental maps, the best mental pictures or images, of what is occurring outside of the body.

At this moment your brain is being fed electrochemical impulses from activities occurring at your sense receptors and sense organs. Various energies are hitting your body carrying information about what is happening in the surrounding world. People with a survivor style are, apparently, the best at constructing an accurate internal representation of the outside world in their brains.

In contrast, those people who are not able to survive well, if left to their own devices, tend to have incorrect or distorted constructions of what is happening in the world outside their bodies. When you listen to some people talk and watch what they do—how they act, think, feel, and describe things—it becomes clear that their perceptions do not match well with what is going on in the world. Their quick emotional reactions tend to overwhelm their cerebral cortexes and/or have them jumping to inaccurate conclusions about what is going on.

To Survive an Emergency: Stay Calm

What can you do in highly emotional moments? Take some combination of these actions:

- Tell yourself to stay calm.
- Take a deep breath and relax.
- Repeat a saying.
- See something amusing about the moment, if possible.

Telling yourself "stay calm" and "relax" is a useful reflex. Several deep breaths will help. Blind rage, screaming, panic, or fainting are not good solutions to a crisis unless done out of choice as a way to affect others.

John Paul Getty was a self-made billionaire. He gave as his number one rule for dealing with a crisis:

> No matter what happens, do not panic. The panic-stricken individual cannot think or act effectively. A certain amount of trouble is inevitable in any business career—when it comes, it should be met with calm determination.

Kathy Plunk tells of an amusing moment during the first night. RK had her in the bathroom and was resting his chin in his hand while thinking about how he would rape her next. Kathy mimicked him. She placed her chin in her hand and waited to see what he would decide. This did not prevent his next assault but it shows that she was not overwhelmed or panicky. She was focused outward on her attacker like a person trained in the martial arts.

Humor Improves Mental Efficiency

Playful humor enhances survival for several reasons. *First*, mental efficiency is directly related to a person's general level of emotional arousal. People are less able to solve problems and make precise movements when strongly worked up. Laughing reduces tension to more moderate levels and efficiency improves. Plotted on a graph, the relationship between efficiency and tension looks like this:

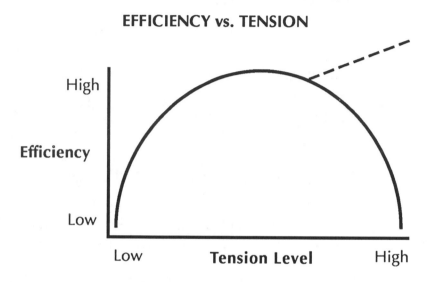

EFFICIENCY vs. TENSION

At low levels of arousal a person is slow to respond. Many people can't get going without their morning coffee. At high levels of arousal a person makes mistakes. He or she reacts too fast, panics, and loses control.

The exception, indicated by the dotted line, is for an action requiring simple, powerful muscular effort. Here, the higher the arousal the better such as a father lifting a burning car off his son who was trapped underneath.

During the Vietnam war, four soldiers were driving a jeep along a narrow dirt ridge between rice paddies. They ran into an enemy ambush. Instantly sizing up the situation and knowing that their jeep could not back up fast enough for them to escape, they all jumped out. Each one grabbed a corner of the jeep. They yanked it around, scrambled back in, and raced away to safety.

Back at camp, they told their story, but their buddies didn't believe them. The skeptics said that four men cannot turn a jeep around. The men had done it, so they bet the skeptics they could do it again. When they tried to turn the jeep around, however, they couldn't. To their embarrassment and financial loss, they discovered that they didn't have the same physical strength back in camp that they had summoned in a life-threatening emergency.

Playfulness is Powerful

Second, playing with a situation makes a person more powerful than sheer determination. The person who toys with the situation creates an inner feeling of, "This is my plaything; I am bigger than it. I can toy with it as I wish. I won't let it scare me. I'm going to have fun with this."

The owner of a high cash volume business says that occasionally a government agent will walk in and demand immediate access to all his records. Having gone through this many times in over 30 years, he sits back and thinks to himself: "I'm paying your salary. Come on, give me your best shot. I want to see how good you are." He listens and jokes with the agent about how much time the agent will spend only to end up with nothing. He does not reveal that he has a law degree and knows exactly what government agents can and cannot do. He also knows that he runs an honest business, so he remains relaxed and enjoys playing with each encounter.

Playfulness Provides Perspective

Another advantage of playful humor is that it gives a person a different, less frightening perspective. It redefines the situation emotionally. For example, a woman told me that while she and her husband were away on an overnight trip their house had burned to the ground. It was a total loss. The next morning she and some neighbors stood looking at the smoldering ruins. The neighbors were tense and quiet. She said, "That's hell-of-a-way to get rid of the cockroaches and mice." When they looked at her strangely, she just shrugged.

The person who makes humorous observations is relaxed, alert, and focused outward toward the situation to be dealt with. When former President Ronald Reagan was shot in an assassination attempt, the bullet entered through his left arm pit at a vulnerable spot above his bullet proof vest. His bodyguards shoved him into the limousine and slammed the door. As the limousine sped away, heading for the nearest hospital, Reagan said, "Did anyone find out what that guy's beef is?"

The surgeons were scrubbed and ready when Reagan was wheeled into surgery. He looked at them in their masks and gowns and said, "I hope you're all Republicans!"

When his wife, Nancy, visited him in the recovery room, she asked how he was. He answered with a famous quote from a W.C. Fields movie: "All things considered, I'd rather be in Philadelphia."

And finally, another benefit of playful humor is that it leads to the discovery of creative solutions.

Experience Counts, There is no Formula

The value of laughing depends upon the situation at hand. Sometimes laughing is the right thing to do, other times it is not suitable. There is no formula for it; it's a matter of experience and judgment.

Some situations may be so upsetting that laughing is not possible. If so, the person with a survivor orientation may swear to reduce tension and bring emotions under control. The purpose, as with laughing, is to free one's mind to understand and find practical ways of responding to the crisis.

The survivor reaction to a crisis, then, is like side-stepping a charging bull. One reads reality rapidly by asking clusters of questions nonverbally, relaxing strong emotions, and looking for something amusing to laugh at.

At the same time, total attention is on surviving and turning the situation around. The person makes an emotional commitment of the total self and devotes all energy toward finding a way to succeed. The solution, the action, is usually creative and comes out of playfulness.

A Total Commitment to Do One's Best

When problems or setbacks occur, the better survivors recover quickly from feeling discouraged. They don't waste time dwelling on the past or on what they've lost. Their energies are directed to getting things to turn out well. The following statements typify their attitudes: "There's no going back—go on the best way possible." "No one can tell me what I can't do." "Life isn't fair. Big deal. You play the hand with the cards you draw." "What would I do if my life was totally disrupted by disaster? Start over again."

Such statements reveal that emotional survival includes overcoming feelings of anger at the world for not treating them fairly. The best survivors spend almost no time, especially in emergencies, getting upset about what has been lost, or feeling distressed about things going badly. They can let go and start over. They know that if they lose everything, they will still have themselves. For this reason they don't usually take themselves too seriously and are therefore hard to threaten. In fact, they may be amused at threats to their jobs, property, or reputations.

The Power of Commitment and Self-Confidence

The survivor way of orientating to a crisis is to feel fully and totally responsible for making things work out well. The better your self-confidence, the more you can face up to a crisis believing that you can handle it without knowing exactly what you will do. When you keep at it, play with it, and allow yourself to do something unpredictable, you usually discover or invent a way to deal effectively with what has developed.

Self-confidence lets you feel comfortable in ambiguous situations. You can move into unknown territories—mental, physical, or emotional—and be curious about what you will discover. This ability to operate in the unknown comes from being able to demand a great deal from yourself. You can count on your own stamina, creativity, and ability to hold up in the worst situations.

Terry Anderson and the other hostages in Lebanon were told that they could not talk with each other but they did not accept the limitation. They circumvented the prohibition by inventing a way of "talking" by blinking their eyes.

TRY THIS: Think back to a crisis or emergency you went through. Describe what happened, how you reacted, and what you did. Without criticizing yourself, think about (1) what you could do to avoid a similar crisis again; (2) how you could handle yourself better if something like that were to happen again.

The Survival Style

The everyday habits of life's best survivors include curiosity, playfulness, empathy, needing to have things work well, feeling completely responsible for their lives working well, and learning how to influence events to result in good outcomes. The paradox is that this style of living one's life is also the best style for handling survival situations. Self-talk stabilizes emotions. Questions draw in essential information. Playfulness reduces tension, provides perspective, and can lead to a practical course of action. Life's best survivors will act logically or, if no reasonable alternative seems available, may do something irrational. Somehow they sense how to act even when they don't really know what they are doing.

Surpassing the Limits of Circumstances

Watching someone with a survivor personality perform under pressure is like listening to a good pianist improvise. If you want to hear good music, you need a well-tuned instrument and someone who can play it well. The artist is more important than the instrument, however. A beginner playing on a perfectly tuned, concert grand piano is not easy to listen to. But a concert pianist can play on even a badly-tuned piano and produce beautiful music.

The most enjoyable piano concert of my life was performed by pianist David Smith in a church camp dining room. It was late in the evening. A group of us were sitting around talking when David announced that he would play for us. The piano was an old upright, badly out of tune, with some of the ivory broken off the keys. Without any warm-up, he played pieces by Chopin, Grieg, DeBussy, and Rachmaninoff absolutely flawlessly. The music was better than the piano. David's total commitment to a perfect performance allowed him to transcend the imperfections of the instrument.

Using All Capacities and Then Some

Having all human capacities available makes possible a wide range of responses and, when organized around the motivation to make things work well, increases the probabilities of survival. It is important to understand, however, that there are exceptions to the general rule that people who *intend* to survive have a better chance than others. Sometimes people survive when they do not believe they will. A World War II combat veteran, Paul Mico, told me his company was on the front line during some of the fiercest fighting during the war in Europe. As the fighting raged on he became scared because so many of his buddies were being killed. Day by day he became more and more fearful about losing his own life.

Tired of the constant fear, Paul decided that because it was so certain he was going to die in combat, he might as well enjoy himself and have a good time during his last days on earth. At that point, he said, he began shooting and fighting with joyous enthusiasm. He kept this up until a peculiar quietness caused him to stop. He stood up and looked around. The battle was over. The Germans were retreating. Out of his company he was one of only three men still alive.

The point of Paul Mico's story is that people with better chances of survival are people who use all of their faculties. They can be logical, analytical, objective, rational, linear, time-oriented, verbal, calm, empathic, and understanding. They can be irrational, creative, visual, nonverbal, and intuitive. They can be complex or simple, wise or primitive. They can be fully committed to surviving, and they can abandon all hopes of surviving. Every function of every brain center is available whether the person is playing at a computer or responding to danger. In other words, the people who are life's best survivors react to emergencies and crises with the same habits they use in everyday life.

CHAPTER FIFTEEN

SURVIVING DISASTERS: MOTHER NATURE VS. HUMAN NATURE

As a resident of Portland, Oregon, I witnessed the eruption of Mt. St. Helens and all the events surrounding it. Observing the behavior of the public and public officials before, during, and after the big eruption, I saw how human nature creates the biggest survival challenges in trying to deal with mother nature.

The big Mt. St. Helens eruption occurred two months after the mountain first started venting. There had been many warning signs that the devastating blast would happen. Yet the 57 men, women, and children killed by the eruption made Mt. St. Helens the most lethal volcano in North America's recorded history. Afterwards I found myself wondering:

- With so many warnings, why did so many people die?
- What are the important lessons to be learned?
- What can we learn about handling other major life disruptions from studying how to survive natural disasters?

What follows are some answers to those questions.

Humans Beings Deny Danger if it is Inconvenient

Contrary to impressions created by movies and television, communities do not panic at disaster warnings. It is just the opposite. In communities with no recent history of a major disaster, a major problem for public officials is that most citizens do not take warnings seriously. Even if they hear and believe the warnings, very few take protective action—especially if doing so would require leaving jobs and homes.

Why do they not act? Partly because when people receive threatening information, they check with each other to verify whether or not the news seems to be accurate and legitimate. A sort of informal voting takes place about whether or not the message should be believed.

Sometimes lack of experience is the reason for the inaction. Those with more experience are more likely to take self-protective action. The U.S. Forest Service, for example, has a healthy respect for the power and unpredictability of the forces of nature. This respect comes from years of experience fighting forest fires. That is why the Forest Service moved its employees and their families out of the area when Mt. St. Helens gave early indications that serious trouble could be developing. As a result no Forest Service employees were killed when the volcano erupted. Neither were there any deaths in the County Sheriff's department nor among the Washington State Police.

Experts Disagree and Seem Uncertain

It is not in the nature of science for any group of scientific experts to completely agree on anything they are studying. They are even less able to agree with certainty about probable future developments.

On March 20, 1980, a huge vent of steam and pumice particles shot up from the long dormant crater on top of Mt. St. Helens and churned thousands of feet into the blue skies above. Vulcanologists immediately flocked to the mountain and started measuring its condition like a patient in a critical care unit.

During the weeks that followed, there were more rumblings deep within the mountain as a dome of lava started building in the crater. One afternoon, while sitting in my living room making a cassette tape letter to a friend, I noticed a huge plume of steam and ash rising about 20,000 feet up from the mountain. Such venting had become so common, I mentioned what I saw and went back to talking about other matters.

Our daily papers and daily news broadcasts routinely contained statements from scientists predicting an imminent eruption. These were followed by statements from other scientists or a government agency assuring there was no serious or immediate danger to anyone. As described in a special report on the eruption by *The Oregonian*, "Throughout the weeks of April and early May, officials responsible for dealing with Mt. St. Helens became increasingly schizophrenic about its potential danger to human life." The scientific waffling about the danger of Mt. St. Helens continued throughout the month of April and is given as one reason why Washington's governor Dixie Lee Ray did not declare an off-limits Red Zone in the vicinity of the mountain until April 30.

Business as Usual

Mount St. Helens is surrounded by forests. Those immediately west of the mountain are largely owned by Weyerhaeuser Company. The U.S. Forest Service controls most of the mountain itself. The State of Washington holds title to forest lands to the north.

At the first indication of dangerous volcanic activity, the U.S. Forest Service closed the mountain above the timberline to all public access. On April 1, the Forest Service moved all employees, their belongings, and household goods out of the danger area.

Weyerhaeuser, however, continued its logging operations and kept over 1,000 employees at work in their forests below the mountain. Logging operations also continued in state-held lands because Washington State officials told Governor Ray the revenues were needed to pay for public education.

When the mountain became increasingly dangerous, the County Sheriff's department and Washington State Police set up barricades to keep sightseers out of the area. Barricaded state roads did not deter people who wanted to get closer to the mountain, however. Without a legal declaration of emergency by the Governor, the police had no authority to arrest or ticket anyone who went past the barricades.

Weyerhaeuser maintains a good relationship with the people in the region by keeping its lands open for hunting, fishing, and camping. Anyone could stop at a local service station for a free copy of a Weyerhaeuser map showing all Weyerhaeuser and Forest Service logging roads. Some local residents earned money as guides by taking tourists through back roads for a close look at the mountain.

It is understandable, then, why many people believed the situation could not be too serious because the Governor had not declared an emergency and Weyerhaeuser was still running its timber-cutting operations.

Politically Influenced Decisions

On April 30, Governor Ray finally declared an area designated as the "Red Zone" off-limits but left an area designated as "Blue-zone" open to access. The red and blue zones, however, did not conform to the map of highest-danger areas drawn up by the geological scientists.

Virtually all Weyerhaeuser and State of Washington lands were designated as being in a less risky "blue-zone" while the U.S. Forest Service lands were in the red zone. The meetings at which the red and blue-zone boundaries were drawn up were closed to the public and the press. Later, when reporters asked to read the minutes of the meetings, they were told that the notes and tapes were lost.

Denial by Vested Interests

Disaster research emphasizes denial on the part of the public, but it seldom documents denial in business leaders or government officials. During the early part of May, such denial seemed to be clearly at work. Lumber crews working near the base of the mountain smelled the rotten-egg odor of sulfur and could feel the numerous earthquakes that preceded the eruption. Men who requested a transfer to logging areas farther away from the mountain, however, were told by Weyerhaeuser supervisors they either had to work where they were assigned or they wouldn't work at all.

It didn't do any good for the loggers to try to get help from the Washington State Division of Industrial Safety and Health. In April, after the mountain started frequent venting, loggers began telephoning to complain that they were being asked to work in areas near the mountain considered too dangerous for the general public. The calls averaged about three per day. The senior state inspector who received the calls said later: "I thought that most of the complaints were from people who wanted a way to get out of work, frankly I thought they were out to get unemployment [compensation]. Now I wouldn't want this to get out in the press, but that is what I thought."

On Friday, May 16, a group of loggers working near the base of the mountain threatened a work stoppage. The Union's safety representative drove up to the work site, met with 50 of the men, and learned from them that Weyerhaeuser had not followed through on commitments to provide specific escape routes from logging operations.

Individual Rights Limit Government Powers

The Constitution and other laws limit the government's power to intrude into a person's life. Owners of summer homes and cabins at Spirit Lake and other areas near the northern base of the mountain, demanded access to their properties in the Red Zone. Governor Ray was in the middle of a difficult fight for re-election. She received letters and telephone calls from people angry that Weyerhaeuser was being allowed to continue logging on nearby lands while they, the taxpayers, could not have access to their homes and cabins.

At a gathering on Friday night, May 16, the property owners were in a sour mood. They decided to form a caravan Saturday morning and drive in to their properties. According to *The Oregonian*, "Reports had filtered back to the Sheriff's office that some hotheads planned to arm themselves and run the roadblock. Anticipating trouble, the Washington State Patrol sent in eight extra cars."

From the beginning of the developing danger with Mt. St. Helens, Harry Truman, a long-time resident at Spirit Lake refused to leave the home that he and his late wife had built. Harry stayed year-round, even when deep snow isolated his cabin from the rest of the world for months at a time. Because his home was in the off-limits area, the County Sheriff deputized Harry Truman to make it legal for him to remain in the Red Zone.

Free Entertainment: the Dangers of Curiosity

The phrase "dying of curiosity" is not just a figure of speech. Curiosity does kill people. Humans are drawn to dangerous, exciting experiences. Firefighters report that one of their main problems in trying to put out a major fire is dealing with the crowds attracted to the blaze. People get too close, and if a building collapses or there is a sudden shift in the wind, spectators get hurt or killed.

As warnings of an eruption increased, more and more people gathered at a large gravel turnaround near the roadblock on State Highway 504, eleven miles west of the Mt. St. Helens summit. *The Oregonian* reported, "Souvenir hawkers and food vendors had joined the crowd that gathered in the turnaround Saturday. Smells of food and campfire smoke filled the air. Radios blared music and people mingled in small groups. There were hitchhikers of several nationalities, photographers, painters, amateur geologists and vacationers of wide description." Camper vans made the area appear to be a makeshift campground. Dozens of people left their vehicles at the turnaround in order to take trails in to camp, fish, hike, or take photographs.

The mountain was calm on Saturday. There were no eruptions, no steam or ash vents, no earthquakes. Except for the strange sight of deer and other wild animals standing motionless out in the open, there were no obvious indicators of the devastating eruption that would soon occur.

Saturday morning the assembled group of property owners received word that governor Ray had ordered a National Guard Helicopter unit to stand by in Yakima and that a convoy escorted by the State Highway Patrol would be allowed to enter the Spirit Lake area. The conditions were that permits must be issued, waivers signed, and promises made that the convoy would be back out by dark.

The property owners cooperated. They filled out the permit forms, and a complete list identifying every person in the convoy was compiled.

The police escorted convoy reached the Spirit Lake area Saturday afternoon. At dusk, a few hours later, as they were departing, they were told another convoy could go in on Sunday.

The Eruption

At 8:23 AM, Sunday, May 18, 1980, Mt. St. Helens erupted with the destructive force of 26.5 megatons of TNT, a force 500 times more powerful than the atomic bomb dropped on Hiroshima. Thirteen billion gallons of water within the mountain, super-heated from 300 to 424 degrees Fahrenheit, pulverized solid rock and hurled the stone particles across the nearby forests at 100 miles per hour. The waters of Spirit Lake, directly in the path of the eruption, were blasted out of the lake bed and splashed onto the upslopes of the surrounding ridges—much like what happens when the front wheel of a car hits a rain puddle.

Huge trees in the path of the blast were vaporized, turned into powder. Farther out, trees weighing tons apiece were snapped off at the base and laid over in rows like dominoes. Ten miles away the hot blast of pulverized stone stripped the tracks and blades off D-8 Caterpillar tractors, shredding the hardened steel like confetti.

The massive eruptions of gray steam and ash boiled and churned 12 miles up into the sky and then drifted northeast. Measurements later showed that in the eruption the volcano discharged more than one cubic mile of material into the air, a volume in weight equal to one ton for every living person on the planet. Measurements revealed that 1,277 feet had blown off the top of the mountain. The eruption and subsequent flooding laid waste to 120,000 acres of forest land. The wall of mud, water, and logs that swept down the river flowing by the base of the mountain knocked out every bridge for 30 miles, and the volume of mud carried into the Columbia river silted up the channel and closed it off to shipping. The total economic damage to the region—timber, agriculture, shipping, fisheries, property, and clean-up costs—amounted to an estimated 1.2 billion dollars.

Disbelief Prevails Over Reality

Scientists had predicted, accurately, that the eruption would cause landslides that would send millions of gallons of water from lakes and reservoirs in huge waves down the nearby rivers. How did people respond? A helicopter pilot reported that he flew down the Toutle River ahead of the 30-foot-high wall of churning water, mud, and trees, warning people below with his loudspeakers to evacuate the area immediately. He said that people sitting in lawn chairs on the bridges raised their beer cans to him and waved as he went by overhead. The watery wall of mud and trees that followed wiped out all the bridges.

Being Useful Has Many Benefits

In the first few minutes after the devastating impact of a disaster, people react in many different ways. Most people are stunned, dazed, and helpless. They do and say strange things. Some people scream, cry or run around frantically. Some people are immediately useful.

The people taking effective action are usually those who have specific, assigned jobs in an emergency. When Mt. St. Helens blew, the people *not* overwhelmed by shock or panic were firefighters, police officers, rescue teams, medical people, radio and telephone operators, and volunteers with vital, life-saving assignments.

Dougal Robertson, in his book *Survive the Savage Sea*, talks about how he reacted in the first few seconds after the sailboat he and his family were traveling on was rammed by whales. He says that people do odd things in emergencies. "Instant disaster allows no time for ponderous decisions, and actions should be taken in order of importance. Important time was wasted by myself in attempting to stem the influx of water into the yacht. The extent of the damage by one whale was irreparable and sufficient to sink us. We were hit by three...when I first shouted 'Abandon ship,' my son Douglas ran towards the sails while I was wasting time looking at the hole." Robertson says that little of what he did was useful in the three minutes it took for the boat to sink. He credits his wife for quickly gathering the items they would need on the life raft.

Denying How Bad it Is

In disasters people tend to deny the gravity of the circumstance. Immediately after the disaster, people tend to expect a quick rescue. They are slow to accurately evaluate their situation. It is typical for people to thoughtlessly consume most of the available food and water, without planning on how to survive and protect themselves if no help arrives.

In a mining disaster study, Rex Lucas described the way six miners reacted when they were trapped 12,000 feet underground after a major upheaval. The six men were experienced miners. After freeing themselves from the rubble, they gathered together in a small underground chamber. Although the devastation was extensive and many of their co-workers were dead, they anticipated that they would be out in a short time.

The miners actively searched for a way out of the area and drank freely from their water supply both the first and second days. They took great risks in moving to places where there was loose, unsupported rock. Because of their exertions and the dust, they continued to drink the available water without regard to its limitations. It wasn't until the third day that they began to realize that they could not escape through their own efforts and that they would have to wait for rescuers to reach them. Only at this point did they began rationing water.

At a different level, 13,000 feet down, another group of twelve men was trapped. Two of the men were injured and, from the start, acted in ways to conserve their water and their energy. The other ten, however, behaved like the group described above. They spent three days in efforts to tunnel out and took great risks in dangerous areas filled with loose rocks and pockets of gas which could easily have exploded. During this time they drank almost all of the available water supply.

Altering Human Customs to Survive

All 18 miners were eventually rescued. Both groups, after facing up to the prospect of being trapped for many days without food or water, had to cope with the growing awareness that they would be forced to drink their own urine. Some were more willing to try than others, and after an initial period of extensive discussion, adjustment, and some experimentation, they discovered ways to make the consumption of urine an acceptable action.

(Note: When interviewed, none of them indicated they knew that urine is sterile in the body, or that in combat, urine has been used to clean wounds before bandaging.)

The 28 people still alive after their airliner crashed high in the Andes mountains in 1972 followed a sequence very similar to that of the coal miners. They expected to be rescued quickly. During the first few hours after the crash, they had a party. They drank liberally from the supply of wine that had survived the crash and ate most of the food and candy available.

They made little effort the first two nights to protect themselves from exposure to sub-zero temperatures and icy winds. Several people died. The third night they erected an inadequate barricade to protect themselves.

As the reality that they would not be rescued quickly sank in, they rationed themselves to a small taste of wine and several chocolate squares each day. They obtained drinking water by reflecting sunlight from pieces of metal onto cups of snow. They erected a more substantial barricade.

On the tenth day on the mountain the food supply was running out; they were starving and knew they could not survive much longer. At their altitude, over 12,000 feet, there was no plant life and no animals or birds to catch.

For some days several of the young men with the rugby team on the flight had realized they might have to eat flesh from the frozen remains of those who had died in the crash. As people got hungrier, a discussion of this possibility spread throughout the group. On a portable radio the survivors heard an announcer report that the air search for their downed aircraft was being called off.

For the next two months, the group survived on human flesh. When the winter storms were over, two of the strongest young men were able to find their way to civilization and send help back for the others. Sixteen people survived the ordeal.

(For survivors of extreme experiences, the tests of their survival skills do not end with rescue or freedom. They must now survive being survivors. The Andes group, after they were rescued, had to deal with people's reactions to what they had done to survive. A later chapter will cover more about surviving being a survivor.)

Organizations Also Ignore Expert Advice

Public and private agencies do not follow expert advice any better than individuals. County, state, federal and regional officials met frequently during the two-month period between March 20 and May 18. Their public information releases created the impression that they had the situation well in hand and that plans had been developed for handling any forthcoming emergencies. As subsequent events revealed, that was not the case. They ignored a wealth of valuable information that had been compiled over the decades by the Disaster Research Group, a national organization of scientists.

In 1962 the Disaster Research Group published a book about the way organizations react before, during, and after disasters. In it James Thompson and Robert Hawkes point out that before a disaster, various public agencies private and community service organizations all reach decisions through discussions that allow each group to maintain control over its own resources and activities. After a disaster has hit a community, organizations tend to fragment. Then over a period of a few days, they come together in a single, unified, synthetic organization. "At first the independent actions of two or more disaster-ready organizations may duplicate one another, resulting in over-concentration of resources in one part of the impact area and underdeployment in another. Inaccurate and contradictory messages have been issued, both within the community and from it to elements of its environment. Assistance in various forms is expected, but when and where it will arrive is unknown." Once the community becomes synthesized into a single organization, various emergency groups become "subordinated to a central headquarters, which allocates resources and integrates them through a master plan or program."

In 1964, disaster researcher George Baker wrote "Approved disaster roles for all relevant social units should be identified prior to a disaster and the position of these roles and the power structure of the total community should be assessed....Special attention should be focused on the development of procedures for rapid stock-taking after crisis events."

Did the people responsible for coordinating the disaster plans for Mt. St. Helens identify disaster roles for "all relevant social units"? No. Did they establish procedures for rapid "stock-taking" in the event of an eruption? No. A review of events immediately after the eruption shows that none of the responsible officials or agencies seemed to know about the existence of a rich body of practical information about what to do.

Murphy's Law Was Suspended, Fortunately

It was incredibly good fortune that Mt. St. Helens erupted when it did. Being Sunday, hundreds of Weyerhaeuser loggers were not at work in the forests. Because it was early in the morning, only a few people were at the turnaround. The caravan of property owners had not yet arrived to go into the Red Zone when the torrent of pulverized stone blasted through it.

On that particular Sunday, the Portland-based U.S. Air Force Reserve 304th Aerospace Rescue and Recovery Squadron was conducting a routine training exercise only 64 miles south of the mountain. When the mountain blew, the 304th was able to begin the helicopter rescue efforts immediately. The 116th Armored Cavalry helicopter unit of the Washington Army National Guard was on standby in Yakima but they were in the path of the falling ash from the volcano. When the mountain erupted they were able to get only 20 of their 32 helicopters off the ground.

Disorganized Search and Rescue: "Who's In Charge Here?"

According to *The Oregonian*, "No one thought to plan for air search and rescue operations before the day the mountain blew apart. No one thought to take charge after it happened. No one thought to establish a central command center, from which search and rescue teams could be dispatched. No one thought to assign a single radio frequency, so helicopter crews from different military units could communicate with one another. No one thought to make certain that aviation fuel supplies would last more than a few hours."

Throughout Sunday and Monday help poured in from many military and emergency units around the West, but a central organization did not exist to coordinate their efforts. Helicopter pilots from different units could not work together easily because no one had thought to provide them with identical maps. Even into Tuesday, duplication of missions was still a major problem. As one helicopter would leave a search sector, another would enter it and go over it again. A pilot complained of "confusion at upper levels. I don't know if it was from somebody wanting to get their name in the paper, but that's what we thought. Some of the pilots got pretty upset about that. There were too many controlling agencies."

A reserve sheriff reported that "For the first few days people were all running around being in command. Everybody was trying to be in charge and nobody wanted to spend time getting organized." Phone calls were flooding in from concerned relatives. According to *The Oregonian*, "No one thought to establish a central clearing house for reports of missing persons, from relatives who thought their loved ones might be among the victims. No one thought to enlist the aid of relatives or friends, even though many knew exact locations where the dead, injured, or missing had camped Saturday night. In several cases, search commanders failed to act on such information when they received it. No one thought to organize the loggers who were intimately familiar with the terrain and who volunteered to start ground searches for survivors."

Since no ground searches for missing people had been organized by Tuesday, loggers began to develop a search plan and asked the County Sheriff for permission to go in to look for people they knew were in the area.

It took until Tuesday night for a sense of coordination to begin to emerge among the multiple commands. The National Guard built a headquarters which became the search center for the next ten days. Army units from Fort Lewis started arriving and an operations office was established to coordinate air search. Efforts were made to eliminate duplication, but "the growing concentration of military brass only added to the headaches for the sheriff's department. It seemed that every officer wearing silver eagles or oak leaves of whatever color wanted to be in charge. The constant infighting slowed decisions and caused more duplication, the very thing the new organization was supposed to correct."

Thus it was that ignorance of existing knowledge about how organizations react in disasters prevented a swift, coordinated, effective response.

Meanwhile, People Help Each Other

The sick, injured, and homeless were helped by a generous outpouring from the community. Neighbors and strangers helped people living near the mountain. Citizen groups set up emergency shelters for people who had to leave their homes. Although people may seem to be concerned about their own interests in ordinary times, in times of disaster they typically gather together and help out each other in ways that are extraordinarily generous. People showed up at temporary emergency centers with boxes of canned and frozen food, blankets, bedding and other items.

Avoiding Blame and Claiming Credit

After the emergency rescue work is over, there is a strong tendency for disaster organizations to compete for social credit for their roles. As described by Thompson and Hawkes:

> For the disaster-ready organization, social credit for its role in disaster would seem to be indispensable. Generally speaking, these organizations gain their support indirectly, rather than by direct exchange through explicit contract. Rather, there is an implied contract that, in exchange for tax payments or voluntary contributions, the disaster-ready organization will act if necessary. If these organizations are to obtain support in the future, then it becomes vital to them to make clear to the community that they did perform as promised.

President Jimmy Carter arrived on Thursday to fly over the destruction area. At a press conference later that evening he stated: "One of the reasons for the loss of life that occurred is that tourists and other interested people, curious people, refused to comply with the directives issued by the governor, by the local sheriff, the State Patrol and others." Governor Dixie Lee Ray and other officials made similar statements over the weeks that followed. For example, Governor Ray later said that "The fact is we were prepared and because we were prepared, there was very little loss of life."

Would President Carter or Governor Ray have been able to claim this kind of credit if the mountain had erupted on the previous Friday or the following Monday or even several hours later on Sunday? The answer is "No," because hundreds of Weyerhaeuser loggers would have been caught in the blast area and neither the 304th nor the 116th would have been assembled to commence quick rescue operations.

If the volcano had erupted in the afternoon on Saturday, could such credit have been claimed? No. The entire caravan of property owners would have been killed, as well as the crowd of sightseers and other people at the turnaround near the blockade because the stone wind blasted through the turnaround at full force. The loss of life would have also been much higher on Sunday afternoon because of the caravan and the crowd at the turnaround.

Thus the search for an answer to the question "Why did so many people die?" leads to a disturbing answer: It is was extremely good fortune that so few people were killed. Only three people are known to have been in the off-limits Red Zone when the mountain erupted, and all three of them were there by permission—Harry Truman and two geological observers from Portland State University. All other people known to be killed in the blast were in the Blue Zone and other areas not officially declared as dangerous enough to be off-limits.

Learning from Experience

Now that it's over, regional officials have developed a good disaster-response system. The county sheriff can interrupt local radio and television broadcasts to give warnings. A well-coordinated disaster-response plan is in place which coordinates Army, Air Force, National Guard, the Forest Service, police, and other units. Shelter and supply sources have been designated.

They are ready for the next one.

Lessons Learned

We live in a time when we receive threats about many possible dangers. One can hear warnings that nuclear reactor plants are not as safe as claimed amidst reassurances that the plants are very safe. Geologists issue warnings about major earthquakes but nothing serious happens for years. People hear warnings about health hazards from toxic wastes in our soil and water, about dangers from nuclear waste, about air pollution, and antibiotics fed to livestock as potentially dangerous to our health.

We hear so many warnings it is easy to become indifferent. What is a person to do?

Some lessons that can be learned about our human nature, from observing the activities and events surrounding the Mt. St. Helens eruption, are these:

Most experts are not as expert as we hope they are. People who specialize in a field see many possible developments. Thus they talk of probabilities, not certainties. Because there are many variables which can influence the timing, duration, and severity of a possible event, other experts studying exactly the same situation may develop different perspectives and have differing opinions about what may or may not happen.

In determining how much credibility to give to an expert's perspective, it is useful to ask: "Does this individual have first-hand experience? If so, how much? When this person speaks, am I being told what to think and feel, or am I being taught about what is going on?" True experts are good teachers.

When warnings are issued, many people dismiss the threat if it has never happened before. People tend to think that because this has never happened before, it won't happen now. (As in some marriages where one spouse warns the other many times that if certain changes aren't made the marriage is going to end. The other spouse tends to dismiss each warning as merely something that has to be put up with, only to be shocked later when served with divorce papers.)

On the other hand, it is legitimate to ignore threats because we all hear many warnings about things that might happen but never do. The survivor response is to actively seek information about the possible danger and to evaluate for oneself what the risks are.

Just because public officials have not prohibited us from going someplace does not mean it is safe. Police officers at the barricade on the highway leading to Mt. St. Helens said people would come up to the barricade and seem to think they were safe standing on one side but that it was dangerous to go three feet past it. Boundaries and barricades are determined more by where it is convenient and manageable to establish boundaries than by where the limits of the actual danger may lie.

When people are curious and drawn to an exciting, once-in-a-lifetime event, they tend to assume that "if it was really dangerous for me, they would keep me away." That just isn't true. Even after the volcano erupted, pilots frequently had to interrupt their search for bodies to rescue people who entered the area afterwards. Part of being a survivor is learning how to keep your curiosity under control.

Even when people know that a disaster might occur, they seldom make plans for dealing with it if it does. Few people knew what to do when Mt. St. Helens blew; they had not imagined, let alone rehearsed possible courses of action.

In contrast, the survivor orientation is to spend time asking "What if?" "If such and such would happen, what would I do?" Thinking ahead gives a person possible ways of reacting in an emergency and it gives something useful to do that helps keep you from being overwhelmed by powerful emotions.

When I was in the paratroopers, they drilled us week after week on the use of our parachutes and weapons. Our actions became reflexes. For the trainees the endless repetition was boring. It led to many complaints and grumbling. Such training is invaluable, however, because thoroughly practiced actions help a person perform well even when terrified.

In an article describing the psychological responses of the Mercury astronauts, George Ruff and Sheldon Korchin state: "One feature of the astronauts' response to stress deserves special emphasis. This is their apparent capacity for the conscious control of emotion arising from extreme danger. Although each man knows of the diverse possible malfunctions which might end his life, this knowledge fails to elicit a disrupting effect. The capacity to control emotion seems to be gained through experience in mastery of stress and through confidence in training and technical readiness."

People die from viewing danger as a divine test. A cause of deaths from "acts of nature" is traceable to the belief that faith, more than action, determines one's survival. Many years ago, public officials in charge of tornado warning systems were puzzled by a disturbing fact. Even though the potential for casualties caused by tornadoes in Alabama is half that in Illinois, Alabama had twice the death rate when compared to Illinois.

Many variables were examined. Neither severity of the tornadoes, types of buildings, availability of shelters, nor warning systems accounted for the difference in death rates. When researchers Sims and Baumann studied personality differences they found that Illinoisans felt more responsible for directing their own lives and more self-confident about actions to survive a tornado. On the other hand, Alabamians were found to feel themselves primarily moved by external forces—fate, luck, and particularly by God. They had less confidence in their ability to take action to avoid being harmed and *did not try*.

There is no one entity called "The Government." Our society has many different official organizations rather than one massive central government. The various governing bodies have overlapping responsibilities that put them into competition and conflict at times. The human beings who attempt to run this hodge-podge of influence are in some instances given the impossible task of both preventing us from hurting ourselves and, at the same time, protecting our rights to individual freedom. Then, when they don't succeed at doing the impossible, we get angry at them.

And finally, on a lighter note: when the electricity goes off and you can't leave the house, enjoy yourself. Many of those in the Mt. St. Helens region did. Nine months later, in mid-February, 1981, the hospital maternity wards in eastern Washington were swamped with baby deliveries!

CHAPTER SIXTEEN

LEARNINGS FROM SURVIVORS OF TORTUROUS CONDITIONS

What is it like to survive the worst conditions that humans can be subjected to, the tortures that humans inflict on each other? How is it that some survivors are so warm and joyful instead of being bitter and emotionally crippled?

To answer these questions, I did extensive research. In particular, I focused on survivors of the WWII battles of Bataan and Corregidor, and Jewish survivors of the Nazi holocaust. I wanted to know what they went through, how they managed, and what might be learned from how they survived.

Bataan

Within hours of the Japanese bombing of Pearl Harbor on December 7, 1941, Japanese forces assaulted the shores of Luzon island in the Philippines. The Japanese wanted to capture Luzon because its main port, Manila Bay, is a huge, strategic harbor able to hold hundreds of large warships.

The American and Filipino troops could not beat back the invasion. The Japanese troops penetrated inland. General Douglas MacArthur's forces were in danger of being split in two. He decided to withdraw the 80,000 soldiers and 26,000 civilians under his command into the Bataan peninsula, a huge arm of jungle covered, extinct volcanoes that forms one side of Manila Bay.

But MacArthur had not prepared for retreat as a possibility. The Bataan peninsula was not provisioned with desperately needed food, supplies, or munitions. The exhausted troops were placed on half-rations.

The soldiers struggled across sheer volcanic cliffs and treacherous rivers. They hacked their way through thick jungles infested with snakes, and insects. They became sick with dysentery, malaria, beriberi, hookworm, and other illnesses. At night the Japanese disrupted their sleep with firecrackers, shell fire, and obscene taunts shouted through megaphones.

To make matters worse, the troops were handicapped in combat because they had been issued old, deteriorated, World War I weapons to fight with. About 70% of the 25 year old mortar rounds fired were duds. Most hand grenades failed to explode. Bill Garleb, then an eighteen year old army private, tells of throwing ten hand grenades into an enemy machine gun nest. He says "seven did not go off and the other three merely fizzled."

Betrayed and Abandoned

During December and January, MacArthur received messages from President Roosevelt and the US Military Command assuring him that massive amounts of supplies and troops were on the way, but none were sent. With each new telegram and each new promise, rumors and hope spread through the troops only to be followed by the realization that nothing was being done for them. They were abandoned.

Bill Garleb says the troops on Bataan felt betrayed by their country. Some GIs wrote "V" on their helmets—for victim. Some made up poems and songs about their plight. Here is one stanza from such a song:

We are the battling bastards of Bataan:
No mama, no papa, no Uncle Sam,
No aunts, no uncles, no nephews, no nieces,
No rifles, no planes, or artillery pieces,
And nobody gives a damn.

The jungle fighting continued week after week. The sick, starving troops became increasingly exhausted. Their rations were again cut in half and then in half again as food supplies dwindled. During the three days before the final battle, the 135 men in Bill Garleb's company had only one dishpan of rice and three cans of salmon to eat.

"In the end," Garleb says, "the situation was so desperate that sick and wounded soldiers were taken to the front lines and propped up against trees. Rifles were placed in their hands and pointed in the direction of the enemy."

The Bataan Death March

The troops on Bataan surrendered April 8, 1942. They were starved, exhausted, wounded, sick, bitter, and demoralized.

It took the Japanese several weeks to bring the defenders out of the jungles. The men were given little food or water and no medicine for their illnesses. Stragglers were shot, bayoneted, or clubbed to death. Those attempting to escape were killed. The prisoners were sometimes made to stand for hours in the hot tropical sun while the Japanese soldiers ate and rested. If prisoners wanted to relieve themselves, they had to do so where they stood.

Most of the captured Americans were sent to Camp O'Donnell, roughly 100 miles away. When the forces on Corregidor, a large island that guards the entrance to Manila Bay, were surrendered a few weeks later, most of them were also taken to O'Donnell.

At Camp O'Donnell the crowded conditions, lack of medical treatment, inadequate food, and physical abuse by the guards caused many deaths. Official records indicate that of the 8000 Americans interned at O'Donnell, approximately 1500 died during the first six months of captivity. But Bill Garleb, who worked on the burial detail, says the actual death figure is much higher.

At least 90% of the POWs received some form of physical savagery from their captors. Scarcely a man escaping at least one beating during his internment. Being struck by hand, rifle, or sabre was quite common. Fingernail torture, water torture, and other forms of torture were used. Prisoner executions were often in the form of beheadings. Garleb says that "at night it was almost impossible to sleep on the hard bamboo floors of the huts because of pain from untreated diseases, mosquitoes, and ants which swarmed on the men's open sores to eat the blood and pus."

Survivors do whatever they must to stay alive. Garleb says that "men with lips and tongues infected and swollen from scurvy would force food into their mouths. When they threw up because of malaria, they would catch their vomited food and force it into their mouths again." He says that "during the day the strongest had to walk barefoot on rocky roads for as far as five miles to and from the labor details. We lost so much weight we looked like walking skeletons."

"Give-Up-Itis"

In those conditions it was easier to die than to live. *Staying alive was something a person had to choose to do every day, even every hour.*

Thousands of men did give up and die. The POWs called it "give-up-itis." To stay alive was an act of personal will; to die, all a person had to do was reach the point of deciding, "I can't take this anymore." Some members of the American Defenders of Bataan and Corregidor told me that dying was "as easy as letting go of a rope." Once a man had decided to give up the struggle to stay alive, he was usually dead within a few hours. During the war the total number of Americans who died in Japanese POW camps, according to Garleb, was about 11,500.

Muselmänner—The Walking Dead

Survivors of the Nazi holocaust refer to those who had given up the will to live as "Muselmänner." In Germany, before the outbreak of World War II, Jews were taken from their homes at gun point, and hauled in unheated railroad box cars to extermination camps. At the camps they had to deal with the horror of discovering that they were targeted for genocide. As families were herded off the trains arriving at Auschwitz, Dachau, or the other death camps, most women and children were separated from the men and put to death immediately. Jewish men strong enough for work details had to carry the dead out of the gas chambers and bury them in huge trenches. Later, when cremation in furnaces was determined to be a more efficient means for disposing of bodies, they were forced to do that gruesome job.

John VanCleef, a Jew who spent three years in Nazi labor camps, emphasized in his talks with me that the Jews were not prisoners of war. They were not trained as soldiers nor prepared for capture, resistance, and survival. Unlike soldiers, police, or others who have had military training, they were totally unprepared for the Nazi brutality. The horrors of genocide over-whelmed them. John, who attributed his survival to his training as a police officer, said that the ones most likely to become "Muselmänner" were former community leaders who were stripped of their nice clothing and ridiculed about their social rank.

What Made the Difference?

One Bataan Death March survivor recalled saying to his fellow prisoners, "We must be crazy! Any farm animal treated like this would have died long ago." When I have asked ex-POWs why they continued to go on day after day, they have said, "I always was stubborn," "Just being ornery, I guess," and "I had a stronger desire to live than to die." John VanCleef told me that "Staying alive was an act of defiance; I wanted to prove to them that although they could break my body, they could not break my spirit."

What Can We Learn From Survivors?

Don't Wait to Learn Survivor Qualities

I have asked many survivors of torturous experiences if the will to live can be taught. They all say "No" without hesitation.

This gives us a valuable perspective on survivorship. Survivor qualities can be developed beforehand, but a person cannot be taught the will to live when in a torturous situation.

When Disillusioned, Adapt to the New Reality

The defenders of Bataan had to cope with the reality that they were expected to fight with antiquated, badly deteriorated weapons and that promises made to them were false. The Jews who were not immediately exterminated had to deal with learning that some of their fellow Jews, called Sonderkommandos, were collaborating with the Nazis. To preserve their own lives the Sonderkommandos served as welcoming committees. They greeted the new arrivals and explained to them that they would have to go through a disinfectant process in shower rooms. The Sonderkommandos then led the new arrivals to their deaths in the gas chambers.

Suppress Strong Feelings and Use Common Sense

Survivors do not waste energy feeling like victims. Bill Garleb and John VanCleef each talk about having had strong emotional reactions to the situation facing them. But then they saw they were reacting like everyone else and that being upset would not help them survive. It was at this point, that a key aspect of the survivor style—active questioning—took over. Like most survivors, they asked themselves questions such as: "What is going on here?" "How do the guards see this?" "What must I do to give myself a chance to survive?"

It is worth noting that survivors spend little time feeling sorry for themselves. They successfully control their anger or rage so that they don't go crazy and do something that would lead to death.

John VanCleef had to deal with being kept alive to serve as a laborer for the Nazis while his wife and children were put to death. One of his worst moments was when the Nazis killed his brother before his eyes. He says he would have lost control of himself except that another prisoner came up behind him and held his arms. The man whispered in John's ear that it would accomplish nothing to waste his life at that moment and that there would be opportunities for revenge later.

Bill Garleb similarly talks about how essential it was for him to control his rage at what the guards did to his fellow prisoners. He says "I had to focus my mind on staying alive, rather than wasting my life through a futile action."

Bob Mitchell, a marine who fought first on Bataan and later on Corregidor, told me that many of the POWs who gave up were unable to cope with the cruelty and hostility directed toward them by the guards. He said that many prisoners tried to influence the guards by feeling upset, expressing pain, pleading, or trying to win them over. When this didn't work, they had nothing left. Many gave up and died.

Be Able to Function Alone Without
Confirmation of Perceptions or Actions

According to Bob Mitchell, survivors are people who can make their own decisions and take action without asking for approval from other people. That was certainly true for VanCleef. In one of the labor camps the prisoners were given bowls of soup that tasted to him like boiled crankcase oil. Most of the prisoners went ahead and ate the soup, but he refused to. His impression was that the "soup" was another Nazi "medical" experiment. Many of the men who ate the soup later died

In *Surviving*, a book about his experiences in the Nazi camps, Bruno Bettelheim argues that loners did not make it. The people who survived were those who banded together in a joint effort to keep as many people alive as they could. His conclusion is correct, insofar as it applies to the Nazi labor and extermination camps. There the Nazis had the Jews operate the camps themselves. Some Jews were appointed as commanders, or Kappos, and they in turn appointed other Jews to handle administrative matters. In these circumstances, the ability to cooperate enhanced the possibility of surviving.

In a book written twenty years earlier, however, Bettelheim himself provides a good example of the survival value of thinking for yourself. Like many prisoners at Buchenwald, Bettelheim suffered from frostbite. "At first I was discouraged from trying to get medical care by the fate of Jewish prisoners whose attempts had ended up in no treatment, only abuse. Finally things got worse and I was afraid that waiting longer would mean amputation, so I decided to make the effort." When he got to the clinic, there were many prisoners lined up for treatment and talking about the chances of being admitted to the clinic. Most had planned what they were going to say in detail. Some thought it best to stress their service in the German army during World War I—wounds received or decorations won. Others planned to stress the severity of the frostbite. A few decided it was best to tell some "tall story," such as that an SS officer had ordered them to report to the clinic.

Eventually they asked Bettelheim what he was going to say. " I said I would go by the way the SS man dealt with other Jewish prisoners who had frostbite like me and proceed accordingly. *I doubted how wise it was to follow a preconceived plan, because it was hard to anticipate the reaction of a person you didn't know."* (Emphasis added.)

Bettelheim's fellow prisoners did not appreciate his strategy. "The prisoners reacted as they had at other times when I had voiced similar ideas on how to deal with the SS. They insisted that one SS man was like another, all equally vicious and stupid...so in abusive terms, they accused me of not wanting to share my plan with them, or of intending to use one of theirs; it angered them that I was ready to meet the enemy unprepared."

Did his strategy work? Here is what he reports: "No Jewish prisoner ahead of me in line was admitted to the clinic. The more a prisoner pleaded, the more annoyed and violent the SS man became. Expressions of pain amused him; stories of previous services rendered to Germany outraged him. He proudly remarked that *he* could not be taken in by Jews....

"When my turn came he asked me in a screeching voice if I knew that work accidents were the only reason for admitting Jews to the clinic, and if I came because of such an accident. I replied that I knew the rules but that I couldn't work unless my hands were freed of the dead flesh. Since prisoners were not allowed to have knives, I asked to have the dead flesh cut away. I tried to be matter-of-fact, avoiding pleading, deference or arrogance. He replied, 'If that's all you want, I will tear the flesh off myself,' and he started to pull at the festering skin. Because it did not come off as easily as he may have expected or for some other reason, he waved me inside the clinic.

"Inside he gave me a malevolent look and pushed me into the treatment room. There he told the prisoner orderly to attend to the wound. While this was being done, the guard watched me closely for signs of pain but I was able to suppress them. As soon as the cutting was over, I started to leave. He showed surprise and asked why I didn't wait for further treatment. I said I had gotten the service I asked for, at which he told the orderly to make an exception and treat my hand. After I left the room, he called me back and gave me a card entitling me to further treatment and admittance to the clinic without inspection at the entrance."

Clearly Bettelheim used good judgment to come up with a strategy that would give him the best chance of getting the medical treatment he so desperately needed. He refused to give in to the stereotyped and unsuccessful thinking of the other Jews about the Nazis.

Make a Deep Emotional Commitment to Keep Going

To function alone means to accept complete, total, and absolute responsibility for one's personal survival. Bill Garleb's desire to stay alive was so strong that he decided to "study" people with give-up-itis. He wanted to thoroughly understand who gave up and why, so that he could recognize and avoid developing any of those attitudes, characteristics, or beliefs.

He learned that those who prayed for God to somehow rescue them, and then waited passively for help, did not make it. He says that those who survived prison camp experienced "a life force from within." Some described this force as the spirit of God, others as an intangible 'will to live' that enabled them to survive in the same circumstances in which so many of their comrades died.

In a study of POWs done for the U.S. government, the interviewers characterized the surviving ex-POWs as having high morale even under the most trying circumstances, having a never failing hope of rescue, being able to repress hostility, being physically adaptable to a strange environment, and being willing to eat anything.

The commitment to somehow, some way survive, to live through the experience if at all possible, gives a person an extraordinary capacity to adapt and keep going. Garleb says that with the will to live, you would eat whatever food was given to you. Some men died because they refused to eat food which contained maggots, weevils, and other insects.

The will to live is different from hopefulness or optimism. The survivors I have interviewed have not talked about being sustained by hope. Researcher and author Terrance Des Pres, as a result of his studies of holocaust survivors, reached a similar conclusion. He said "the chances for survival and freedom were so logically improbable that no hope, as we know hope, could be allowed into consciousness." The attitude he found in survivors is that, "They might make it, they probably won't but *they will not stop trying*." What keeps survivors going after all vestiges of normal civilization have been stripped away? According to Des Pres, it is that "survivors fall back on life itself."

He found that survivors report "something other and greater than personal ego, a reservoir of strength and resource which in extremity becomes active and is felt as the deeper foundation of selfhood." When survivors reach their personal limits they discover within themselves "a deeper knowledge, an elder wisdom, a substratum of vital information biologically instilled and biologically effective." Stripped of everything but life, survivors fall back on some "biologically determined 'talent' long suppressed by cultural deformation, a bank of knowledge embedded in the body's cells."

Develop Disillusioned Empathy

Empathy for others, even for guards, leads people who survive to an awareness that the oppressors are not all the same. Some guards even have compassion for prisoners. To be open to this development required being able to give up the stereotyped notion that all guards were sadistic and cruel.

Bruno Bettelheim said "Some SS men never made anti-Semitic remarks. Others risked their lives by smuggling out letters for prisoners without expecting any reward."

Trained in psychiatry, Bettelheim saw that the Nazis had stereotyped ideas about Jews and that many of the Jewish prisoners had stereotyped ideas about the Nazis. In his encounter with the guard at the clinic, Bettelheim was able to look at things through the eyes of the German soldier assigned to duty outside the clinic door. The soldier assumed that "whenever Jews approached him on the basis of their stereotyped depiction of the SS, he dealt with them on the basis of his stereotyped picture of the Jew."

By acting in a way contrary to the soldier's stereotyped notions, Bettelheim got a much different response. "A matter-of-fact statement was the kind that was acceptable to an SS soldier," Bettelheim says. "To reject a prisoner who behaved this way would have meant rejecting his own scheme of values and his own way of acting and thinking. This he either could not do or felt no need to do."

Bill Garleb was part of a large group of prisoners transferred to another island. He saw that the tin-roofed train cars that would haul them to the new prison camp would be stifling hot inside and that each car was being packed very full. He held back until he was one of the last men into the freight car. This left him very close to the door, which the car's guard left slightly ajar in order to provide a little bit of air.

Garleb saw that much more air was needed for the soldiers inside, so he started asking the soldier questions about his family back home. The guard, who could speak English, asked Bill several questions, and Bill got the guard laughing with a comical explanation of how he got captured. As the guard relaxed and saw that there would be no problems with this group, Bill asked him to open the door wider so that more air could come into the car. The guard did so and, as a result, fewer men died from suffocation than occurred in many of the other cars.

Some of "The Enemy" are Kind

John VanCleef says that to survive you must study your enemy. You must thoroughly understand how he thinks, feels and acts. Survivors see that their captors are not all the same. They discover that some of "the enemy" do not like what is happening either.

Bill Garleb says that each day an older Japanese sergeant would take a work detail outside the camp to cut wood. On the way back, if the men had done their best, the sergeant would bring the prisoners to a halt at the side of the road. The sergeant would turn his back and take himself a long smoke break. He did this within a few feet of a small Filipino store. While his back was turned some of the men would go inside and purchase food. On the way back to camp, the sergeant acted as though he did not hear the cans of food clinking in their clothing.

Shlomo Breznitz tells how his mother took himself and his sister to Czechoslovakia and put them into a catholic orphanage to hide them from the Nazis. One Christmas evening, as the children were singing carols, the Commandant of the nearby German garrison walked in. The mother superior explained to the children that the Commandant was a devout catholic, wanted to spend the evening with them, and had brought them a special present—a large chocolate cake.

After listening to the children sing "Silent Night" in the Czech language, the Commandant asked if anyone could sing it in German. Shlomo's sister stood up and walked over to him. Shlomo joined her. They stood singing the song in German when Judith suddenly stopped with terror in her eyes. She had realized the Commandant must know why they were the only two children able to sing the German version. The Commandant motioned them closer. Speaking in a soft voice, he said to them "Don't be afraid, your mother and father will come back." The Commandant then continued his evening at the orphanage as though everything was normal.

In both these examples the survivors had to be alert to quietly accept the secret act of kindness. They had to be smart enough to collude, as it were, in the pretense that the kindness was not taking place. An ability made possible by seeing that all of "the enemy" were not alike.

Imagine Yourself in the Future

Based upon his experiences in Nazi concentration camps, Viktor Frankl says: "It is a peculiarity of man, that he can only live by looking to the future...and this is his salvation in the most difficult moments of his existence, although he sometimes has to force his mind to the task."

He relates a personal experience in which he had become disgusted with the state of affairs which compelled him daily and hourly to think of very trivial things having to do with day-to-day existence: "I forced my thoughts to turn to another subject. Suddenly I found myself standing on the platform of a well lit, warm and pleasant lecture room. In front of me sat an attentive audience on comfortable upholstered seats. I was giving a lecture on the psychology of the concentration camp! All that oppressed me at that moment became objective, seen and described from the remote viewpoint of science. By this method I succeeded somehow in rising above the situation, above the sufferings of the moment and I observed them as if they were already of the past. Both I and my troubles became the object of an interesting psychoscientific study undertaken by myself."

Frankl knew that he was able to endure because he had a mental picture of a good future ahead for him. "The prisoner who had lost faith in the future—his future—was doomed. With his loss of belief in the future, he also lost his spiritual hold; he let himself decline and became subject to mental and physical decay."

For Frankl, faith in the future seems to mean faith in oneself to live through present danger or grief or any other trouble and to carry oneself forward into a time to come. This is not "hope" in the sense of a passive desire to be rescued or treated better; rather it is a process of steeling oneself to handle the dilemmas of the present in order to make possible a good future for oneself and others. Hope creates two possible outcomes; what one wants and what one doesn't want. Faith holds the desired outcome constant regardless of developments. This singularity of vision has an important effect.

Escape into Fantasy

Prisoners held in solitary confinement report surviving the ordeal by losing themselves in vivid fantasies. Green Beret officer, Jim Thompson, for example, was a prisoner in Viet Nam for four years. He had a broken back, was sick with malaria, and spent months at a time in an isolation cell. "To pass the time and to save his sanity, he engaged in demanding mental exercise. Mainly this involved the design and construction of houses; he did not merely think about these creations, he actually put them together in his head, idea by idea, piece by piece, step by step, using knowledge he had gained years earlier while working for a building contractor. Each house took months to design and build, for it was vital that everything be perfect. He would dwell for long periods on every detail, computing the precise amount of board feet of lumber he would need, the number of bricks, the flagstone, the plastering, the electrical wiring, plumbing. "In his mind Jim first built houses. But after five of these, he "built a church, a small rustic chapel...." Each Sunday he would meet his wife and children at the chapel and they would attend services. "Having been a faithful, lifelong attender [sic], Thompson knew the entire order of worship, and would listen in memory to his favorite hymns."

Henri Charriere, known as Papillon, the Butterfly, was convicted of murder in Paris at age 25 and sentenced to life imprisonment in the penal colony of French Guinea. He escaped to the nearby islands but was recaptured and placed in solitary confinement for two years. He managed to survive by taking "flight into the past." He lost himself in vivid recollections—of walking along the ocean shore and being reunited with his native woman, Lali. He totally lost himself in experiences of eating, talking, and making love with her. He walked for hours in his cell until he was exhausted. "Once I was truly exhausted, I stretched out on my back and wrapped the blanket around my head…what indescribable sensations! I spent nights of love, more intense than the real ones. I could sit down with my mother, dead these 17 years…I was there; it wasn't imagination."

Appreciate Life

Even in torturous circumstances, where one's total personal resources must be devoted to staying alive hour by hour, there are moments of extraordinary joy. To survive in the jungle fighting, Garleb says he had to turn himself "into an ear." He completely shut off the thinking and talking activities of his mind and turned himself completely outward to the world he was in. As a result, he became extraordinarily attuned to the sounds, sights, and smells around him. He talks about the joy he experienced from the sound of a bird singing, the vibrant, shimmering greens and browns of the jungle, and the smell of the wind. All his senses were alert to the strange life of the jungle. During the death march through small Filipino communities, he recalls joyfully watching a young Filipino mother walk by with her baby on her hip.

Sustain a Controlled Defiance

Every survivor I have interviewed is a person who refused to accept the situation on the terms of the people working to control them. John VanCleef said he could usually tell whether or not a person new to the camp was going to make it. The survivors were people who would, in some small way, test and break rules. An ex-POW from the Korean war tells of being told by a guard to sit at one end of a four foot long bench without moving and how, with the guard watching him, he moved very, very slowly until he was eventually sitting on the other end.

Eugene Heimler attributes his survival, and the survival of other Jews at Buchenwald and Auschwitz, to such acts of resistance. "The world is wrong in thinking that we on the receiving end did not resist. When we extended a helping hand to someone in need, it was a serious act of resistance; when we slowed down at work, that was resistance, too."

This resistance took many forms. Once Heimler and about 2000 other men, having survived Auschwitz, were assembled in a large cinema hall at Buchenwald to await shipment to yet another camp. "Then one of the SS men decided he wanted a more cheerful atmosphere, and ordered onto the stage a few of us outcasts, with instructions to sing. It was pathetic to listen to these songs, Hungarian songs of bygone days. Then the idea struck me; why should I not get up and recite a poem of resistance? The Germans would not understand it. I went to the SS man who had demanded amusement and asked him in German for a pencil and paper to produce something for entertainment. He gave me what I asked for and there and then, in the corner of that cinema, I wrote 'The Song of Buchenwald.' Then I went up to the platform and read it in Hungarian...the SS guards looked at me and at my audience. They could not make out what it was all about. There was an uncanny silence for several minutes, and everyone started to clap and many of them cried." He says the guards never knew what he had said, and that nothing adverse happened as a result of his actions.

Heimler, of course, did more than resist his captors. And he did more than defy them. He managed to find a way to outsmart them in order to reach out to his fellow Hungarians and stir their hearts. In the midst of their collective despair, Heimler found a way to enable them to feel connected to one another and thus to redouble their individual and collective desire to survive.

Maintain Contact with Others

Survivor researcher Julius Segal emphasizes that communication with others is the lifeline of survival. He says that "In every episode of captivity in recent American history, POWs and hostages have been sustained by ingeniously improvised lifelines of communication. In Vietnam, a clever tap code, in which the number and sequence of taps spelled out letters of the alphabet, became the prisoners' chief means of communication."

Segal describes how this code sustained Vice Admiral James Stockdale during almost 7 ½ years as a POW in North Vietnam. "On one occasion the North Vietnamese handcuffed Stockdale's hands behind his back, locked his legs in heavy irons, and dragged him from his dark prison cell to sit in an unshaded courtyard so the other prisoners could see what happened to anybody who refused to cooperate."

Stockdale was kept in that position for three days. "The guards would not let him sleep. He was beaten repeatedly. After one beating, Stockdale heard a towel snapping out in prison code the letters GBUJS. It was a message he would never forget. 'God Bless You Jim Stockdale.'"

Gerald Coffee was a navy pilot shot down over Vietnam. He was taken to Hanoi, and subjected to excruciating torture during his seven years as a POW He says "Few things are more basic to our survival than to communicate." In talking about the tap code he says that "by applying our communication system persistently and creatively, we would breach barriers of brick and concrete and vast spaces in between. We would console, encourage, sympathize with and even entertain one another."

Find the Humor

Most accounts of people who have been through torturous circumstances include only the horrors. There are moments of joy and humor, however. If you ask survivors of horrible experiences how they managed day after day to keep on going, you will probably learn that even under the most desperate circumstances, they were able to maintain a strong sense of humor. During the battle of Bataan, soldiers would joke about the grenades not exploding and keep on throwing them because, being hunks of iron, they might conk the enemy on the head.

The Pacific War POWs often referred to the Japanese bayonets as "vitamin sticks," explaining that a poke from a Japanese bayonet provides as much energy to keep on moving as a vitamin pill. At Bill Garleb's camp, the Japanese guards wanted to know why the Americans were so much taller than themselves. Some prisoners answered that it was because the Americans took growth pills. A few guards wanted the pills, so some enterprising soldiers made tablets out of aspirin and toothpaste, lime, or dried beans, which they dyed and then sold to the Japanese guards. These transactions often led later to sessions of uproarious laughter. Garleb also tells of hilarious camp shows at which they "roasted" the Japanese officers and doctors.

In Buchenwald, Auschwitz and other camps the women stopped menstruating and the men lost all sexual urges. This provided material for many humorous remarks. When newly arriving male prisoners asked if survival was possible the standard answer was "Yes, but you won't want to sin with women."

Toward the end of the war in Germany, many bombs were falling on German factories and military installations. Sometimes the bombs didn't explode and had to be removed. Jews were used for bomb removal squads. One day John VanCleef was taken with a small group of men and told by a Nazi SS officer that they had to remove a bomb that had landed on top of a munitions storage area.

VanCleef saw an opportunity to bargain for much-needed food. When he made his request, the officer said they would be given food after they finished. John said they needed to eat before they worked in order to have enough strength to lift the bomb out. The officer finally agreed. John vividly remembers the deep amusement he felt but could not allow to show when he saw the SS officer coming out of the mess hall with two SS troopers carrying a large steaming pot of chicken stew and having them stand by while he and the other men ate their fill.

Viktor Frankl emphasizes the role of humor in survival. "Humor was another of the soul's weapons in the fight for self-preservation. It is well known that humor, more than anything else in the human makeup, can afford an aloofness and an ability to rise above any situation, even if only for a few seconds. I practically trained a friend of mine who was next to me on the building site to develop a sense of humor. I suggested to him that we would promise each other to invent at least one amusing story daily, some incident that could happen one day after our liberation. He was a surgeon, and had been an assistant on the staff of a large hospital, so I once tried to get him to smile by describing to him how he would be unable to lose the habits of camp life when he returned to his former work."

Gerald Coffee says "Laughter sets the spirit free to move through even the most tragic circumstances. It helps us shake our heads clear, get our feet back under us and restore our sense of balance and purpose. Humor is integral to our peace of mind and ability to go beyond survival."

Coffee says one of his best laughs came shortly after he arrived at the infamous prison in Hanoi called "Heartbreak Hotel." He was taken to a small, damp, slimy, shower room strewn with garbage and told to wash. As he lathered up under the trickle of cold water coming out of an old rusty pipe he realized it had been three months since his last shower. He says "I thought back to the previous months…I hadn't done as well as I should. I was disappointed, devastated."

He slowly rinsed the soap from his body and stood, he says, holding "the pipe in both hands, head lowered in pensive dejection. Finally, I raised my head. And there at eye level on the wall in front of me…were the words 'Smile, you're on Candid Camera!' Well, I couldn't not smile…I smiled broadly. I laughed out loud, enjoying not only the pure humor and incongruity of the situation, but also appreciating the beautiful guy who had mustered the moxie to rise above his own dejection and frustration and pain and guilt to inscribe a line of encouragement to those who would come after him."

Dougal Robertson survived a shipwreck and spent many days at sea in a life raft with his family. He says, "If any single civilized factor in a cast-away's character helps survival, it is a well-developed sense of the ridiculous. It helps the cast-away to laugh in the face of impossible situations and allows him or her to overcome the assassination of all civilized codes and characteristics which hitherto had been the guidelines of life. A pompous adherence to precedence, an assertion of physical superiority, the inability to abandon prudish reserve, these and many other traits are as deadly as thirst and starvation in the confines of a survival craft."

How a person lives everyday life and what people do to survive torturous circumstances seem to be very similar. Quick adaptability, curiosity, disillusioned empathy for attackers, humor, and playfulness enhance one's innate survival abilities. Cooperative resistance while thinking for one's self, taking an action that has not been tried by others, or taking an action contrary to what companions are doing, are merely continuations of what the person does every day.

Be Alert to the Unexpected

By being open to what is going on in the surroundings, by not withdrawing or engaging in self-pity, and by having the deep commitment to somehow and in some way survive, a person becomes more open to unique possibilities.

Samuel Pisar, only 12 years old at the time he was put into a Nazi camp, survived because of his reaction to something very unexpected. "One evening, after an endless roll call, an order was read to us: 'All who are tailors by trade remain standing at attention. The others fall out.' If they needed tailors, I reasoned, they would keep them alive. My instincts told me to stand still." When the officer came by to question him about being a tailor, Pisar said that he was a buttonhole maker. Pisar says that somehow the idea that, "Wherever tailors are needed, buttonhole makers are needed too—must have impressed the SS Officer because he waved me to one side, the side of life." The others who were not picked went out to the death chamber.

John VanCleef says that for the three years that he was working in the labor gangs, he tried to remain as invisible as possible. He obediently did whatever he was told. He always knew in the back of his mind, however, that sometime in the future an opportunity to escape would occur. Toward the end of war as the allied troops were moving into Germany, John and several hundred other Jews were on a train heading for the interior. When the train pulled over onto a siding and stopped to wait for a troop train pass, the guards allowed people to get out to relieve themselves and to rest on the ground. When it was time for everyone to get into the train again, VanCleef saw that from his position where he was resting behind a bush none of the guards could see him. Here was the opportunity he had known would occur. He remained hunched down and out of sight while the train loaded up and moved up the track. When it was out of sight he calmly walked into the next town, where he obtained food, clothing, and shelter.

Some Missing Stories

It would be a distortion to give the impression that people who have been through torturous circumstances are the best examples of survivor personalities. Many of life's best survivors anticipate trouble before it develops and take steps to avoid it. They avoid getting trapped.

When the Nazis took Samuel Pisar from his home and placed him in a railroad car with other Jews, a few people did not believe they were, as told, merely being relocated. Since Samuel was the smallest—he was only 12—he was held up to look out the small hatch in the roof of the car to see when the coast was clear. When there were no guards nearby, people from his car would scramble up out of the car onto the roof , and jump off of the train.

Some Jews who escaped from the death camps returned at great personal risk to their old neighborhoods to warn people about what was happening. Many people refused to believe the stories, denying that such a thing could possibly occur. A few people did listen, however, and got out of Germany early.

The Nazis, at first, allowed some Jews to leave the country but with no money, jewels, or anything of value. One man sold all his personal and other property, went to a bank, and purchased Swiss "bearer" bonds. He memorized the numbers and then burned the bonds. After he had taken his family out of Germany and into Switzerland, he went to the issuing bank and had the destroyed bonds replaced.

When the Nazis imposed curfew on the Jews, one of Bruno Bettelheim's relatives joined a group that went to Budapest in Hungary to have a better chance of escaping detection. He says " From among them they selected typically 'Aryan' looking men, who, equipped with false papers, immediately joined the Hungarian SS so as to be able to warn of impending actions, to report in advance when a particular district would be searched, etc."

According to Bettelheim, this tactic "worked so well that most of the group survived intact…a few of the Jews who had joined the SS were discovered and immediately shot. Probably a death preferable to one in the gas chamber. But, even among their special group, a majority survived, hiding within the SS up to the last moment."

Another story not include here is one of the most incredible survival stories of all, that of Native Americans. The Indians in North America have survived hundreds of years of efforts by the white settlers to eradicate them. The U.S. Government has broken treaties with them, taken away their lands, ruined their sources of livelihood, taken their children, destroyed their cultural treasures, and suppressed their customs, beliefs, and religion.

How have Indians survived and endured? Despite everything done to them, why have Indian men and women always served in the United States armed forces with honor? It will take a long time to understand, but their survival comes in part from a deep spirituality, knowing how to sustain their communities through the worst conditions, and living in a way that is in harmony with all life on earth. Ironically, this people the whites have been unsuccessful in coercing into adopting white ways, may prove in the centuries ahead to be an invaluable source of guidance on how to keep the earth a habitable place.

Survivors Are Not Better People

Nothing in my research suggests that survivors are better people than those who do not survive. No one can be faulted for deciding to not remain alive in torturous conditions. And many people who commit themselves to staying alive don't make it. Survivors know that *almost everyone is just like them.* The problem is that most people do not know what they are capable of until forced to survive in extreme conditions.

Charlie Plumb titled his book about his experience as a POW *I'm No Hero.* He says he is no different than "millions of Americans who have applied heroic principles in overcoming hardships....These ordinary Americans are not held in esteem as heroes, yet they have suffered grave misfortune and have recovered as have I."

The Worst Experiences Bring Out the Deepest Strengths

The fires of an emotional hell refine some people into their purest essence. One of the most spiritually beautiful, warmly compassionate women I know is Edith Eva Eger, an Auschwitz survivor. The Nazi officers kept her alive while the rest of her family were killed because she was a slender sixteen year old ballerina and they made her entertain them with her dancing.

Now a psychologist in private practice in California, Edith is known for her quiet, healing presence and deep understanding of people going through emotional crises. She says "Everything I know I learned from Auschwitz."

When I asked her how she resolved her feelings and memories of her past she said, "It took me 40 years. I can't erase the experience but I can integrate it, come to terms with it. In Auschwitz I learned to become compassionate and forgiving. You must be strong to forgive. Forgiveness is not condoning or excusing. Forgiveness has nothing to do with justice. Forgiving is a selfish act to free yourself from being controlled by your past."

"At the end I remember feeling sorry for the German officers and soldiers as I watched them flee through the open camp gates. I remember thinking to myself, 'I will have painful memories of what happened, but they will always have to live with memories of what they did.' I lost my family in Auschwitz. It was very traumatic. But I have integrated the experience, and I'm the person I am because of it."

Many people have memories of horrible experiences—sexual abuse during childhood, violent beatings, friends stabbed, loved ones shot or killed. Your past experiences will always be a part of you. You can't eradicate them, but even the most horrible experiences can be dealt with so that they do not ruin your life. It is possible, also, that by working to overcome your emotional trauma, you go beyond recovery. You may develop a higher, better, stronger version of yourself than you suspected could exist.

CHAPTER SEVENTEEN

THE SERENDIPITY TALENT: TURNING MISFORTUNE INTO GOOD LUCK

John and Jane Youell reached out and held hands as the airplane started down the runway. They smiled at each other as the pressure from the steep climb pushed them back into their soft, first class seats. They were finally taking the vacation of their dreams, a trip to the South Pacific and Thailand.

The year was 1950. There were no wars. Tourist rates were reasonable. It was a good time to travel.

This was their first real vacation in almost twenty years. John's trucking company, a firm that specialized in hauling automobiles from Detroit to West Coast dealers, had demanded his constant attention. His trucks and drivers were scattered along a 2000 mile route. To keep operations running smoothly he had to build and manage his own truck stops. To control costs, he had designed and built trucks that a driver could load and unload without assistance or special equipment. His dispatchers had to coordinate deliveries to all the automobile dealers in the Northwest with each automaker's assembly plant production schedules.

Running any business has its irritations. He especially disliked having to pay a tariff, a vehicle use tax, to every state every time one of his trucks drove through. And even though he treated his employees very well, it hurt him during contract negotiations to have the unions antagonistic toward him. John was a survivor, however. He had a hand-lettered sign over the workbench in his basement at home: "If you think it can't be done, you will stand by and watch someone else do it."

John maintained an easy, gentle contact with every person in his company and everything that happened. When he was at his headquarters in Portland, he would spend about an hour each day walking around the yard and through the buildings. He knew every employee by name and something about them. He told me his "Howdy" rounds were the main reason why his company ran so well.

Now, after many years, his managers and supervisors could run the company on their own. "At last" he thought to himself as the plane headed across the Pacific ocean, "a *real* vacation!"

At their first destination, a quiet resort in the Philippines, John tried to relax, but couldn't. He felt restless. He paced around. During an evening show he was distracted, he couldn't enjoy it. Jane urged him to forget about his concerns.

During the next several days John tried his best to put all concerns about the business out of his mind, but he had a gnawing feeling something was wrong. Jane insisted he had just been working too hard too long. She kept trying to get him to relax. Finally, to settle the matter, she agreed to let him call the office to see how things were going.

His vice-president was in a panic. He yelled over the telephone, "John, we're ruined! The railroads have announced they are building auto transport trains that will haul automobiles to all points in the country! We're wiped out. We're ruined!"

John asked, "How soon will the new service start? When will they be ready to go?" The vice-president did not know. John told him to not make any announcements to the newspapers or the employees until he got back.

When John returned to his wife, she asked "What did you find out?" He said, "Well, you won't hear me complaining about those interstate tariffs anymore!"

On the flight back to Hawaii John silently asked himself questions about this new development. He looked at things from the perspectives of the auto dealers, the railroad officials, and the automobile manufacturers.

In Hawaii, John called his vice-president. He learned that it would be six months at the earliest before the first train would be ready to haul automobiles. John told the vice-president to immediately arrange for appointments with the auto company and railroad officials in Detroit. The vice-president wasn't sure the officials would agree to meet with him. John said they had to because if he stopped his trucks, the automakers would be hurting very badly.

In Seattle, he stopped briefly to see that Jane was safely on her way home, and then proceeded on to the meetings. In Detroit, the first meeting with auto company executives was tense. John thanked them for agreeing to meet with him and then asked a question. He said, "When trains loaded with automobiles arrive at the West Coast terminal points, how will you get the cars from the train yards to your auto dealers in Astoria, Pendleton, Bremerton, and the hundreds of other cities on the Northwest?

The executives looked at each other.

John sat and waited.

One executive whispered to another, "Have you thought about how we will do that?"

John sat and waited.

More whispering. Finally one of the executives said, "We don't know. We hadn't thought about that."

John said he had a solution. He explained "I can reorganize my company. We will build unloading facilities for the trains. I have the trucks and drivers, the dispatchers, and all the office systems in place to get the right automobiles to the right dealers."

The executives were delighted that he had solved a problem they hadn't anticipated. John said he and his people could guarantee a smooth transition with no disruption in deliveries if they would give him an exclusive contract. The auto and railroad executives agreed.

Within 30 days from hearing the news, John had reorganized his company, had architects designing new facilities, and started negotiations for the purchase of industrial property with railroad sidings.

Years later, when he told me about this incident he said, "It was the best thing that ever happened to me."

"In what way?" I asked.

"It cut my costs. I needed fewer drivers and fewer trucks. We had lower fuel bills. I could sleep in my own bed almost every night." He grinned and added, "And I didn't have to pay interstate tariffs anymore!"

The Good Luck of Misfortune

John Youell's story shows how and why some people are better survivors than others. When misfortune strikes, life's best survivors not only cope well, they often turn a potential disaster into a lucky development.

How they do it is not a mystery. Review the sequence: John Youell sensed that something was wrong and trusted his intuition. He reacted to bad news with questions. He found an amusing benefit to the loss of his business. He adapted to the new reality very quickly. He had empathy for all other parties. He retained his self-confidence. He searched for a way to make things work out well for everyone. He was tough in calling for a meeting. He succeeded in turning the business disaster into a stroke of good luck.

Walpole's Term

The English writer Horace Walpole coined a word for the ability to convert what could be a disaster into good fortune. He named the talent "serendipity." His idea for the term came from his memory of an old Persian story he read during childhood about the "Peregrinations of the Three Sons of the King of Serendip."

The story is about three princes banished from their homeland by their father, King Giaffer. Each had received the best possible education, but their father knew they needed to be seasoned by real life. He used a trivial incident as an excuse to become furious at them. He had them thrown out with no servants, no horses, no jewels or money.

In their various adventures together, the three princes used their powers of observation and deduction to make difficult circumstances turn out well. As fairy tales usually go, so goes this one; each eventually married well, became emperor of his own kingdom, and reconciled with the King.

Serendipity is not good luck, it is, according to Walpole, an ability in which "sagacity" is used to convert an accident into good fortune. According to Walpole, three elements must be present to qualify as an example of serendipity. (1) Something accidental must happen, (2) in response to which a person uses his or her good sense or wisdom, (3) to discover a beneficial outcome.

I've learned that the best indicator someone has a survivor personality is when they talk about their worst experience and then add, "It was one of the best things that ever happened to me."

You Never Know

Imagine renting a rustic wooden cabin in a beautiful forest setting for your honeymoon. The place is delightful. At dawn, however, a woodpecker starts it's loud, rat-a-tat pounding on the roof. The noise is so loud you couldn't sleep. It happens at dawn the second morning, again on the third morning, and so forth. What would you do?

Many people say they'd shoot the bird. Some say, "Who cares? It's your honeymoon."

This incident with a woodpecker happened to Gracie and Walter Lantz on their honeymoon. They were a happy, playful couple and they discovered an opportunity. By the time they had returned from their honeymoon, they were inspired to create the cartoon character "Woody the Woodpecker." Walter was the illustrator, Gracie the voice. Many years later, when interviewed on their fiftieth wedding anniversary, Gracie said, "It was the best thing that ever happened to us."

Many valuable scientific discoveries have been made serendipitously. Wilhelm Roentgen noticed that radiations passing through an object left an image on unexposed photographic negatives. This led to his discovery of x-rays. Arthur Fleming's observation that in certain bacteria cultures a fungus was killing the bacteria, led to the discovery of penicillin.

Look for Serendipity in Your Past

When you think about one of the most difficult experiences in your life, do you see value in it? Do you feel that you gained or benefited in some way from what happened? When telling others about one of your roughest experiences, do you include why it was good for you?

If not, spend some time taking a close look at past difficulties and distressing experiences. Have you ever lost your job through no fault of your own? Had to live or work with a very negative person? Have to deal with angry people? Been forced to cope with a distressing, disruptive life change?

Explore these experiences with questions. Ask yourself questions such as:

- Did I learn something useful?
- Did I gain new strengths? Develop more self-confidence? Become more understanding for others?
- Why can I be thankful that I had that experience? Why was it good for me?

Learn About Serendipity from Survivors

If serendipity is not one of your practiced skills, you can learn about it from interviewing survivors that you admire. Think of people you know who have been through incredibly difficult experiences. These may be Vietnam combat veterans, survivors of childhood sexual abuse, or survivors of head or spinal injuries. Talk with survivors who have a strong, playful, spirit. Find out how they manage to be happy and why they aren't bitter considering what they went through. (Note: before conducting your interview, it may help to review the "Guidelines for Interviewing Survivors" in Appendix A.)

The Serendipity Personality

Life's best survivors are better than most people at quickly turning a disruptive event or adversity into a desirable development. Their reaction to almost anything that happens is "Good! I'm glad this happened! Look what we can do now. Let's play!"

If distressed by an unexpected crisis, they do not let themselves feel victimized. They go from being emotionally upset to coping to thriving to serendipity with amazing speed.

Thus it is that the phrase "The Serendipity Personality" could have been selected instead of "The Survivor Personality." In my mind they are interchangeable. (As would be the phrase "The Synergistic Personality.") The better one understands how the serendipity talent is integrated into the survivor style, the easier it is to understand why life's best survivors spend less time surviving than others.

Serendipity Guidelines

The talent for landing on one's feet comes from mental and emotional habits a person can develop. Here are basic guidelines:

- **Learn to welcome adversity.** There is an old saying that "Good mariners are not made on calm seas." Adversity and misfortune can be catalysts for discovering astounding strength of character. Extreme tests can bring out your deepest strengths if you keep repeating "Somehow, someway I am going to handle this and make things turn out well." The more extreme the difficulty, the greater the eventual benefit.

   When caught off guard by bad news or misfortune, one of the best ways to focus your energies is to remind yourself of your natural ability to pull through. People responding to survivor personality surveys report that when knocked off balance they frequently repeat sayings to themselves, sayings such as:

   "When the going gets tough, the tough get going."
   "Every dark cloud has a silver lining."
   "When life hands you a lemon, make lemonade."
   "When trouble comes in the door a blessing comes in the window."

- **Laugh or cry.** Laughter is great for getting you more relaxed. Remember how John Youell's first comment to his wife, after hearing the bad news, was "Well, you won't hear me complaining about inter-state tariffs any more!" If you can't laugh, then cry. One way or another, get your emotions calmed. Your mind will work more effectively when strong feelings aren't welling up to override your ability to think. Do whatever you must to regain emotional balance quickly.

- **Ask survival/coping questions.**
   What would be useful for me to do right now?

What is the new reality?

- **Be playful and curious.** Toy with the crisis. Poke fun at it. Experiment with your perspective. What are other people thinking and feeling about this situation?
- **Ask serendipity questions.**

    Why is it good that this happened? Is there an opportunity here that did not exist before?

    How did I get myself into this anyway? (Not in a blaming way. In an observing way that looks for cause and effect.) Next time what will I do differently?

    What am I learning from this?

    What could I do to turn this around and have it turn out well for all of us?
- **Take Action.** Do something different, anything that might in some way lead to a good outcome. Remember: When what you are doing isn't working, do something else!

The Outcome

People hit by adversity or misfortune react in different ways. Some go numb. Some become very emotional in ways that solve nothing. Some become victims. They feel ruined by the misfortune and complain "if only that hadn't happened, my life would have been better."

The serendipity choice is to focus on finding a way to make things turn out well. Life's best survivors react to a disruptive change forced on them as though it is a change they desired. The same crises or disruptive changes that some people feel victimized by are turned into good fortune by people with the serendipity talent.

CHAPTER EIGHTEEN

SURVIVING
BEING A SURVIVOR

"I knew I was right," the thin pale man wearing an old blue sweater declared, grinning at me. His eyes glowed with joy. "The other managers at my company say I'm negative, but I'm not. I'm more determined to be successful than they are. Your workshop today proves that I'm right. I've tried to tell them that for us to succeed with a new product we should try to anticipate all the problems we might encounter. But they don't listen. They dismiss me as a pessimist and then make big blunders." He shook his head and looked down. "It's strange. I know I'm better at anticipating and avoiding problems than they are but they're convinced that their gung ho way of thinking is superior to mine."

Coping With the Challenges of Being a Survivor

It is not unusual for people with survivor personalities to be misunderstood by others. Some feel like misfits. The key issue is whether to *act right*, trying to stay within the comfort level of others, or, to *act in ways that work well* even when it means that others do not comprehend.

Life's best survivors know that their way is not the norm but, they must be the way they are despite the drawbacks. The following is a partial list of some of the disadvantages they encounter:

Confuse others. Others may misunderstand your paradoxical traits. People who think in either/or ways are not able to appreciate your ability to think in both one way and the opposite. If you don't remain quiet and tell people who hold only one perspective that you agree with them, they may label you a negative person, a trouble maker, or someone who is not a team player.

Empathy is misinterpreted. Others seldom comprehend how you can empathize with an unpopular view while not agreeing with it. A person who listens with understanding to an opposing group runs the risk of becoming an outcast.

In a face-to-face situation, if you see merit in another person's point of view, he or she may mistakenly think you will do things their way. Some people cannot comprehend how you can understand how things look to them and still not agree to the solution they want.

Learning about yourself isn't always fun. Learning about yourself through empathy for the effect you have on other people, may lead you to discover hypocrisy, faults, and defects in yourself. You may feel stupid and experience periods of remorse. Remember: keep learning in life your number one priority. Make the most of all your self-discoveries and insights.

Experimentation is uncomfortable. You never feel "finished" or grown up. When you try new actions, feelings, and thoughts, you may make mistakes and may feel very uncomfortable during the transition.

Give up labelling and scapegoats. Developing more survivor qualities may require giving up illusions about your upsetting opposites. You may now find yourself acting, thinking, or feeling in ways you previously condemned in others. People who have ridiculed others for reporting ESP experiences, for example, usually find it very hard to accept their own ESP experiences. You may have to stretch your self-concept to accept new things about yourself and discover that qualities that you criticized in others are valuable for them.

Invalidated by others. When you answer questions about what you did to survive, many people, instead of listening and learning, will tell you that you didn't do it right. Paul Plunk says that most men hearing about his family's kidnapping ordeal, say to him "What I would have done is..." and explain how they would have grabbed a gun or run the van off the road. Men seldom give him emotional support or congratulate him for doing what he thought was best in that situation and *succeeding*!

Offering helpful advice can backfire. Following the Golden Rule can make people angry at you when you point out to them how they are acting in self-defeating ways or could be doing something better. What you wish more people would do with you is not what they want you to do with them. Many people do not want solutions when they complain about a problem. They just want an audience. The fact that your suggestion is practical and could work strains the relationship.

Seen as disloyal for trying to make things better. Responsible, ethical, loyal employees who go through proper organizational channels to report concerns about organizational misconduct fraudulent reports, unsafe products, unethical or illegal activities, often get into trouble. Instead of being thanked, they are told to not "rock the boat." If they don't heed the warning they are seen as disloyal or as "not a team player."

Become a "whistle-blower." An employee whose conscience requires him or her to "go public" about organizational wrong doings usually gets into serious difficulties. As has been well documented, organizations typically react in very punitive ways to a person who "blows the whistle." The managers acting in unethical/illegal ways typically react in a manner consistent with the charges against them. They do anything they can to cover-up, invalidate the charges, and discredit the whistle-blower.

The consequences of whistle-blowing are so potentially damaging to everyone (including the accused) that Ralph Nader, the famous consumer advocate, has developed a list of questions he recommends that any person take time to answer before going public with charges. (Some laws now exist to protect whistle-blowers, and support services are avilable. See "Notes.")

Reject help or advice, won't talk with others. A highly self-sufficient person can be so determined to go it alone, he or she may refuse help which could be very useful. Many Vietnam combat veterans went for years refusing to talk with counselors or participate in rap groups, even though they were not dealing well with their memories and feelings about their war experiences.

One reason why so many military veterans and survivors of abuse have troubled relationships is that they have never relived their feelings about what they went through. Talking *about* the feelings is not enough. To overcome Post Traumatic Stress Disorder, *the feelings must be re-experienced.* Most veterans Outreach Centers have a sign that says "No Pain, No Gain." It takes more courage to deal with PTSD than it took to go into combat, and it is the *only* route back home. A wounded spirit does not heal when kept hidden from exposure. The only way to heal the festering wound and turn it into a scar is to expose the wound to others who have healed their wounds.

People plead for help from you. Survivors who get publicity receive many requests for help. People write and telephone asking to be rescued from their desperate situations. They somehow think you have some survivor energy you can magically bestow on them. This can be a difficult challenge, especially when you care about others. After Joy Blitch spoke at conferences about how she recovered from cancer she would be awakened at two and three in the morning by telephone calls from people wanting her to help them help someone else who had cancer.

Envied by others. When you become good at making things work well in your life, some people claim you are just lucky. You have to brace yourself for some jabs and cheap-shots from those who believe that because you make it look easy—it is. A solution: Accept them as part of a noisy planet and *give yourself credit*.

Must always be strong. Some people may expect you to be strong all the time. They won't allow you to have moments of weakness. They won't reverse roles with you, even when asked, and give you the nurturing or support they always expect you to give them.

Suggestion: Practice asking for help from those close to you when you need support. Inform others about your needs. Learn how to speak up about what you need.

Must get tough. To make things work well may require not being "nice." Sometimes you may need to refuse to help a person who creates his or her own problems. Sometimes the best course of action is to let others struggle. Sometimes you will need to hold back and let others suffer the consequences of their actions.

Will not quit. By being so determined to master something, you may refuse to give up, even when it would be wise to do so. Suggestion: make it part of your strategy to periodically review how worthwhile an effort is. What would happen if you let it go?

You outclass yourself. Becoming too competent, effective, and professional may mean that some employers will not want to employ you. They know they can't out-think you or control you.

People who have once owned and run their businesses, for example, seldom fit in as employees in large corporations. Vietnam veterans, who at the age of 19 were making fast, life and death decisions and handling thousands of dollars worth of supplies, could not, at the age of 21, tolerate sitting in long meetings listening to a whimp of a manager lecture them about the cost of using too many paper clips.

Too sensitive. Empathy exposes you to distress and pain in others. Having too much subliminal sensitivity can set you up to pick up other people's fears and distress without knowing the feelings are not yours—a confusing emotional state when trying to monitor your own intuition. You feel something but you aren't sure what it means.

Give yourself time to discern the meaning and origin of feelings you sense. For example, the next time you are stuck in traffic check to see if angry feelings are yours or may actually be coming from the many other drivers nearby. You may need to do some "insensitivity training" with yourself.

Outgrow others. When you develop better and more well-integrated ways of thinking, feeling, and acting, you may outgrow friends and loved ones. This may even mean that a marriage partner or a partner at work is no longer someone you want to maintain emotional contact with. You may find that the person's ways of thinking, feeling, and acting are no longer attractive have now become energy draining. You may want to alter a relationship to avoid being drained or exploited. If altering the relationship is not possible you may need to re-evaluate it with regard to your future.

You get criticized for taking care of yourself. When you attempt to pull out of a desynergizing situation, one in which people have been gaining attention for their pain, distress, problems, and difficulties, they may attempt to keep you in it by becoming even more extreme at what they've done in the past. They may try all manner of tricks to make you feel responsible for their well being and take advantage of your sensitivity to them.

Taking steps to change things for the better in your life may throw other people out of their habit patterns and force them to make changes they didn't want to make. They may blame you for their distress and your empathy habit will have you seeing their point of view. Doing what you must is a lot easier when you are blithely unaware of the feelings of others. It requires a unique form of courage to act when you sense the distress other people experience from your actions. Just keep in mind that their insensitivity to you and their inability to handle difficulties is partly why you are pulling away.

Feel lonely. Because of your unique, complex nature you may feel a special kind of loneliness, a longing for someone who really understands you. If it is any consolation, remember that as you become stronger and more well developed, the more unusual you become. Highly competent, intelligent women, for example, typically find that the better they get, there are fewer and fewer men equal to them. Unfortunately, in today's world an exceptional person is often looked at as being something of a freak.

Being Abnormal is OK

In my introductory psychology course, I would give the students the following assignment, "Write a short paper explaining why an exceptionally mentally healthy person is abnormal." Most students would frown, look puzzled, and say, "Huh?"

Usually, however, by the time they had completed the paper and we had discussed the issue in class, most of them came to realize that *normal* does not mean "good" or "right" or "healthy." It means "average." Anyone who deviates far from the norm is, technically speaking, an *ab*-normal person.

Men, for many decades, have made a big mistake in believing that because women are so unpredictable there must be something wrong with them. The psychiatric nurse who said she appreciated learning about the paradoxes said "It's good to know it's not weird—I used to puzzle myself."

It is ironic how often people with well developed survivor qualities fear they are mentally unstable when they are in truth, exceptionally mentally healthy. Fortunately, the trend is in their favor. Indications are that in the decades and centuries ahead the survivor personality may become the norm.

CHAPTER NINETEEN

OUR TRANSFORMATION TO THE NEXT LEVEL OF DEVELOPMENT

Looking Back From the Future

A thousand years from now this period in history will be seen as the time when the human race awakened from the dark ages of its consciousness. Students taking tests will write: "The start of the 21st century marked the transformation to integrated consciousness. Until then, human societies were dominated by a child's way of thinking...."

Our Transformation

"Transformation" means to change from one form to another. When one looks, it is easy to see many signs that the human race is transforming to its next stage of development. People are finding that their survival and well being depends on breaking free from old ways of thinking and functioning that are no longer useful. In the *old form*, or pattern, human societies have been controlled by a child's thinking pattern that based each person's identity on an external frame of reference. The *new form* is emerging as humans achieve a higher level of development based on each person's internal frame of reference.

The Old Form: To Be a Certain Kind of Noun

The *old form* traces back to the experience of each baby as it learns to talk. It is coached to learn the names for things. The names are called nouns. Once it gets the idea, a young child loves showing that it has learned the names for its ear, the clock, mother, and water. It learns that its identity is "boy" or "girl" and that a name for one thing cannot be used for another.

Names and labels for people, the nouns people become, are derived from *an external frame of reference*. For thousands of years adult humans derived their identity from their tribal, ethnic group. One's identity was as a Watusi, Cree, Slav, Basque, Viking, Mongol or one of the many other ethnic groups scattered around the planet.

Later, when religions swept through civilized lands, people identified themselves as being a new kind of noun. They became a Buddhist, Hindu, Muslim, Jew, Catholic, and so on.

Many people became the name of their occupation—Carpenter, Butler, Fisher, Hunter, Weaver, Tailor, Smith, Miller, Baker, Cook, and Shoemaker, would be examples from English speaking countries. In more recent times individuals kept their family and given name but worked to also be turned into a doctor, lawyer, electrician, policeman, plumber, senator, teacher, or other occupational noun. And throughout all the centuries, each person received gender identity instructions from his or her culture on how to be "a man" or "a woman."

Cooperating with the cultural process of becoming a noun helped others. They could quickly determine who a person was. It reduced ambiguity for them. They did not have to learn individuals. Hear the noun, know what the person is like. Know what one noun is like by contrasting it against an opposite noun.

A Problem With the Old Form

Here is an example of a problem that developed from the old habit of thinking of people as nouns. Most organizations, following the long-standing tribal custom of having a dominant male be in control of a group, promoted men into management positions and kept women in subordinate positions. Experienced, capable, well qualified women were passed over for promotions into management.

In workshops I conducted twenty years ago, when I asked participants to describe the characteristics of an excellent manager, the descriptions were close to descriptions of what a good man is like. Descriptions of what a good woman is like did not match what an excellent manager is like. You can see the problem. How could a woman be a manager and still be a woman?

Further, male executives said they would not promote women into important managerial positions because women were too irrational. This belief, not being supported by facts, was irrational thinking on men's part. So why the irrational resistance in men? Why the "glass ceiling" put up against women? Why did men persist in acting in ways not in the best interests of their organizations, when they kept higher qualified women working for lesser qualified male managers?

The root of the problem stemmed from males needing their job titles, impressive labels, to feel like men. The presence of women in management positions triggered an identity crisis in many men. The irrational and sometimes desperate resistance of many males against women coming into management was much more than a power issue. If a woman can be a manager, executive, or president as well as a man, what happens to the frame of reference men base their masculinity on? How can a man feel like a man if a woman is a better at being "a manager" than he?

The Personal Price is High

The price one pays by trying to be a noun following an externally based set of instructions, is an inability to function when something happens outside the role instructions. Acting like a noun blocks learning and adapting. Psychologist Herb Goldberg says "masculinity and femininity are psychological disorders." Efforts to act like "a man" or "a woman" work only when a person who has learned one role can find someone else to play the complimentary role as instructed. Marital problems occur when a person doesn't play his or her role in the way that supports the other person playing his or her culturally assigned role. In other words, a person trying to act like "a man" or "a woman" is emotionally a child attempting to act like what a child thinks an adult man or woman is like.

A person prevented from natural development acquires and adheres to only the approved traits. A person with a trained, or imposed personality pattern is more fragile, does not handle change well, and learns little from experiences.

An imposed personality pattern locks a person into a frustratingly limited existence. When difficulties with others develop, they tend to believe (sometimes unconsciously) that the other person isn't following instructions.

The Futility of Being a Good Noun

A person whose identity is based on being a good, or aggrandized noun must have people in the world who are bad, or pejorative nouns to provide a frame of reference or contrast. It is an indirect way to build up one's feelings of esteem at the expense of others. The identity of individuals in many religious groups, for example, is inseparably linked to their perception of being surrounded by "sinners"—which is why they can never succeed in eliminating or converting those so seen, no matter how vigorously they try. Any person whose identity is based on being against others viewed as undesirable nouns is guaranteed a never ending supply of those he or she is against because it is a self-defeating child's way of thinking. People with a "good noun" identity can never eliminate the bad nouns that provide the frame of reference for their identity.

The New Form: From Nouns to Descriptions

People raised to be good boys and good girls carry inner prohibitions against acting like the person in the opposite role. Good boys learn that to be a man is to not be like a woman. They develop a masculine identity that is based on not being feminine. They put energy into *not developing* what the culture traditionally has identified as feminine traits.

For many centuries, when an infant was born the first question the parents usually asked was, "Is it a boy or a girl?" From birth on, the infant's biological gender drew actions from adults that selectively suppressed the traits deemed undesirable for a child of that sex and encouraged the development of traits deemed desirable. The process can be drawn this way:

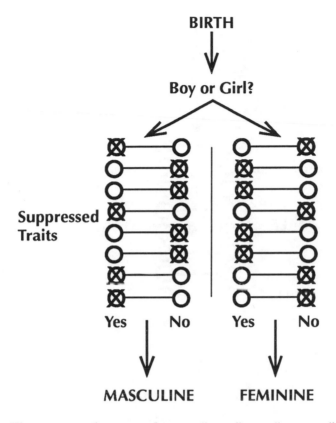

GENDER QUESTION

BIRTH

Boy or Girl?

Suppressed
Traits

Yes | No   Yes | No

MASCULINE   **FEMININE**

The way a culture produces a "man" or a "woman" or a "good child" is to take a potentially complex person and selectively suppress certain qualities deemed undesirable. This is a deeply ingrained cultural habit passed on from one generation to the next. Children who did not succumb were seen usually seen as bad, sick, deviant, or some kind of misfit—all of which reflected badly on the parents.

In recent times a significant change has taken place in child rearing practices. Now when an infant is born, the first question usually asked by mothers and fathers is, "Is it healthy?"

The emerging new way of thinking is that each person is larger than biological gender, that every person has many qualities, traits, and attributes with maleness or femaleness only making up part of the person. The process can be represented this way:

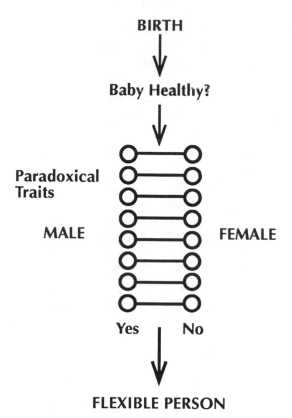

HEALTH QUESTION

BIRTH

Baby Healthy?

Paradoxical Traits

MALE

FEMALE

Yes | No

FLEXIBLE PERSON

A healthy personality develops when the emergence of a child's inborn nature is facilitated rather suppressed. The child's interests and explorations are encouraged rather than stifled when they run contrary to old role models. In today's world, more children are growing up assuming it is natural to be both trusting *and* cautious, selfish *and* unselfish, intuitive *and* logical, and so on.

A New Form: The Professional Manager

One of the best examples of how humans are evolving from the old form to the new can be found in modern organizations. Nowadays descriptions of a professional manager are not based on sex roles. There is widespread recognition that professionalism is not gender specific. Competent women and competent men manage in the same way. Women in management, for example, are expected to be forceful when it is called for, while their male counterparts are learning facilitating skills and developing intuition. Here is a list of characteristics workshop participants typically produce when asked to describe today's professional manager:

- Asks questions and listens well. Quickly grasps what others say and feel.
- Can admit ignorance, and is not ashamed to admit what they don't know.
- Is strong on production *and* people, tasks *and* relationships
- Is open to unpleasant information, is not thrown by bad news, and remains stable in emergencies.
- Has time for you, yet doesn't let people waste their time.
- Is self-confident and optimistic, creates a positive atmosphere.
- Will make tough decisions and commit to a course of action.
- Is flexible. Can get a job done in several different ways.
- Can usually explain what he or she is doing, how, and why.
- Will do the unpleasant parts of the job. (Like having to fire someone.)
- Has good working relations with people in allied jobs and treats them with respect.
- Keeps updated in the field, is self-motivated to learn, and is always trying to improve.
- Has a personal style—a unique way of doing things.
- Can coach a team and leave it alone when things are working well.
- Is effective; gets results with minimum effort.
- Monitors results, welcomes feedback or criticism, accepts blame, and learns from mistakes.
- Can laugh at themselves.
- Expresses appreciation to others.
- Is farsighted, anticipates well, yet expects the unexpected.
- Is not "married" to the job; has other important interests such as family, recreation, hobbies, community, or church activities.
- Has strong inner standards and ethics.

This list is free from sex role stereotypes and reflects how much change has taken place in only several decades. One of the most clear signs of the transformation in the world of management is that *the best managers no longer manage with instructions, they manage with questions.* Managers no longer act as they should, they act according to what results they get.

Organizational Transformation

Can organizations develop survivorship skills? Yes. Organizations are living systems. In their efforts to survive and thrive in today's world, corporations are undergoing major transformations. They are striving for more inner flexibility so they can respond quickly to changes in technology and changes in consumer needs. They ask more questions and are developing more empathy for the consumers of their products and services. Instead of making customers buy the way they want to sell, they now sell the way the customer wants to buy. They value customers who tell them what they have done wrong. They learn from mistakes instead of placing blame.

They convert difficulties into opportunities. Job titles have become less important than effectiveness. Employers who previously regarded minority workers as a hassle, have found that cultural diversity strengthens the work force.

A Living Example of the Old Form

One of the best examples of an old, outmoded form can be seen in the psychiatric profession. The public does not know it, but there is no proof in the psychiatric literature that schizophrenia is a disease or illness. After 100 years of intense study, psychiatrists still do not know what schizophrenia is. With over 100,000 articles and books published on the topic, the psychiatric research literature has documented that who will get schizophrenia is unpredictable, there is no immunity from it, there is no risk of catching it from another person, the symptoms differ from person to person, people with it often have to be talked into thinking they are sick, there is no cure for it, people treated for it in psychiatric facilities are generally worse off, no one dies from it, people can recover from it on their own, and some people are better off for having had it.

What is going on here? The situation is not a matter of professional incompetence. It is a cultural reenactment of a child's way of labeling people as bad or good, depending on its experience of them. Someone who talks or acts in upsetting ways is seen as a pejorative, "bad noun" and is turned over to an aggrandized, "good noun" who, like mother, is all powerful, all knowing, and all caring. In Europe for many centuries, the special class of good nouns were "priests." Their identity was defined by their efforts to rid the world of "heretics" and "witches."

In our society the most powerful, all knowing, all caring good nouns are called "psychiatrists." The identity of the psychiatric profession is inseparably linked to its struggle to cure people designated as "schizophrenics." It is our society's way of acting out the child's "good noun—bad noun" pattern of thinking, a pattern held onto despite the protests of thousands of ex-patients.

Years ago, I naively told some psychiatrists that the perception of mental illness is mostly a stress reaction in the mind of the beholder. They were not good listeners. I subsequently learned why they do not have to be. Our society gives psychiatrists more control over patients than any other medical speciality and then excuses psychiatrists from having to be effective. In hospitals and clinics they are the only medical doctors allowed to blame their patients when their prescribed therapies do not work. Every state has laws granting psychiatrists immunity from lawsuits for harm done to mental patients. Effort is all that our society wants with "schizophrenics," not results, because maintaining the illusion of "good" and "bad" nouns is more important.

Schizophrenia: A Transformation

There is a specific reason for selecting psychiatry and its ineffective struggle with schizophrenia as an example of the old form of thinking. When I searched through historical writings for early accounts of people with survivor qualities I made a fascinating discovery. The first writings containing descriptions similar to my survivor personality findings were made by Wilhelm Nietszche in Germany at the same time schizophrenia was first observed. About 100 years ago, while Nietszche was describing what he called a new, "higher human," German psychiatrists were puzzling over a new kind of mental disturbance, one never before seen in humans. It was a condition in which healthy young adults suddenly became demented. Because the main feature of this mental disorder was "a splitting of the mind," they decided to use "schizo-phrenia" as the diagnostic term for the condition.

Nietszche's famous statement, "that which does not kill me makes me stronger," shows that he was very aware of the ability to gain strength from extremely distressing experiences. In his writings he described a new human who lived according to inner judgement, not socially imposed rules. He described many combinations of contradictory traits in the new human.

Now, a hundred years later, the contradictory or paradoxical qualities of people who have reached this new level of human development are more well defined. Life's best survivors demonstrate pessimistic optimism, flexible stability, tough sensitivity, selfish unselfishness, loving anger, self-critical self-appreciation, moral lust, disillusioned hopefulness, cooperative non-conformity, responsible rebellion, and many more paradoxical combinations.

In other words, *the survivor personality appears to be a successful form of schizophrenia*. Both schizophrenia and paradoxical traits were first observed in humans at the same time in the same part of the world. As portrayed in the story of blind men attempting to describe an elephant, Wilhelm Nietszche and German psychiatrists were apparently describing the same new phenomenon from different perspectives. It seems likely that schizophrenia will eventually prove to not be a horrible scourge afflicting modern humanity, but rather as a natural transformational stage leading to a better level of development.

The Human of the Future

When silva culturists with the U.S. Forest Service want to predict the dominant tree in an area in several hundred years, they look at the undergrowth in the forest. They know that when a percentage of saplings of a new species reaches a certain point, it will be the dominant species in the future.

Survivors who make the news may appear to be rare exceptions, but there are now so many people with survivor personalities in the "undergrowth" I believe we have a glimpse if not a clear view of the human of the future. The loosening of centuries old, restrictive, masculine and feminine roles as well as the good child role is freeing people to benefit from their inborn capacity for lifelong learning.

To give up an act forced on one as a child can be frightening and painful, as when the women in China unbound their feet. But people *are* doing it. More self-managed emotional healing is taking place now than has ever happened before. Self-help groups have been formed for survivors of rape, incest, alcoholic parents, physical abuse, and other traumatic experiences. We are recognizing that horrible experiences often produce post-traumatic stress disorders, and that people can overcome the constricting effects of those experiences. Thousands are examining and freeing themselves from co-dependency roles. Adults are releasing themselves from inner prohibitions that have kept them from getting better and better throughout their lives.

Jonas Salk, famous for developing a polio vaccine, believes we are in a major, worldwide transformation from "Epic A" to "Epic B." He characterizes the two epics as follows:

EPIC A	EPIC B
Anti Death	Pro Life
Anti Disease	Pro Health
Death Control	Birth Control
Repression	Self Expression
External Restraint	Self Restraint

In *Survival of the Wisest,* Salk says "These lists contain sets of opposed complementaries which have to be reconciled by an *and* rather than by an *or* attitude." He goes on to say that "As in nature generally, there will be (people) who will endure and those who will not—groups and types that survive and those that will not. Nature has its own way of choosing...it does not take too much wisdom to predict who will be favored, since Nature, and *not man* will in effect have the last word."

Our transformation to the next level of development is being driven by the forces of nature. Humans determined to have their lives and their world work well are breaking free from old instructions that thwart, inhibit and constrict their inborn capabilities.

Learning What Can't Be Taught

No book written, no workshop, no training program can teach you how to have a survivor personality. The more you allow some workshop program, or an author who has never met you, to shape you into being a more ideal person, the *less* chance you have of developing your own survivorship style. Keep in mind also, that my report, like all writings about surviving, resiliency, hardiness, thriving, coping, or whatever, describes what I have found has worked in *the past*, for *others*, in *situations that may never exist again*.

What *you* may be confronted with in the future, and what you develop as *your* unique combination of strengths and capabilities—are for you to discover. Only you can do it. Survivorship often depends on how well you can comprehend a new reality and do something unusual that works—for you.

What you can do is create a self-managed plan for acquiring qualities and skills that will improve your ability to handle change, unexpected developments, and disruptive crises that come your way. In your personal plan you may want to include some of the following:

- **Ask questions!** Respond to change, new developments, threats, confusion, trouble, or criticism by asking "What is happening?" Develop a curiosity reflex. Practice reading each new reality rapidly.
- **Increase your mental and emotional flexibility.** Tell yourself "It is all right to feel and think in both one way and the opposite." Free yourself from inner voices from your past that say you shouldn't feel or think a certain way. Develop many response choices for yourself.
- **Assume that change and having to work with uncertainty, ambiguity, and unknowns are a way of life from now on.**

Learn to handle these with self-confidence. Practice making new developments work out well. In today's world getting good results counts more than working hard.

- **Become useful quicker and in more ways than other people.** Ask yourself "How can I interact with this so that things get better for everyone?" Your ability to find ways to be useful *makes you valuable*. In every situation make it a habit to make your area of responsibility more valuable than anyone thought it could be. Consider such efforts an investment in yourself.

- **Develop empathy skills, especially with difficult people.** Put yourself in the other person's place. Ask "What do they feel and think? What are their views, assumptions, explanations, and values? How do they benefit from acting as they do?" Govern your actions not by your good intentions, but by the actual effect you have on others.

- **Learn how to learn from experience.** That way you are *always* becoming more capable and more employable. Practice thanking people who give you unpleasant feedback. Consider viewing difficult people as your teachers in the school of life. Instead of trying to get difficult people to change, ask yourself "Why am I so vulnerable? What are my blind spots? How could I handle myself better with such people?"

- **Resist labelling others; practice observing and describing what others feel, think, say and do.** Use negative nouns when you want to swear and positive nouns when you want to put someone on a pedestal, but recognize that the labels you put on others reflect *your* emotional state.

- **Pause occasionally to silently observe what is happening.** Take several deep breaths. Scan your feelings. Be alert to fleeting impressions. Notice little things. Be alert to early clues about what might be happening.

- **Take time to appreciate yourself for the helpful things you do.** Appreciate your accomplishments. Feelings of positive self-regard help blunt the sting of hurtful criticism. Your self-esteem determines how much you learn after something goes wrong. The stronger your self-esteem, the more you learn.

- **When hit by adversity, no matter how unfair it seems, follow the survivor sequence:** regain emotional balance, adapt and cope with your immediate situation, thrive by learning and being creative, then find the gift. The better you become, the faster you can convert disaster into good fortune.

So, my friend, I hope you see how circumstances that almost break your spirit can be converted into good fortune, and that adversity may lead to the discovery of wonderful new abilities within you.

Guidelines for Listening to Survivors of Extreme Experiences

More than once after a survivor has talked with me, the person's family has said, "What did he tell you? He's never talked to us about it." The following guidelines show how to be a good listener with people who have survived distressing experiences.

- **Do not ask about a person's experiences unless you can handle honest answers.** When Vietnam combat veterans returned home, they found that very few people had the emotional strength to listen to their stories. Many Gulf War combat troops saw gruesome sights when they went into Iraq and Kuwait. Women who were sexually abused as children seldom find anyone who can handle listening to their story.

- **Do not open someone up and then "chicken out" when the story gets too rough.** Tell yourself that a reasonably strong human being ought to be able to at least *listen* to what another person has *lived through*. Survivors of major, distressing experiences will usually talk to a person who has the courage to listen.

- **Give the person lots of time**. Survivors of deeply painful experiences seldom find anyone who can listen to their complete account. Ex-POWs report that the average person who asks about their experiences can listen for only several minutes. So, if you inquire, plan to listen for hours. If a Gulf War veteran, for example, is willing to talk to you, it is important to allow him or her plenty of time to talk. Don't interrupt to share your feelings and opinions about the war.

- **Be an active listener**. When they were growing up, most children of alcoholic or abusive parents were forced to put on a front of having a normal, happy family. Now, years later, it may not be easy for them to drop that act. You can encourage them and get a better picture of what they had to cope with by being an active listener. When you feel puzzled about facts or incidents, ask questions. With war veterans, do a "walk-through" of their combat duty from start to finish. Ask about their feelings while getting ready to go into combat. What were the person's first impressions on arrival? Ask for details. Use a similar approach with survivors of corporate battles or reorganizations, and the down-sizing of public agencies. Find out what happened, what it was like for them, and how they felt in each circumstance.
- **Do not force the person to have negative emotions**. Use the interviews to learn an important reality about surviving: *It isn't the situation, it is how a person reacts to it that counts*. For example, the teen-age girl I mentioned in the chapter on paradoxical traits, told me she had been kidnapped by her father when she was five. Rosyann's parents had been divorced and she was living with her mother at the time. One afternoon when school let out her father was waiting for her. He put her into his car. He told Rosyann that her mother had died, and then drove them to another state.

  They lived in poor neighborhoods. The father was usually broke, drank when he had some money, and sometimes didn't come home at night. Rosyann said that when she was hungry or didn't have enough clothing to wear, she would search around the neighborhood for "good ladies" like her mother. She would ask them for clothing or food and would almost always get what she needed. She learned to get money by knocking on doors and asking for empty cans and bottles to cash in.

  To avoid suspicions in the neighborhood, the father would take her to the nearest school, tell the principal that they just moved from out-of-state and give misleading information about how to obtain her records. Weeks later, when school authorities would call or write and ask too many questions, he would put their things in his car late some night and move to another city. He managed to evade authorities in this way for eight years, until he was finally arrested when Rosyann was thirteen.

When I asked her how she felt about all this, she glanced at me and shrugged. Her easy smile and the sparkle in her eyes went away. Why was she cautious about answering my question? She said that the case workers, school officials, and others kept insisting that it must have been an awful experience. They wouldn't let her be honest. In truth, she didn't feel bad. She was proud of herself. She was self-sufficient. She made friends easily and had a lot of good times. She had learned how to deal with her father. She laughed and said she was the "Dear Abby" at her new school. Her classmates come to her for advice on how to handle angry parents, mean teachers, and bullies.

The point here is that not everyone reacts with self-pity or grief to the difficult events that happen to him or her. A drawback for those who survive well is that they encounter people who need to rescue and help others. People who have an identity built on rescuing people seen as victims often force help and sympathy on others, even when it is unwanted and is inappropriate. As a consequence, people who survive well tend to avoid or clam up around people who need to have others feel bad or victimized.

If you want to get an accurate story, you need to be an honest listener. This means you must be open to learn that another person may not be distressed about experiences that would upset you. Don't force negative emotions onto him or her.

- **Listen with compassion but minimize sympathy.** It is easier for people to talk about the rough part of an experience if they don't have to put up with sympathy. Expressions of sympathy such as "How awful!" or "You poor soul!" may be well intended, but they can sidetrack the person or inhibit them from being fully open with you. Survivors of horrible experiences talk more easily to a person with calm concern. Control your imagination and resist letting their feelings become your feelings. Don't make the person have to handle your emotional reactions as well as his or her own. If you need emotional support, seek it elsewhere. If the person relives moments of distress, don't tell them to not feel what they are feeling. Just sit with them and breathe.

- **Ask what he or she sees that is positive in the experience.** It is not accurate to think of most war veterans as having a post-traumatic stress disorder. Some do. The majority do not. Research shows that many Vietnam combat veterans became significantly more mature and developed a healthy personal identity during their tour of duty. Do not assume that an adult child of alcoholic parents or survivor of abuse is emotionally crippled. One of the purposes of your interviews is to discover for yourself how the same extreme circumstances that are emotionally traumatic for some people can cause others to become stronger. Ask if they believe that one thing contributed to their survival more than any thing else.

- **Take notes afterward and talk with others about what you learn.** To increase your learning, write down what you remember soon after your interview. Reflect on what the person's experience means to you. Talk about what you are learning with someone else who has the same interest. Ask new questions about resiliency, survivorship, and thriving.

Guidelines for Thriving During Job Loss and Job Search

Losing your job can be very difficult. And to make matters worse, if you feel wiped out emotionally, how do you find the energy to search for work? How can you be pleasant, relaxed, and cheerful in an interview? Here are some guidelines for handling the *emotional* challenge of searching for new employment.

- **Spend lots of time writing out how you feel about what has happened.** Include all the things you would like to have said to your bosses in the past but didn't. Continue expressing your feelings over and over until you get tired of it and can put it behind you. Prospective employers are turned off by a person who complains about a previous employer.

  James Pennebaker, psychologist, had one group of unemployed people write down their feelings about being laid off for twenty minutes, five days in a row. He had another, similar group write about time management for twenty minutes, five days in a row. In the months that followed a significantly larger number of the people who wrote about their emotions found employment.

  TRY THIS: If you have not fully expressed your feelings about losing your job, consider doing so now. Get a pad of paper. Write "I feel..." over and over. Doing this a few minutes every day could be very useful.

- **Form a small support group.** Link up with others like yourself. Telephone each other frequently to find out how you are doing. As Barbara Sher and Annie Gotlieb point out, people have more courage for each other than they have for themselves. Hold brainstorming sessions. Arrange for conference calls. Help each other discover good opportunities.

Devote one or two meetings to grieving what you have lost. Talk about what you miss. Talk about your best experiences in your former job. What will you always be proud of?

- **Rebuild your self-esteem.** Make a list of everything you like and appreciate about yourself. Include all the things you've done in the past year that you like yourself for doing. A good way to boost your self-esteem and self-confidence is to *obtain letters of appreciation* from recent co-workers and managers about how great it was to work with you. These may be short paragraphs describing either specific or general contributions you made. True, it takes an ounce of courage to ask people for these endorsements, but you will be astonished and touched by people's eagerness to help. You will be moved by their appreciation of things you may not have realized anyone noticed.

  After obtaining these endorsements, type three or four paragraphs from them on a single sheet and attach it to your resume. Remember: employers in the process of hiring are concerned by the one factor most difficult to predict: *What would this person be like to have around on a day to day basis?* By providing an "endorsement" sheet, you help prospective employers resolve their dilemma and provide a more complete picture of yourself. In addition, you dispel the illusion that unemployed people have something "wrong" with them. These endorsements document the value you had to people you worked with and will help to remind you of all that you contributed.

- **Write a detailed description of what you do well.** Describe specific projects or assignments you feel proud about. Describe your people skills. Describe what equipment or software you run well.

- **Practice talking about your reliable strengths.** Describe your abilities with a friend. One executive told me, "I ask job applicants why I should hire them. I figure if they can't sell themselves to me, how can they sell my company to prospective customers?"

- **Make finding a job your new job.** Get out and talk with people. Nine out of ten job openings are never advertised in the newspaper. Make appointments to conduct informational interviews to find out what is happening in places where you would like to work. Don't hang around the house as if you are on vacation.

- **Be persistent.** Research has shown that the main factor leading to getting hired is the number of potential employers contacted. *But* make certain you are contacting the right decision makers. The personnel manager for a large school district said that every week a woman who had applied for a teaching position called in and every week they tried to explain to the woman that all hiring decisions are made by school principals who select from the list of applicants. The woman created a negative impression in the personnel office for wasting their time and being so dense.

- **Focus on each employer's needs, more than yours.** No one except your cousin is going to hire you because you need a job. When you find a position you would like to have, research what the managers need to have happen. Then customize your resume and application to fit exactly with what this employer needs. They must see you as *uniquely* qualified for the position.

- **Before your job interview take a few minutes to meditate on your past successes and reliable skills.** If you become preoccupied with the fourteen times you've been turned down you might as well not show up. The attitude "You probably won't want to hire me either" gets results just as does the attitude "You are going to be very fortunate if you hire me."

- **Be open to unexpected opportunities.** A man who had worked as an inventory control specialist for a large electronic firm was in a convenience store one Saturday about noon. Behind him was a tired looking man with an arm load of sandwiches and soft drinks. "Going on a picnic?" he asked the man with the sandwiches.

"No," the man said. He nodded toward the building across the street, "we're doing our annual inventory. We'll be here all week-end working late."

"Don't you have a database program to do all that?" the specialist asked.

"The company has one but the person who knew how to run it left for another job. We're doing it by hand."

The specialist said he believed he could help, walked across the street, and after a quick demonstration of his skills was hired on the spot.

- **Take creative action.** Professor Howard Stephenson, author of a book about people who were survivors during the Depression in the 1930s. said that one of his favorite examples was about a red-headed young man who answered a newspaper ad for an office assistant. When the young man showed up at the business he found a long line of job applicants ahead of him. Sizing up the situation, he went to the nearest Western Union office and had the following telegram delivered to the employment interviewer: "Don't hire anyone until you talk to the red-headed kid at the end of the line." Shortly after the telegram was delivered the interviewer came out of his office with the telegram clutched in his hand. He found the red-headed sender of the message and took him into the office. The interviewer said "You are exactly the sort of assistant we need here," and hired him.

- **Pay attention to your recent employer's new situation.** Some environmental specialists with a state agency had their jobs eliminated even though their work was mandated and partially funded by the federal government. In a problem solving session, a few of them saw that their work had to be done by someone even if the state had to hire a consulting firm to do it. The solution? They formed a consulting firm and obtained the contract—at a higher rate of pay for them all!

Chapter Notes and References

Chapter 1   **Life is Not Fair**
Walt Disney story in *The Art of Walt Disney*, by Christopher Finch; Harry N. Abrams, publisher, 1975, Chapters 1-2.

Charlie Plumb quote from transcript of interview on NBC "1986," June 24, 1986. His book, *I'm No Hero*, can be obtained by writing to: Charlie Plumb, P.O. Box 223, Kansas City, MO 64141.

"self-help authors..." for example, a famous author of self-help books states in the first sentence in one of his books "This is the last self-help book you will ever need to read."

Julius Segal, *Winning Life's Toughest Battles*, Ivy Books, 1986, p. 130.

Chapter 2   **Learning About Survival**
E. James Anthony, *The Invulnerable Child*, The Guilford Press, 1987, p. 147. See also *Vulnerable But Invincible: A Longitudinal Study of Resilient Children and Youth*, by Emmy E. Werner and Ruth S. Smith; McGraw-Hill Book Company, 1982.

Lee Iacocca, *Iacocca: An Autobiography*, Bantam Books, 1984, pp. 96-97.

Chapter 3   **Playful Curiosity**
Selma Fraiberg, *The Magic Years*, Scribner's, 1959, pp. 23-62.

Maria Montessori, *The Absorbent Mind*, Holt, Rinehart & Winston, 1967. Also Delta Books, soft cover, 1967, p.180.

Robert W. White, "Motivation Reconsidered: The Concept of Competence," *The Psychological Review*, Vol. 66, Sept., 1959.

Robert Fulghum, *All I really Need to Know I Learned in Kindergarten*, Ivy Books, 1986, p. 9.

"IQ problem" The psychologists' solution was to engage in a sort of professional slight of hand. They decided to say the average score for each age group would be equal to an IQ of 100. Thus, even though the average eighteen year old gets a higher score than the average forty year old on the same test, they are both given an IQ score of 100.

Chapter 4   **Flexibility**
"What Makes An Ideal Man?" *Psychology Today*, March, 1989, pp. 58-60. (A copy of Al Siebert's response letter is available on request.)

T.C. Schneirla, "An Evolutionary and Developmental Theory of Biphasic Process Underlying Approach and Withdrawal," *Nebraska Symposium on Motivation*, Vol. 7, Marshall R. Jones, editor, 1959. Reprinted in *Selected Writings of T.C. Schneirla*, W.H. Freeman Co., 1972.

"long-term AIDS survivors..." *Parade Magazine*, January 31, 1993, pp. 4-7.

"two biologists..." Lorus J. Milne and Margery Milne, *Patterns of Survival*, Prentice-Hall, 1967, p. 4.

The Life of General H. Norman Schwartzkopf, by Roger Cohen and Claudio Gatti; Berkeley Books, 1992, pp. 1, 281, 303, 333.

Abraham Maslow, *Eupsychian Management*, Dorsey Press, 1965, p. 72.

Moshe Feldenkrais, *Awareness Through Movement*, Harper & Row, 1972, p. 85.

Chapter 5   The Synergy Imperative

Mihaly Csikszentmihalyi, *Flow: The Psychology of the Optimal Experience*, Harper & Row, 1990.

"Synergy: Some Notes of Ruth Benedict," edited by Abraham Maslow and John Honigman, *American Anthropologist*, Vol. 72, 1970, pp. 325-326. This is the only publication containing Ruth Benedict's thinking on synergy. It was published after her death from a compilation of notes taken by students in her classes.

"synergistic personality..." an excellent portrayal on television is the character Paul Forrester played by Robert Hayes in the *Starman* series. Paul Forrester's gentle way of converting threats and danger into things turning out well for everyone, stirred such a powerful response in viewers, they formed a national Starman organization. For newsletter or membership information contact: Lil Sibley, 4945 "U" Street, Sacramento, CA 95817-1528.

Jose Ortega y Gassett, *The Revolt of the Masses*, 1932, p. 69.

Abraham Maslow, *The Farther Reaches of Human Nature*, Viking Press, 1971, p. 210.

Anthony Robbins, *Sharing Ideas* newsletter, Dec., 1992/Jan. 1993, pp. 5-6.

Whistle-blowing! Loyalty and Dissent in the Corporation, by Alan F. Westin; McGraw-Hill, 1981, p. 2.

Chapter 6   Empathy

For a complete account of Kenneth Donaldson's story, see his book *Insanity Inside Out*, Crown Publishers, 1976.

Arnold Toynbee, *Surviving The Future*, Oxford Press, 1971, p. 152.

Walter Toman, *Family Constellation: Its Effects on Personality and Social Behavior*, 2nd Edition, Springer, 1969.

"How Not to Get Conned," booklet from the Office of Justice Assistance, Research , and Statistics, U.S. Department of Justice, Washington, DC 20531.

American Cæsar: A Biography of Douglas MacArthur, by William Manchester; Little Brown and Company, 1978.

Chapter 7   The Survivor's Edge

Roy Rowan, *The Intuitive Manager*, Little, Brown and Company, 1986, p. 11.

Weston H. Agor, "How Top Executives Use Their Intuition to Make Important Decisions," *Business Horizons*, Jan/Feb, 1986, pp. 49-50. For information about the Global Intuition Network write to: Weston H. Agor, Ph.D., The University of Texas, P.O. Box 614, El Paso, TX 79968

Winston Churchill: An Intimate Portrait, by Violet Bonham Carter; Harcourt, Brace and World, 1965, pp. 42-46.

Robert Godfrey, *Outward Bound: Schools of the Possible*, Anchor Books, 1980, p. 130.

Harold Sherman, *How to Make ESP Work for You*, Fawcett-Crest, 1964, pp. 85-87.

Creativity test answers:

1. *cheese*: blue cheese, cheese cake, cottage cheese
2. *hand*: hand made, hand cuff, left hand
3. *slow*: slow motion, slowpoke, slow down
4. *hard*: hardwood, hard liquor, hard luck
5. *stone*: keystone, stone wall, precious stone

E. James Anthony, *The Invulnerable Child*, The Guilford Press, 1987, p. 149.

Marcia Sinetar, *Developing A 21st Century Mind*, Villard Books, 1991, p. 5. Sinetar's observations are similar to mine about essential skills for thriving in the years ahead but she labels people "creative adaptives." For easier reading, mentally substitute the phrase "persons with creative adaptive abilities" whenever you encounter the label.

Psychologist Sarnoff Mednick was developing the "Remote Associations Test" while I was in graduate school at the University of Michigan. His copyrighted version has high validity.

Howard Stephenson said that imagination is only the first step, however. As he expressed so clearly in his 1937 book, *They Sold Themselves*, Depression survivors also had "nerve" and "tact."

Alex F. Osborn, *Your Creative Power*; Dell, 1948. For information about Osborn's book and the Creative Education Foundation he founded, write to: 1050 Union Road, #4, Buffalo, NY 14224-3402.

Emile Coué quote in *How to Use Autosuggestion Effectively*, by John Duckworth; Wilshire Book Company, 8721 Sunset Blvd., Hollywood, CA 90069, p. 105.

Chapter 8   The "Good Child" Handicap

"good boys and good girls vs. bad kids..." special thanks go to Larry Mathae, a warmly remembered friend and colleague, who alerted me to this pattern with his unpublished manuscript "The Good Guy, Bad Guy Code of the West." See also the passages on "being nice" in *Creative Aggression*, by George Bach and Herb Goldberg, Avon Books, 1974

"ain't men awful..." from conversations with Susan Carlson.

Anne Wilson Schaef's pioneering activities and her books *'Women's Reality,"* and *"Co-Dependence,"* gave rise to the co-dependency movement. There are now dozens of books on the subject. For current information contact: Wilson-Schaef Associates, P.O. Box 18686, Boulder, CO 80308.

"constructed personality..." from conversations with Shale Paul and from his book, *The Warrior Within: A Guide to Inner Power*; Delta Group Press,1983, Chapters 2 and 7. For information write to: The Delta Group, 245 Ponderosa Way, Evergreen, CO 80439.

Chapter 9   Thriving

"gaining strength..." a good book on the thriving process is *Resilience: Discovering A New Strength At Times Of Stress*, by Frederich Flach, M.D.; Fawcett Columbine, 1988.

James Pennebaker and associates, employment data from unpublished research report.

"emotions journal..." James Pennebaker, *Opening Up*, Avon Books, 1990, Chapters 7 and 10.

Hanry W. Taft quote in "Preface," p. viii, *Outward Bound: Schools of the Possible*, by Robert Godfrey; Anchor Books, 1980.

Internal-external test adapted from sample test in "External Control and Internal Control," by Julian B. Rotter, *Psychology Today*, June, 1971, p. 42.

Jim Dyer, personal communications.

Hans Selye, *The Stress of My Life: A Scientist's Memoirs*, 2nd edition, Van Nostrand Reinhold, 1979, p. 70.

"stress vulnerable and stress resistant..." see *The Self-Healing Personality*, by Howard S. Friedman, Ph.D.; Henry Holt and Company, 1991, Chapters 5 and 6. See also, *The Hardy Executive*, by Salvatore Maddi and Suzanne Kobasa; Dorsey Press, 1984.

Chapter 10   Negative People

Martin E.P. Seligman, Ph.D., *Learned Optimism: How to Change Your Mind and Your Life*, Knopf, 1991, pp. 44-47.

Irving Janis, *Victims of Groupthink*, Houghton Mifflin, 1972, p. 198. *Decision Making*, by Irving Janis and Leon Mann; Viking Press, 1977, pp. 130-131.

Chapter 11 Angry People

A good book on anger is *The Dance of Anger*, by Harriet Lerner, Harper and Row, 1985. See also *Prescription for Anger—Coping With Angry Feelings and Angry People*, by Gary Hankins, Ph.D.; Warner Books, 1992.

George Bach and Petrer Wyden, *The Intimate Enemy*, Wm. Morrow and Company, 1968. See also Chapter 20 in *Creative Aggression*, by George Bach and Herb Goldberg, Avon Books, 1974.

"I feel..." Dr. Thomas Gordon developed this technique for parents in the 1960s. His book on *P. E. T. Parent Effectiveness Training*, (Wyden, 1970,) and his workshops led to Teacher Effectiveness Training (T.E.T.) and Leadership Effectiveness Training (L.E.T.)

Chapter 13 Self-Managed Healing

Siegel references in this chapter are from *Love, Medicine and Miracles*, Harper and Row, 1986, and from his workshops. For information about books, tapes, and ECaP groups, write to 1302 Chapel Street, New Haven, CT 06511.

For a copy of a 14 page special report by Brendon O'Regan on "Healing, Remission, and Miracle Cures," send $4.00 to: Institute of Noctic Sciences, P.O. Box 909, Sausalito, CA 94966

W. C. Ellerbroek, "Language, Thought, and Disease," in *The Co-Evolution Quarterly*, Spring, 1978, pp. 30-38.

Barbara Marie Brewster, *Journey to Wholeness*, Four Winds Publishing Company, P.O. Box 19033, Portland, Oregon 97219.

Larry King, "How a Heart Attack Changed Me," *Parade Magazine*, January 15, 1989, pp. 10-11.

Ian Gowler...from newspaper articles obtained from Australian Cancer Foundation, 59A Canterbury Road, Canterbury, Australia.

"Self-sickening..." See *The Self-Healing Personality*, by Howard S. Friedman, Ph.D.; Henry Holt and Company, 1991.

"research in Europe..." see "Health's Character," by Hans J. Eysenck, *Psychology Today*, December, 1988, pp. 26-35.

Ed Roberts, "How It's S'pozed to Be," *This Brain Has a MOUTH*, July/August, 1992, pp. 22-23. *Mouth* is an exceptionally useful magazine for people with head injuries and other challenging conditions. For information write to: 61 Brighton Street, Rochester, NY 14607.

Anne Seitz, personal communications.

Moshe Feldenkrais information from Feldenkrais practitioners.

Norman Cousins, *Anatomy of an Illness*, W.W. Norton & Co., 1979, pp. 130-148.

Bonnie R. Strickland, "Internal-External Control Expectancies: From Contingency to Creativity," *American Psychologist*, January, 1989, pp. 4-7.

"A Doctor..." from conversations with William Meagher, Certified Insurance Rehabilitation Specialist.

"What is Christian Science Treatment?" The Christian Science Monitor, August 3, 1990, p. 17.

O. Carl Simonton, M.D., Stephanie Matthews-Simonton, and James L. Creighton, *Getting Well Again*, Bantam Books, 1980, p. 10.

John D. Evans, "Imagination Therapy," *The Humanist*, Volume 41, No. 6, Nov./Dec., 1980, pp. 32-36.

Louise L. Hay questions and results with PLWA group from public lectures and her book *You Can Heal Your Life*, Hay House, 1984.

Maxwell Maltz, *Psycho-Cybernetics*, Essandess Special Editions, 1960.

Emile Coué's work is described in *How to Use Auto-Suggestion Effectively*, by John Duckworth, Wilshire Book Company, 8721 Sunset Blvd., Hollywood, CA 90069; 1965, p. 104.

Paul Pearsall, Ph.D., *Making Miracles: A Scientist's Journey to Death and Back*, Prentice Hall Press, 1991.

Norman Cousins, *Head First: The Biology of Hope*, E.P. Dutton, 1989.

Mind/Body Medicine: How to Use Your Mind for Better Health, edited by Daniel Goleman and Joel Gurin, Consumer Reports Books, 1993.

American Holistic Medical Association, 4101 Lake Boone Trail, Suite 201, Raleigh, NC 27607.

Dee Brigham, personal communications. For information about the Getting Well program, write to: 823 Mendez Court, Orlando, FL 32801.

Burt Reynolds and Loni Anderson story, "Shades of Burt Reynolds," by Bart Mills, *Saturday Evening Post*, March, 1992, pp. 38-41. "What Love Means," by Dotson Rader, *Parade Magazine*, March 8, 1992, pp. 4-7.

Dorothy Woods Smith, personal communications and article in *Orthopædic Nursing*, Sept./Oct., 1989, pp. 24-28.

Jeanette Hafford, personal communications. For information write to: Tiny's Books for Children, 174 Main Street - Apt. 401 West, Bangor, ME 04401.

Donna Cline story in *Ordinary Women, Extraordinary Lives*, by Marcia Chellis; Viking Penguin, 1992, pp. 23-49.

Chapter 14   Surviving Emergencies

Paul and Kathy Plunk information from interviews and feature story in *The Oregonian*, July 14, 1991.

John Paul Getty, *How to Be Rich*, Playboy Press, 1966, p. 107.

"soldiers in Vietnam..." a Reader's Digest story.

Terry Anderson story from television and newspaper reports.

Chapter 15   Surviving Disasters

Mt. St. Helens information and quotes from media reports and "Mt. St. Helens Special Report" by Alan K. Ota, John Snell, and Leslie L. Zaitz; *The Oregonian*, October 27, 1980.

Although 61 deaths were reported, the count was reduced to 57 after four missing persons were located. (One of them was an opportunistic traveler who took advantage of the eruption to leave his wife.)

George W. Baker, "Present and Future Disaster Research," in *The Threat of Impending Disaster*, edited by George H. Grosser, Henry Wechsler, and Milton Greenblatt; The M.I.T. Press, 1964, p. 317.

Dougal Robertson, *Survive The Savage Sea*; Bantam Books, 1973, pp. 15-1.

Rex A. Lucas, *Men in Crisis: A Study of a Mine Disaster*; Basic Books, 1969, p. 53.

Piers Paul Reed, *Alive: The Story of the Andes Survivors*, J.B. Lippincott and Company, 1974.

James D. Thompson and Robert W. Hawkes, "Disaster, Community Organization, and Administrative Process," in *Man and Society in Disaster*, edited by George W. Baker and Dwight W. Chapman, Basic Books, 1962, pp. 268-300.

George W. Baker, *op. cit.*, pp. 324-325.

James D. Thompson and Robert W. Hawkes, *op. cit.*, p. 295.

John H. Sims and Duane D. Bauman, "The Tornado Threat: Coping Styles of the North and South," in *Science*, 176, June, 1972, pp. 1386-1392.

Chapter 16 Surviving Torturous Conditions

"Philippines invasion..." see *American Cæser: A Biography of Douglas MacArthur*, by William Manchester, Little, Brown & Company, 1978.

Bill Garleb quotes from personal communications. Portions of his story are reported in *Death March—The Survivors of Bataan and Corregidor*, by Donald Knox; Harcourt, Brace, Jovanovich, 1981. Bill Garleb is a hearty, cheerful, ebullient man who speaks to various groups about survival. He can be reached at 2123 Glen Ridge Road, Escondido, CA 92027; tel: (619) 745-7129.

"number of deaths..." the original reports of Americans dying on the "Death March" were exaggerated, apparently influenced by the slaughter of over one million Filipinos and 2 million Chinese.

John Van Cleef quotes from personal communications.

"Sonderkommandos..." in *War and Remembrance*, by Herman Wouk; Pocket Books, 1978, p.355.

Bruno Bettelheim's experiences described in *The Informed Heart*, Free Press, 1960, and *Surviving and Other Essays*, Knopf, 1979.

Bob Mitchell quote from personal communications.

Study of Former Prisoners of War, Studies and Analysis Services, Office of Planning and Program Evaluation, U. S. Government Printing Office, 1980, Stock Number 06254555.

Terrance Des Pres, *The Survivor: Anatomy of Life in the Death Camps*, Oxford University Press, 1976, p. 187. In my opinion, this book is by far the best at capturing the essence of the survivor spirit. Des Pres uses his skills as an English professor to show how humans are equal to the worst that can happen.

Shlomo Breznitz, *Memory Fields*; Knopf, 1992. See also *Parade Magazine*, December 20, 1992, pp 4-5.

Victor Frankl, *Man's Search For Meaning*, Washington Square Press, 1963, p. 115.

Jim Thompson story in *P.O.W., A Definitive History of the American Prisoner of War Experience in Viet Nam, 1964-1973*, Reader's Digest Press, 1976, p. 409.

Henri Charriere, *Papillon*, William Morrow & Company, 1970, pp. 225-226.

Eugene Heimler, *Resistance Against Tyranny: A Symposium*, Praeger, 1966, pp. 157-158.

James Stockdale story in *Winning Life's Toughest Battles*, by Julius Segal, Ivy Books, 1986, pp. 13-14. See also "You Can Find The Courage," in *Parade Magazine*, April 8, 1990, pp 8-9.

Gerald Coffee, *Beyond Survival*, G. P. Putnam's Sons, 1990, pp. 130, 133, 144.

Dougal Robertson, *Survive the Savage Sea*, Bantam Books, 1973, p. 240.

Samuel Pisar, *Of Blood and War*, Little, Brown & Company, 1980, p. 52.

Charlie Plumb, *I'm No Hero*, Independence Press, 1973, p. 287.

Edy Eiger, personal communications.

Chapter 17   Serendipity

John and Jane Youell, personal communications.

For an account of Horace Walpole's coining of the word "serendipity," see *Serendipity and the Three Princes: From the Peregriniaggio of 1557*," edited by Theodore G. Reemer; University of Oklahoma Press, 1965. The original Persian story is in *Peregrination of Three Princes of Serendip*, by Theodore Reemer. (In some libraries the book is listed under the name of the Italian translator, Christopher Aremno.) Note: It turns out that Walpole's childhood memory of an English translation of German translation of an Italian translation of an old Persian story did not accurately reflect the original. But, of course, this turned out to be a fortunate distortion.

Gracie and Walter Lantz story from an *NBC Today Show* interview on their 50th wedding anniversary.

Chapter 18   Surviving Being a Survivor

Whistleblowing, by Ralph Nader, Peter Petkas, and Kate Blackwell; Grossman Publishers, 1972.

For an excellent summary of questions to ask before becoming a whistle-blower, see "Blowing the Whistle," by Eldon C. Romney, *Mensa*

Bulletin, June, 1990, pp. 4-6, or send a self-addressed, stamped envelope to Eldon C. Romney, 1771 Portal Way, Sandy UT 84093. (Romney founded and ran a whistle-blowing clearing house for Mensa.)

Dr. Donald Soeken, himself a whistle-blower, provides a whistle-blowers support service. An article about him appeared in *Parade Magazine,* August 18, 1991. He can be contacted at Integrity International, Suite 102, 6215 Greenbelt Road, College Park MD 20740; Telephone: (301) 953-7358.

To learn more about both ends of the normal distribution curve being "abnormal," look through several introductory psychology textbooks.

Chapter 19   Our Transformation

Herb Goldberg quote from a lecture. He is author of *The Hazards of Being Male,* Signet, 1976, and *The New Male,* Signet, 1979.

"schizophrenics…" as stated in DSM-III-R, the Diagnostic Manual of the American Psychiatric Association officially adopted in 1980, "A common misconception is that a classification of mental disorders classifies people, when actually what are being classified are disorders that people have. For this reason DSM-III-R avoids the use of such expression as 'a schizophrenic.'" (p. xxiii.)

"schizophrenia first observed…" *Schizophrenia Genesis,* by Irving I. Gotterman, M.D.; W. H. Freeman and Company, 1991, p.4.

I am referring primarily to hospital psychiatry and the practice of forcing people with upsetting thoughts and feelings to go, involuntarily, to "hospitals" and required to take "treatments" that could not pass Federal Drug Administration (FDA) standards for being *effective, safe,* and *appropriate.* This situation helps explain why the American Psychiatric Association is the only medical specialty that, at its conventions, must arrange for police protection from demonstrations by former patients.

For a copy of "Successful Schizophrenia: Nietzsche's Uebermensch," an unpublished paper by Al Siebert, send $3 to P.O. Box 535, Portland, OR 97207.

Jonas Salk, *Survival of the Wisest,* Harper & Row, 1973, pp. 75-78.

Appendix B: Thriving During Job Search

Barbara Sher and Annie Gottlieb, *Teamworks!;* Warner Books, 1989, p. 7.

"unexpected opportunities…" from a CareerMakers talk by Pam Gross. *Want a New, Better, Fantastic Job?,* by Pam Gross and Peter Paskill, is a valuable book for anyone doing a job search. To order a copy by mail, send $11.50 to: RightSide Resources, 30 Greenridge Court., Lake Oswego, OR 97035.

Recommended Reading

The Survivors: An Anatomy of Life in the Death Camps, by Terrance Des Pres.

Winning Life's Toughest Battles: Roots of Human Resilience, by Julius Segal.

Love, Medicine, and Miracles, and *Peace, Love, and Healing,* by Bernie Siegel.

Beyond Survival, by Gerald Coffee.

The Warrior Within: A Guide to Inner Power, by Shale Paul.

Resilience: Discovering New Strength at Times of Stress, by Frederick Flack.

Learned Optimism: How to Change Your Mind and Your Life, by Martin Seligman.

Ordinary Women, Extraordinary Lives, by Marcia Chellis.

More than Mere Survival, by Jane Seskin.

Survival of the Wisest, by Jonas Salk.

Developing A 21st Century Mind, by Marcia Sinetar.

The Will to Live, by Arthur Schopenhauer.

I'm No Hero, by Charlie Plumb.

In the Mouth of the Wolf, by Rose Zar.

Of Blood and Hope, by Samuel Pisar

Staying Alive, by Roger Walsh, M.D.

Anatomy of an Illness, by Norman Cousins.

The Hardy Executive, by Salvatore Maddi and Suzanne Kobasa.

You Can Heal Your Life, by Louise Hay.

Journey to Wholeness, by Barbara Marie Brewster.

Uncharged Battery, by Edra L. Blixseth.

Making Miracles: A Scientist's Journey to Death and Back, by Paul Pearsall, Ph.D.

The Invulnerable Child, (chapter one), by E. James Anthony.

When Smart People Fail, by Carole Hyatt and Linda Gottleib.

Beyond Survival, by Theresa Saldana.

Three Levels of Time, by Harold T.P. Hayes.

The Book of Survival, by Anthony Greenbank.

The Art of Survival, by Cord Christian Troebst.

They Survived: A Study of the Will to Live, by Wilfrid Noyce.

History and Human Survival, by Robert Jay Lifton.

Survivor, by Laurence Janifer, (science fiction.)

INDEX

A

action choices   171–173
adaptability   25
adversity   1
   thriving in   130–132
Agor, Weston   51
AIDS survivors   27
   PLWA group   158
alarm reactions   89
Alda, Alan   4, 21
allergic minds   93
amusing benefit   224
Anderson, Loni   161–162
Anderson, Terry   177
angry people   113
   guidelines with   114–120
   learning/coping reaction   113–14
      observing   114
   success with   121
   victim/blaming reaction   113
Anthony, Mark   118–119
attitude
   changing   109–110
authoritarian   31
awareness   171–173

B

bad   65
bad child   67–68
Baker, George   191
behaviors
   illness resistant   92–94
   illness susceptible   92–94
Berne, Eric   114
best and worst manager   29
Bettelheim, Bruno   205–207, 208,
   218–219
biological
   gender   238–239
   stress   89–91
biphasic
   development   32
   pattern of adjustment   26
   personality traits   27
Blitch, Joy   154–156, 232
born survivors   6–7

brainstorming   62
Brewster, Barbara   142
Breznitz, Shlomo   209–210
Brigham, Deirdre   161

C

Carter, Pres. Jimmy   194–195
catatoxic reaction   93–94
cause and effect relationships   17–18
cerebral cortex   130
change   1–3
Charriere, Henri   212
child's
   personality theory   68–70
   prohibitions   2
   way of thinking   31
choices   27, 122
Christian Science Church   156
Churchill, Winston   55–56
Cline, Donna   164
co-dependency
   therapists   77
Coffee, Gerald   214, 216
combat survivors   4
competence   18–19
constant change   86–88
   list
      now   86–88
      past   86 88
contact with others   214
continental divide principle   80
contrast   76
controlled defiance
   sustaining   212–213
converting misfortune   10
Corregidor Island   4, 4–5
Coué, Emile   63, 159
Cousins, Norman   150–151, 160
crash survivors
   Andes mountains   190
creative action   256
creativity   51, 59–61
   test   60
Csikszentmihalyi, Mihaly   35
curiosity   18
   dangers of   186
   playful   46

D

deepest strengths 220
Des Pres, Terrance 207–208
diseases of adaptation 89
distress 90
doctor/patient puzzle 151–153
Donaldson, Ken 43
dreams 58–59
Dyer, Jim 42, 88–89

E

efficiency vs. tension 174–175
Eger, Edith Eva 220
Eisenhower, General 50
Ellerbroek, W.C. 141, 158–159
emergencies 165–179
  survival 173
emotional
  fragility 73
  handicaps 68
  immunities 93–94
  shock 129
emotional handicap 99–101
empathic listening 125
empathy 42, 43–50, 101, 224
  avoidance 45–46
  development 43–45
  disadvantage 49
  disillusioned 208–209
  early clues 48–49
  less information 47–48
  pattern 46–47
energy draining effect 72
ESP 54
eustress 91
Evans, John 157, 158
Exceptional Cancer Patients (ECaP)
  152
experimenting 15–16, 17
experts disagree 182–183
external frame of reference 236
extraordinary life crisis 169–170

F

Feldenkrais, Moshe 33, 150
femininity 237
Fleming, Arthur 225
flexibility 22, 23, 25, 109
  mental and emotional 26

Fraiberg, Selma 15
Frankl, Viktor 210–211, 215
friendship response 125–126
Fulghum, Robert 18

G

Garleb, Bill 200, 204, 209, 215
general adaptation syndrome 89
getting smarter 19
Getting Well program 161
Getty, John Paul 173
give-up-itis 202
glass ceiling 237
God 155–156
Godfrey, Robert 56
Goetze, Joyce 139, 140, 148–149
Goldberg, Herb 237
good 145
good boys 9, 64
good child 66, 146, 239
  handicap 65
  inner restrictions 94–95
good girls 9, 64
good listening 119
good luck 224
good luck of misfortune 224
good manager 241–242
good noun 238
good people
  energy draining 72–74
good person
  victim 127
good timing 47
Gowler, Ian 142–143
groupthink 109

H

Hafford, Jeanette 163
Hawkes, Robert W. 191
Hayes, Louise 158
Hazel, Joanne 36, 94–95
head injuries 132, 162
healing ritual 155–156
Heimler, Eugene 213
higher human 244
Hitler 50
hunches 54

I

Iacocca, Lee 13–14, 19
identity crisis 130, 237
imagination 62–63
inborn abilities 1
inner prohibitions 9
  overcoming 112
inner resources 130
inner selfs 129–138
Institute of Noetic Sciences 141
intuition 51, 224
invulnerable children 13
IQ tests 19

J

James, E. Anthony 12, 59
Janis, Irving 108
job loss
  guidelines 253–256
job search
  guidelines 253
judgmental 61
  people 61
Julius Cæsar 118–119

K

King, Larry 142, 143
Korchin, Sheldon 197

L

labeling 61, 243
labels 31, 236, 237
Lantz, Gracie 225
Lantz, Walter 225
laughing 151, 174–175
law of reversed effort 159
laws of nature 100
learning 15–16, 246–248
  challenge 8–9, 141
  from experience 19–20, 195–198
  self-managed 16
  self-managed benefits 21–22
  struggle 8
learning/coping 7–8
  reaction 103
lie detector 52
life expectancy 91
life smart 19
life-disruptive change 79–80
life-style 91, 144–145

life's best survivors 1
listening
  guidelines 249–252
living systems 242
Locke, Norman 48
locus of control 153–154
  both internal and external 154–156
  external 85, 153–154
  internal 85, 153–154
  test 85–86
Lucas, Rex 189

M

MacArthur, Gen. Douglas 50, 199–200
Maltz, Maxwell 63
manager
  low synergy 40
  professional 240–242
manipulation 123–124
martial arts 125
  emotional skills 126
martyr 127
masculinity 237–238
Maslow, Abraham 30–31, 80
McClelland, David 112
Mednick, Sarnoff 60
mental efficiency 174–175
mental imagery 157
Mico, Paul 179
mining disaster 189
Mitchell, Bob 205
mode of thinking
  curious, empathetic 101
Montessori, Maria 15
Mt. St. Helens
  eruption 181–187
  lessons 196–198
Murphy's Law 192
Muselmanner 202–203

N

Naito, Bill 79–80
Native Americans 219
needing for things to work well 35–36
negative attitude
  benefits 102–103
  response 103–109

negative people 97–112
  guidelines 103–109
nervous system 130–131
  autonomic 130
  central 130
  somatic 130
new form 238
new reality 224
next level of development 10, 235–245
  transformation 235
Nietszche, Wilhelm 244

O

observing 101–102, 114
observing person 61
old form 235–236
open-brained 61, 172–173
  test 170
The Oregonian 185, 186, 192–193
Ortega y Gassett, Jose 39
Outward Bound 56, 83
overcoming a hidden inner barrier 112

P

Papillon 212. See also Charriere, Henri
paradoxical 32, 154
  qualities 27
  traits 65–68
    women 33
pattern empathy 171
Pearsall, Paul 160
people as nouns 31, 236
perception 76
perceptual 60–61
personality terms
  both/and 31
  either/or 31
physical afflictions 162–163
physical injuries 132
Pisar, Samuel 217, 218
playful humor 174–175
playfulness 15, 17, 20
  powerful 175
  providing perspective 175–176
Plum, Lt. Commander Charles 7
Plunk, Kathy 165–170, 173
Plunk, Paul 165–170, 230

polio 163
positive and negative thinking 110–112
positive attitudes 98
power of love 161–162
prayer 160
premature closure 61
private interviews 11–12
prohibitions 67
  logic 66
psychiatrists 243
psychological principles 9
psychological self-defense 125
public employees 133

Q

questioning reaction 224

R

Rambo 4
rapidly read reality 169
Ray, Gov. Dixie Lee 183–185, 186, 194–195
Reagan, Ronald 164, 176
reliable strengths 254
religious 154–156
resiliency 1, 129–130
response flexibility 109
Reynolds, Burt 161–162
Robbins, Anthony 40
Roberts, Ed 146
Robertson, Dougal 188, 216
Roentgen, Wilhelm 225
Rotter, Julian 85
Rowan, Row 51
Ruff, George 197

S

Salk, Jonas 245
schizophrenia 34, 242–244
  successful 243–244
schizy 23
Schneirla, T.C. 26
Schwartzkopf, Gen. H. Norman 29–30, 50
Scott, M. Peck 96
Segal, Julius 7, 214
Seitz, Anne 146–147
self assessment 134

self-concept 130–132

self-confidence 5, 130–132, 177–178, 224

self-esteem 130–131
developing 134–135
rebuilding 254

self-frazzling 92

self-love 146–147

self-managed healing 139–164, 147
emotional 245

self-managed learning
benefits 21–22

self-management
poor 92

self-sickening 143–145

self-starters 29

self-talk
healing 157–159

selfish 65

selfish-unselfish dichotomy 39–40

Seligman, Martin 101

Selye, Hans 89–92

sense of identity 129

serendipity 2, 10, 163–164
finding 225–226
guidelines 227–228
learning about 226
personality 226–227
talent 221–223

sex role 240
stereotypes 242

Shakespeare, William 118

Sherman, Harold 57–58

Siegel, Bernie 140, 142, 149, 152

Simonton, Carl 156

Simonton, Stephanie Matthews 156

Sinetar, Marcia 59

Smith, David 178

Sonderkommandos 203

spiritual healing 156

spontaneous remission 140

Stephenson, Howard 256

Stockdale, Vice Admiral James 214

strain syndrome 90, 90–91
resistant 93
susceptible 92–93

street-wise 45, 48

stress 89
disability claims 90

Strickland, Bonnie 153

subconscious information 58–59

subliminal perception 52–53

suicide
slow 144

support group 82, 253–254

surpassing the limits 178–179

surviving disasters 181–198

survivor
challenges 229–234
being abnormal 234
questions 5
style 168–170, 178
three basic elements 169
surviving being 229

survivor personality
foul-weather friends 39–40
four criteria 5
ordinary people 6

survivor sequence 248

survivors 4
fast questioning 171–173
inspiration from 163
learning from 203–220
find humor 214
not better people 219–220
not good patients 149–150
questions about 34
warm and joyful 199

sympathy 43–45

synergistic
becoming more 41–42
personality 38

synergy 35, 37–38
high 37
low 37
selfish need 39–40

syntoxic reaction 93–94

T

Taft, Henry W. 83

teaching challenge 8–9

terminally ill 140

theme song of the human race 100

thinking
nonverbal, visual 130
verbal, conceptual 130

Thompson, Jim 211

thriving under life's strains 95–96
thriving under pressure 79
total commitment 177
Toynbee, Arnold 45
transformation 235
  organizational 242
  schizophrenia 243–244
Truman, Harry 185
two-faced 70–71

U
U.S. Forest Service 182, 183–184
underlying principles 9
unemployment 129–130, 253–256
unexpected opportunities 255–256

V
validate 101
VanCleef, John 202–203, 204, 209,
    215, 217
victim/blaming 7–8
victims 129
vitamin C 151

W
wake-up call 142
Walpole, Horace 224–225
White, Robert W. 16
win/win outcome 122
worst experiences 220

Y
Youell, Jane 221–223
Youell, John 221–223

Acknowledgements

While hundreds of people made this book possible, I wish to give special thanks to the following:

Sam Kimball for countless hours of volunteer editing, encouragement, insightful suggestions, and special friendship.

My mother, who left my mind alone.

Mary Karr, my sister, for her unflagging support and volunteer proofreading.

Gillian Holloway for her support, manuscript editing, and helpful suggestions.

Stephanie Abarbanel for her enthusiasm and perceptive feedback.

Don James, the epitome of a writing instructor, for years of unbridled enthusiasm.

Ruth Aley for her warm encouragement when it was most needed.

Kristin Pintarich for her outstanding computer skills, intelligent thinking, and excellence in handling details.

Bill Garleb for his friendship and hundreds of hours of discussions about surviving.

Enos and Charlott Herkshan for their friendship and teachings.

Bill McKeachie, my teaching mentor.

Jim McConnell, my advisor, writing mentor, and friend.

All the survivors willing to answer my questions and tell me about their experiences.

Public employees who keep things running while receiving more criticism and less praise than they deserve.

ALSO AVAILIABLE

Cassette tapes:
"The Survivor Personality: How to Do It During Layoffs and
    Reorganization"
    A talk by Al Siebert, Ph.D. One hour, $12.95

"How to Thrive and Grow During Your Job Search"
    A talk by Al Siebert, Ph.D., at the Northwest Career Fair
    One hour, $12.95

Book:
The Adult Student's Guide to Survival and Success: Time
    For College (2nd ed.)
    Al Siebert, Ph.D. and Bernadine Gilpin, 176 pgs, $12.95

Booklet:
Coping and Thriving During Downsizing and Layoffs
    Al Siebert, Ph.D. and Gillian Holloway, Ph.D., 32 pgs, $3.95
    (Volume discounts available.)

Send orders and requests for information about *The Survivor Personality Newsletter* to:

Practical Psychology Press
P.O. Box 535
Portland, OR 97207
503/289-3295
fax 283-1214

Please add $1.00 postage & handling for books and tapes.
Satisfaction guaranteed.